Critical Theory Between Klein and Lacan

PSYCHOANALYTIC HORIZONS

Psychoanalysis is unique in being at once a theory and a therapy, a method of critical thinking and a form of clinical practice. Now in its second century, this fusion of science and humanism derived from Freud has outlived all predictions of its demise. **Psychoanalytic Horizons** evokes the idea of a convergence between realms as well as the outer limits of a vision. Books in the series test disciplinary boundaries and will appeal to scholars and therapists who are passionate not only about the theory of literature, culture, media, and philosophy but also, above all, about the real life of ideas in the world.

Series Editors
Esther Rashkin, Mari Ruti, and Peter L. Rudnytsky

Advisory Board
Salman Akhtar, Doris Brothers, Aleksandar Dimitrijevic, Lewis Kirshner, Humphrey Morris, Hilary Neroni, Dany Nobus, Lois Oppenheim, Donna Orange, Peter Redman, Laura Salisbury, Alenka Zupančič

Volumes in the Series:
Mourning Freud, Madelon Sprengnether
Does the Internet Have an Unconscious? Slavoj Žižek and Digital Culture, Clint Burnham
In the Event of Laughter: Psychoanalysis, Literature and Comedy, Alfie Bown
On Dangerous Ground: Freud's Visual Cultures of the Unconscious, Diane O'Donoghue
For Want of Ambiguity: Order and Chaos in Art, Psychoanalysis, and Neuroscience, Ludovica Lumer and Lois Oppenheim
Life Itself Is an Art: The Life and Work of Erich Fromm, Rainer Funk
Born After: Reckoning with the German Past, Angelika Bammer
Critical Theory Between Klein and Lacan: A Dialogue, Amy Allen and Mari Ruti
At the Risk of Thinking: An Intellectual Biography of Julia Kristeva (forthcoming), Alice Jardine
Transferences: The Aesthetics and Poetics of the Therapeutic Relationship (forthcoming), Maren Scheurer
The Analyst's Desire: Ethics in Theory and Clinical Practice (forthcoming), Mitchell Wilson

Critical Theory Between Klein and Lacan

A Dialogue

Amy Allen and Mari Ruti

BLOOMSBURY ACADEMIC
NEW YORK • LONDON • OXFORD • NEW DELHI • SYDNEY

BLOOMSBURY ACADEMIC
Bloomsbury Publishing Inc
1385 Broadway, New York, NY 10018, USA
50 Bedford Square, London, WC1B 3DP, UK
29 Earlsfort Terrace, Dublin 2, Ireland

BLOOMSBURY, BLOOMSBURY ACADEMIC and the Diana logo
are trademarks of Bloomsbury Publishing Plc

First published in the United States of America 2019
Paperback edition published 2021

Copyright © Amy Allen and Mari Ruti, 2019

Cover design by Daniel Benneworth-Gray
Cover image: Woodblock print by Furuya Korin, 1904

All rights reserved. No part of this publication may be reproduced or transmitted in any form or by any means, electronic or mechanical, including photocopying, recording, or any information storage or retrieval system, without prior permission in writing from the publishers.

Bloomsbury Publishing Inc does not have any control over, or responsibility for, any third-party websites referred to or in this book. All internet addresses given in this book were correct at the time of going to press. The author and publisher regret any inconvenience caused if addresses have changed or sites have ceased to exist, but can accept no responsibility for any such changes.

A catalog record for this book is available from the Library of Congress.

Library of Congress Cataloging-in-Publication Data
Names: Allen, Amy, author.
Title: Critical theory between Klein and Lacan : a dialogue / Amy Allen & Mari Ruti.
Description: New York : Bloomsbury Academic, 2019. | Series: Psychoanalytic horizons | Includes bibliographical references and index.
Identifiers: LCCN 2019008432 (print) | LCCN 2019017711 (ebook) |
ISBN 9781501352270 (ePub) | ISBN 9781501352287 (ePDF) |
ISBN 9781501352263 (hardback : alk. paper)
Subjects: LCSH: Critical theory. | Klein, Melanie. | Lacan, Jacques, 1901–1981.
Classification: LCC HM480 (ebook) | LCC HM480 .A44 2019 (print) |
DDC 142–dc23
LC record available at https://lccn.loc.gov/2019008432

ISBN:	HB:	978-1-5013-5226-3
	PB:	978-1-5013-7832-4
	ePDF:	978-1-5013-5228-7
	eBook:	978-1-5013-5227-0

Series: Psychoanalytic Horizons

Typeset by Integra Software Services Pvt. Ltd.

To find out more about our authors and books visit www.bloomsbury.com
and sign up for our newsletters.

CONTENTS

Preface vi

1 Subjectivity 1
2 Fusion 33
3 Anxiety 63
4 Affect 95
5 Love 129
6 Creativity 157
7 Politics 187

Notes 214
Index 232

PREFACE

AA: Let me begin by telling the story of how this project came to be. It started as a casual dinner conversation when Mari was visiting Penn State to give a talk on Jacques Lacan's seminar on anxiety. Prior to her visit, I had been working for a while on Melanie Klein as part of a project on the relationship between psychoanalysis and Frankfurt School critical theory. Over the dinner that followed Mari's lecture, we had a lively conversation about her presentation, her work on Lacan in relation to critical theory, and my research on Klein, during which many points of connection and overlapping themes emerged. These convergences surprised us because we had both to some degree accepted without question the conventional assessment that Klein and Lacan are theoretically and ideologically so far apart that trying to bring them into conversation with each other was intellectually implausible.

Before that evening, although I had been interested in Mari's work, I had thought of my choice of Klein as my psychoanalytic touchstone as an *alternative* to the more common critical theoretical engagement with Lacan. That first conversation was the dawning of the realization that the relationship between psychoanalysis and critical theory needn't be framed in terms of an either/or choice: Klein vs. Lacan. At the end of the evening, as we were leaving the restaurant, I said to Mari: "We should write a book on Klein and Lacan together." Mari's enthusiastic response was: "That's a *great* idea!"

Under ordinary circumstances, that would have been the end of it: another engaging post-lecture dinner discussion and an interesting idea for a book that would never materialize. But—and on some level I must have known this when I made the suggestion—Mari Ruti isn't someone who merely talks about writing books: she has published twelve of them. As a consequence, my offhand suggestion became a reality relatively quickly. In an email dated the day after our dinner Mari said: "We should totally write a book about Klein and Lacan. I think that this would be very cool." She then continued to gently encourage and nurture the idea, touching base every so often to remind me of it, until we were able to find time in our schedules to meet for a series of taped conversations that form the backbone of this book.

We chose the following themes to organize our dialogue: subjectivity, anxiety, affect, love, creativity, and politics. The following year we met again to revise the transcripts of our conversations into the exchange that follows. During this revision process, we realized that the question of primary fusion—of whether the baby in the first months of its life is wholly merged with its primary caretaker or whether there's a degree of separation, and therefore of intersubjectivity, from the very beginning—was a prominent and recurring theme that ran through our conversations. We therefore decided to create a separate chapter for the topic.

Citations were a part of our original conversations because our tape recorder was surrounded by major texts of Klein and Lacan from which we frequently quoted in order to elucidate our points. I want to add that I sometimes talked about Lacan and Mari sometimes talked about Klein because, prior to our conversations, we had made an effort to familiarize ourselves with the basics of each other's fields. In the revision process, we added endnotes, including some references to relevant secondary sources. Yet we also strove to retain as much of the conversational and somewhat provisional tone of our dialogue as possible.

The initial idea for the book is also its primary goal: to continue the dialogue that had begun to take shape during our dinner about the relationship between Kleinian and Lacanian psychoanalysis—which has received surprisingly little attention[1]—and to examine the implications of their approaches for critical theory. Three features of our project make it distinctive. First, this book is a genuine dialogue. Rather than merely laying out Klein and Lacan's positions side by side—a method that seems to suggest an either/or choice—the text unfolds as a conversation in which we respond directly to each other's questions, objections, and interpretations; we undertake a rigorous yet generous intellectual exchange in order to explore the similarities and differences between Klein and Lacan. Although the claim that Klein and Lacan aren't as far apart as they have frequently been assumed to be is a refrain that runs through this book, our goal isn't to get rid of the divergences between these thinkers. Rather, our objective is to map out points of convergence between them in such a way that familiar criticisms—for example, Lacan's famous critique of Klein's notion of the integration of the ego—can be reassessed in ways that throw the remaining points of disagreement into greater relief.

Klein and Lacan are among the most influential psychoanalytic theorists after Freud. Their work has had profound implications for how academics from various disciplines—as well as clinicians working in the Kleinian and Lacanian traditions—have understood topics such as subjectivity, intersubjectivity, autonomy, agency, desire, affect, trauma, history, progress, and the potential for individual and collective (and even political) change. Although Lacan's oeuvre has been mined extensively by critical theorists, his work has often been interpreted in an overly negative and antirelational manner. At the same time, the recent recuperation of Klein by critics who are interested in a more "reparative" inflection of theorizing—who have adopted the rhetoric of reparation as an antidote to what they perceive as the destructive (or "paranoid") tendencies of critical theory—has tended to obscure Klein's emphasis on primary aggression, negativity, and ambivalence. We offer alternative interpretations of Klein and Lacan that bring out their complexities while walking the fine line between the negative and the generative.

Second, this book offers an accessible introduction to the theories of Klein and Lacan at the same time as it delves deeply into what we deem to be their major theoretical contributions. Although we both know a fair amount about both Klein and Lacan, the fact that I'm more thoroughly trained in the Kleinian tradition than Mari is—and that Mari is more thoroughly trained in the Lacanian tradition than I am—necessitated lucid explanations regarding foundational concepts, such as Klein's paranoid-schizoid and depressive positions and Lacan's notions of constitutive lack and sublimation. This ensures that non-expert readers will be able to process the text without difficulty. Yet our conversations are comprehensive, detailed, and nuanced enough—not to mention unique in exploring central psychoanalytic themes in a space *between* Klein and Lacan—to cater to the needs of expert readers.

Third, as I've already emphasized, we're interested not only in understanding how Klein and Lacan might speak—or in some instances not speak—to each other but also in thinking through the ramifications of their work for critical theory. In this context, the fact that we're working with different definitions of critical theory, operating within different disciplinary contexts, and engaging with different intellectual interlocutors, adds breadth to our exchange. Indeed, given that a concern with something that we both call "critical theory" is what animates our interest in psychoanalysis and therefore frames our entire dialogue, it makes sense for us to begin with a discussion of how our different intellectual trajectories inform our conceptions of critical theory.

MR: I agree that it's necessary to explain our divergent intellectual formations to clarify that when we talk about psychoanalysis and critical theory, we're approaching the theme from different places of expertise. Amy is thoroughly trained in the Frankfurt School tradition of critical theory, including its Habermasian legacies, whereas my training is in critical theory more broadly defined, in what critics often simply call "contemporary theory," "posthumanist theory," or "progressive theory." By this I mean the kind of theory that has profited from the insights of French poststructuralism, Lacanian psychoanalysis, Foucauldian biopolitics, Agamben's notion of bare life, and other continental philosophical trends, frequently combining these trends with cultural studies, political critique, ethnic studies, postcolonial studies, deconstructive feminism, and queer theory.

We are both familiar with the thinkers who served as precursors to both the Frankfurt School and my broader version of critical theory: Marx, Nietzsche, Freud, Kierkegaard, de Saussure, Heidegger, Arendt, Fanon, Sartre, de Beauvoir, and so on. At the same time, although I know the early Frankfurt School—Benjamin, Adorno, Horkheimer, and Marcuse—relatively well, I haven't read a great deal of Habermas, in large part because my genre of critical theory has flatly rejected him for his rationalist tendencies. I'm in fact more familiar with the scholarship of post-Habermasian feminists who criticize aspects of his work, such as Seyla Benhabib, Nancy Fraser, and Amy herself. Moreover, my engagement with the Frankfurt School stops there, whereas Amy is immersed in the most recent debates in the field—debates that scholars in my version of critical theory don't seem to have much awareness of. Amy also knows Foucault better than I do. Finally, while Amy was trained in a philosophy department, I was trained, first, in the social sciences, and later (and more extensively), in contemporary theory in a comparative literature department that allowed me to focus almost exclusively on continental philosophy, critical theory, psychoanalysis, and related fields. My thanks go to Alice Jardine, Barbara Johnson, Marjorie Garber, Susan Suleiman, Eric Downing, Svetlana Boym—and, well, Julia Kristeva—for making this possible.

Throughout her career, Amy has been making her way from the Habermasian tradition toward my version of critical theory—at least that's how I've understood her scholarship. For instance, she has been trying to convince her peers within the Frankfurt School tradition that the irrational side of human experience—which psychoanalysis is exceptionally capable of exploring—should continue to play a part in post-Habermasian Frankfurt School theory, as it certainly did in the early Frankfurt School tradition. I in turn have chafed against some of the more excessive features of progressive theory, such as its semi-autonomous celebration of the annihilation of the subject and its by now almost ritualistic rejection of everything that even hints at agency, autonomy, or normative justice.

I of course understand the historical reasons for the refutation of these tropes, which have to do with the ways in which progressive theory has positioned itself in opposition to everything that's associated with the Enlightenment, because there's no question that the ideals of the Enlightenment can't be dissociated from problematic notions of self-transparency, sovereignty, rationality, and mastery. From these notions, it's legitimate to draw a link to Western imperialism, slavery, and other atrocities, with the result that the motivations for rejecting them are often politically sound. Nevertheless, I've been uncomfortable with critical-theoretical models that valorize desubjectivation and the pulverization of the subject—what Lacanians call "subjective destitution"—because I can't see how these models help precarious subjects who already feel shattered by collective inequalities, such as racism. I'm also suspicious of these models because their fetishization has become the default position in my field. I believe that when an intellectual orientation becomes habitual, it loses its critical edge: it becomes something that critics say just because they know that they are supposed to say it. As early as my dissertation—which became my first book—I stopped wanting to simply repeat customary positions without thinking them through.

Throughout my career I've been looking for a conceptual middle ground, which psychoanalysis provides in the sense that it gives us a decentered, fragmented, and partly irrational subject without thereby advocating the complete destruction of the subject. That said, some Lacanians have taken Lacanian theory in the direction of destruction by valorizing the death drive. But that's not my Lacan: although I don't ignore the death drive, I simply don't believe that Lacan would have wanted his analysands to either fall into psychosis or damage themselves, which is why my version of Lacanian theory is centered on the question of how to keep living when there's no cure for your constitutive lack, maladaptation, and disorientation. In looking for this middle ground, I've found Amy's work extremely productive and thought provoking because she has been exploring the irrational side of life without thereby abandoning her preoccupation with agency and normative justice.

I've long felt that Amy and I have been approaching the same kinds of preoccupations about subjectivity, psychic life, agency, ethics, and politics from versions of critical theory that many critics see as intrinsically antithetical to each other: I've been making my way from progressive theory's wholesale rejection of the humanist subject—a rejection about which I have significant reservations even if I in principle support it—toward autonomy, reason, agency, and normative justice, whereas Amy has been making her way from the Habermasian Frankfurt School tradition—the tradition of communicative action and normative justice—toward the more irrational side of critical theory, including the early Frankfurt School. This is perhaps most evident in her *The End of Progress*,[2] where she returns to Adorno and puts considerable pressure on the ideal of progress, broadly understood.

As a result, when Amy suggested that we collaborate on a project on Klein, Lacan, and critical theory, I jumped at the opportunity. I then added the idiotic idea that we should tape the book as a dialogue, which placed us in the terrifying position of going about the project semi-spontaneously, without the usual support systems of a scholarly undertaking. I reckon that for both of us the experience has been intense but also extremely rewarding.

AA: I think that recording our conversations and making the transcripts of these conversations the starting point for our book was a *brilliant* approach. It's true that it was terrifying—and not only in the initial stage of our taping sessions but also in reading the transcripts—yet also incredibly liberating and, yes, rewarding.

With respect to our different intellectual trajectories, what you said sounds right to me. I would only complicate a little bit your description of my path to—and through—the Frankfurt School. Initially, when I was in graduate school in the 1990s, I was mostly interested in Foucault and feminist theory and even stubbornly uninterested in Frankfurt School critical theory. This was somewhat self-defeating because at the time, there was a tremendous amount of intellectual energy and excitement around the Frankfurt School at Northwestern, where I earned my doctorate: it was one of the things that my department was best known for. Around that time, Habermas retired from Frankfurt and started coming to Northwestern regularly to offer seminars, and many of the best graduate students in the department were working on Habermas with Tom McCarthy. But for some reason at that time I didn't identify myself as someone who worked in that field.

As a result, my dissertation, which became my first book, barely discusses Habermas. The book addresses feminist theoretical debates about power through the work of Foucault, Arendt, and Butler. It was only later, when I was working on my second book—which grew out of my desire to correct what I thought were significant misunderstandings and misinterpretations of Foucault and Butler by Habermasian critical theorists—that I began to think of myself as engaged in the project of critical theory as the field is understood by the Frankfurt School. However, largely because of my early interest in Foucault and feminist theory, I've always attempted to reconcile mainstream Habermasian and post-Habermasian Frankfurt School critical social theory with what you call progressive theory. For me this has happened primarily through my work on Foucault, but I've also been interested in making broader connections to feminist theory, queer theory, and, more recently, postcolonial theory, with the consequence that my work has always drawn me into a wider orbit of critical theory than what is considered to fit within the parameters of present-day Frankfurt School preoccupations.

For instance, *The End of Progress* aims to open up Frankfurt School critical theory to a conversation with feminist, queer, and postcolonial theory in part by establishing an alternative lineage to the Habermasian vein of the Frankfurt School, one that runs from Adorno to Foucault. Moreover, broadening the conception of Frankfurt School critical theory is something that I've tried to do not just through my own work, but also institutionally, through the book series that I edit for Columbia University Press. This series was envisioned as a space for creating linkages between some of the different wings of critical theory. As I see it, what connects the different understandings of critical theory that you and I have—and what makes them distinct from, say, critical literary studies—is that we strive to critique existing social, cultural, ethical, and political practices, structures, and institutions. As a result, your work on Lacanian ethics and the political implications of Lacanian theory is critical theory in the sense that I define and practice it, even if it doesn't have anything to do with Habermas.

MR: You're right that, despite my training in a literature department, I don't do critical literary studies, which causes consternation among some of my colleagues but which my graduate students seem to appreciate. I'm much more interested in sociopolitical critique and in using theory to examine the fundamentals of the human condition. Furthermore, one reason that our approaches have always seemed so compatible is that both of us are constantly trying to bridge divisions that appear insurmountable. In one of my recent books, *The Ethics of Opting Out*,[3] I attempt to convince colleagues in queer theory that there's no reason to think that Foucault and Lacan are incompatible. Of course there are differences, and of course Foucault, for good reasons, staged an immense critique of psychoanalysis early in his career, but when you look at the main outlines of their theorization over time, there are so many intersections that I think that, much of the time, they lead more or less to the same conceptual place.

You might find this amusing: One of the peer reviewers of my book on Levinas and Lacan was overall pleased with the manuscript[4]—the verdict was "publish as it stands"—but they were enormously exasperated by the fact that in the last chapter I discuss Habermas in the context of the scholarship of Fraser and yourself. Their question was—and I paraphrase—"Why the hell are you even talking about Habermas?" In this sense, veering off the well-trodden path of one's field can be tricky. Sometimes it makes colleagues furious, though I've never understood why. Whatever his failings, it's not like Habermas is a total moron.

This point is relevant for this book because, as you have noted, there are critics who believe that Klein and Lacan have positively nothing in common, and that it's consequently a form of intellectual heresy to even mention them in the same paragraph. However, because both of us are used to attempting to reconcile the irreconcilable, I believe that this book manages to foreground previously ignored convergences in the theories of these two psychoanalytic giants. As you said, our aim isn't to pretend that Klein and Lacan are always on the same page. Nonetheless, our conversations generate nodes of commonality with striking frequency.

AA: I agree that there are risks to attempting to stage conversations between theoretical positions that are generally thought to be opposed. Yet like you, this is what I've always tried to do in my work, starting with my first article on Foucault and feminism, running through my book on the Foucault-Habermas debate, and continuing in my recent work on Frankfurt School critical theory and postcolonial theory. There's no doubt that this approach can anger readers who have a lot invested in certain divisions between fields or within their own field. Ultimately, however, I believe that intellectual work can only remain vibrant and exciting to the extent that we, as intellectuals, remain open to different—sometimes even competing—perspectives and allow ourselves to be transformed by the encounter between them.

The conversations that follow unfold organically, with one theme leading to the next. Nevertheless, it might help to orient the reader to outline the basic organization of this book. Conversation 1 opens with Klein and Lacan's theories of subjectivity, including their understandings of the formation of the subject. Although our discussion traverses a variety of issues—including the different notions of phantasy/fantasy in Klein and Lacan; the Kleinian paranoid-schizoid and depressive positions; the Lacanian emphasis on lack as the foundation of subjectivity; the complex relationship between the intersubjective and intrapsychic; and the importance of the drives—the conversation culminates at Klein and Lacan's divergent conceptions of the ego. Whereas for Lacan the goal of analysis is to weaken an ego that's regarded as overly grandiose and narcissistic, Klein's analytic goal is to strengthen the ego. Although this may appear as an intractable discrepancy between them, our conversation reveals that Klein's distinctive vision of what it means to strengthen the ego—which entails enriching it by incorporating a greater degree of unconscious content and increasing its tolerance for ambivalence, ambiguity, and conflict—is more compatible with Lacanian theory than it initially appears.

Conversation 2 addresses the question of whether either Klein or Lacan accept the concept of primary fusion. Although both Klein and Lacan have been read as endorsing this concept, we argue that such readings are erroneous. Allen maintains that Klein's view that the infant is object related from the start entails a rejection of primary fusion, whereas Ruti draws on Lacan's critique of Michael Balint to show that Lacan doesn't endorse primary fusion either. For both Klein and Lacan, intersubjectivity exists from the beginning of life, albeit in different ways. In the course of this discussion, we also assess Lacan's critique of Klein's biologism, the views of both thinkers on the ambivalence of psychic experiences, and their differing conceptions of the death drive.

In the third conversation, we focus on anxiety, a central theme for both Klein and Lacan. We start with Allen's account of Klein's distinction between persecutory and depressive anxiety and her understanding of the connections between anxiety and the death drive (or primary aggression). We then turn to Ruti's explanation of three varieties of anxiety that she extracts from Lacan's seminar on this topic—each of which, according to Ruti, highlights the importance of intersubjectivity in Lacan's work. After discussing the relationship between Klein's understanding of anxiety and Lacan's three varieties, we consider how love serves as antidote to anxiety for Klein whereas creativity and sublimation play a similar role for Lacan. The conversation closes with an analysis of the distinction between constitutive and circumstantial (context-specific) forms of lack or wounding in both Klein and Lacan.

Conversation 4 considers the relationship between Klein and Lacan in light of the recent rise of affect theory, which in some instances has come to be seen as a politically and collectively attuned alternative to the more subject-centered theories of psychoanalysis. While affect theorists have been inspired by Klein's account of reparation, they have tended to reject Lacan as a practitioner of paranoid critique. Our discussion calls into question the terms and limits of this debate. Allen suggests that Klein's view is more negativistic and therefore more inherently ambivalent than the picture of reparative scholarship that emerges from affect theory. Similarly, while acknowledging the valuable insights that have emerged from affect theory—particularly with respect to circumstantial forms of wounding—Ruti defends the Lacanian emphasis on the subject's constitutive lack-in-being, proposing that constitutive and context-specific forms of traumatization aren't mutually exclusive. Our conversation converges on the idea that critical theory needs a synthesis of Kleinian and Lacanian perspectives rather than an either/or choice.

Conversation 5 analyzes (mostly romantic) love, opening with the question of whether love can function as an antidote to aggression or anxiety. Ruti stresses that for Lacan love is a derailing—even a traumatizing—force, and that this feature of love, coupled with the subject's constitutive lack, explains why Lacan doesn't consider love as a feasible route to psychic integration and harmony. Allen in turn draws attention to the complexities of Klein's account of love, which is ambivalent to the core; this implies that complete integration and harmony are impossible for Klein as well. As a result, Klein and Lacan seem to converge on the idea that love is anything but harmonious insofar as it requires—in Kleinian terms—tolerating ambivalence and—in Lacanian terms—loving what is inadequate, wounded, or disorienting about the other. We argue that for both Klein and Lacan, the ambivalence of love is a function of the centrality and ineliminability of the death drive.

Conversation 6 tackles the relationship between lack, loss, and mourning on the one hand and creativity and sublimation on the other. We start with a discussion of Lacan's scathing but, in our opinion, uncharitable critique of Klein's understanding of sublimation. We note that, like Lacan, Klein believes that creativity is founded upon and made possible by loss. Moreover, although Klein herself tends to view the death drive in negative terms, some contemporary Kleinians have drawn closer to Lacan's argument regarding the death drive as essential for any act of creativity. Similarly, Hanna Segal's application of Kleinian insights to aesthetics opens up interesting connections to Lacan's understanding of creativity as involving the commingling of the signifier and the jouissance of the real. Drawing on Segal's work, we envision a Kleinian analogue to the Lacanian idea that creativity requires riding the death drive as close to the limit of subjective intelligibility as possible—that is, courting the possibility of psychosis—without being destroyed in the process. Although the sociopolitical implications of both Klein and Lacan are discussed throughout this book, our final conversation makes politics its primary theme. For Allen, the critical and political importance of psychoanalysis lies in its realistic theory of subjectivity, its ability to diagnose contemporary political realities, and its conception of resistance. At the same time, while Klein offers powerful insights into the first two of these topics, Ruti's presentation of Lacan—in particular of his conception of the real as a resource for resisting the demands of the hegemonic social order—suggests that his work provides more resources for the third. And yet, as we stress throughout this book, Klein and Lacan converge on the insistence that there's no definitive cure for the subject's aggressivity (Klein) or lack-in-being (Lacan). This idea has profound implications not only for how we envision the contours of human life but also for how critical theorists understand concepts such as progress and emancipation.

1

Subjectivity

MR: We agreed to start our conversations about Klein and Lacan with basic accounts of their versions of how the subject becomes a subject, how the human being becomes a human being. Because I've been more influenced by Lacan, my grasp of the Kleinian story is less precise than it could be. I would appreciate it if you could explain themes such as the body in bits and pieces, splitting, gradual ego integration, the paranoid-schizoid position, the depressive position, and so on.

AA: The core of Klein's understanding of subject formation consists of her account of the two positions: the paranoid-schizoid and the depressive positions. Perhaps the first thing to note about her theory is the language of positions itself. The term *position* is an alternative to concepts such as stages or phases of development, which means that the positions aren't stages that one passes through and leaves behind. Rather, they persist throughout life, and individuals can and do oscillate between them, particularly in times of stress. In other words, the term *position* refers to what Hanna Segal describes as a configuration of object relations, anxieties, and defenses that characterize the individual's entire lifespan.[1] Klein also mentions in several places that the two positions can blend into one another, so that there can be depressive anxieties in the paranoid-schizoid position, and vice versa, which implies that the distinction between them is really more conceptual or analytical than substantive.

Another point to make about the language of positions is that each of the positions is, for Klein, linked to a specific modality of psychological disturbance: the paranoid-schizoid position is connected to psychotic states or anxieties whereas the depressive position is connected to neurotic states or anxieties.[2] And that's interesting because in this sense Klein could be seen as offering an account of what Joel Whitebook, following Hans Loewald, calls the psychotic core of the psyche.[3] The idea is that there's an archaic core of the psyche that persists in all of us that's psychotic in character and that we might learn something about subjectivity by investigating this psychotic core. For Whitebook, the core is psychotic because the infant initially exists in a state of fusion or merger with its mother or other primary caregiver, so that there's no differentiation between self and object, and therefore no coherent or unified self. For reasons that we'll discuss later, I don't believe that Klein accepts this story about primordial fusion. But she does maintain that the core of the psyche is psychotic in the sense that in the paranoid-schizoid position one experiences one's objects and also one's self as unintegrated, incoherent, and split, and that, for her, is what psychosis means. This isn't to say that all children are psychotic, but it does explain why Klein claims that "every child will periodically exhibit psychotic phenomena."[4]

Two more specific ideas are important for understanding Klein's theory of positions. The first has to do with the primacy of aggression, or the death drive. Klein believes that the death drive is in operation from the beginning of life, and that the infant perceives this drive as a threat to its existence. In this respect, Klein took herself to be developing the ideas about the duality of the life and death drives explored in Freud's late work. She once said that she regarded Freud's late drive theory to be "a tremendous advance in the understanding of the mind."[5] But she also thinks that Freud didn't give enough weight to aggression and that he never sufficiently integrated his account of aggression into his overall theory, and that's something she's trying to do.

Unlike Freud, who didn't believe that there could be any content to the fear of death because we don't ever experience anything analogous to it, Klein held that there is from the very beginning of life an unconscious fear of death. This idea follows directly from her conviction that all drives have psychological correlates, which means that if there's a death drive operative from the get-go, it must have a psychological analogue. This psychological analogue, for Klein, is the fear of annihilation.[6] Klein believes that this points to a fundamental and ineliminable conflict between the life and death drives that, in turn, is the initial cause of anxiety. Moreover, since the conflict between the life and death drives is ineradicable, so too is anxiety. This is why anxiety is absolutely central to Klein's conception of the subject. For her, the primary job of the early ego—and for her there's a rudimentary, incoherent, and unintegrated ego in place from the beginning of life—is to try to master anxiety. In addition, mastering anxiety is, for Klein, the main psychological task of the adult as well, as well as the goal of psychoanalysis.

The second key idea to understanding the Kleinian positions is her conception of the object. For Klein, object relations are in place from the onset of life. The first object is the mother, specifically her breast. This way of talking obviously raises important worries about whether or not Klein endorses biological essentialism—a topic I know we'll discuss later. For now I want to emphasize that what's interesting about Klein's claim that object relations are present from the beginning of life is that it appears to entail a rejection not only of Freud's initial conception of primary narcissism—which supposed that the infant was initially in a state of self-sufficiency and only later came to relate to others—but also of his later conception of primary fusion with the mother (which, as I just mentioned, Whitebook accepts).[7] I know that we'll return to this theme as well. At this point, I merely want to say that Klein's rejection of the idea of primary fusion goes hand in hand with her claim that there exists a rudimentary ego from the beginning. Simply put, the infant can't be in a state of undifferentiated fusion, union, or merger because there's already an elementary ego in place that's relating to an object. So, for example, Klein says that "there is no instinctual urge, no anxiety situation, no mental process which does not involve objects, external or internal; in other words, object-relations are at the *centre* of emotional life."[8]

With all of this as background, we can turn to the paranoid-schizoid position, which is the starting point for subject formation for Klein. In this position, as a result of the internal operation of the death drive, the infant finds itself in a state of extreme anxiety. Klein calls this type of anxiety "persecutory anxiety," which consists of the fear of the annihilation of the ego that I alluded to a moment ago.[9] The early ego attempts to master this anxiety in two ways. First, it directs its aggression outward toward the primary object, which is the breast, for example by biting the breast, which Klein interprets as a matter of acting out a phantasy of devouring the breast. Second, it projects its aggression onto its primary object, which it then experiences as a persecutory entity with the power to annihilate it: it's now the object rather than the infant itself that becomes the site of aggression. Although this second strategy may seem counterintuitive, it helps the infant to master the anxiety caused by the death drive by getting rid of or expelling the badness and danger it feels inside itself by projecting it onto an external object. This has the effect of externalizing the internal operation of the death drive, and therefore of putting some distance between the death drive and the ego.

However, this projection also requires, for Klein, a splitting of the breast in order to protect the good breast, which is the object to which the infant is libidinally attached. Klein doesn't particularly stress this point—she puts more emphasis on the primacy of aggression—but aggression has to come together, even at the very beginning, with love or libidinal attachment because otherwise the primary object wouldn't be an object at all. As she puts it, "The power of love ... is there in the baby as well as the destructive forces, and finds its first fundamental expression in the baby's attachment to his mother's breast."[10] Thus, the infant is in a complicated and highly ambivalent situation. Its projection of the persecutory anxiety caused by the fear of annihilation—caused in turn by the operation of the death drive—onto the breast necessitates the splitting of the breast into good and bad parts. This activity of splitting is central to the paranoid-schizoid position. In the wake of this splitting, the good breast becomes the one that nourishes and loves the ego, gratifying its wishes for fulfillment, while the bad breast is the one that hates, attacks, and attempts to destroy it.

But the story is even more complicated than this because there are complex dynamics of projection and introjection involving both the good and the bad breast. As I mentioned, the infant projects its aggression onto the primary object, creating the bad breast, but it also projects its love and libidinal impulses outward, thereby creating the phantasy of the good or gratifying breast. At the same time, the infant *introjects* the good breast, which enables it to defend itself against its anxiety. In this way, the good breast becomes its internal protector, and comes to form the core of the developing ego, the entity around which the ego "expands and develops."[11] Yet the infant also introjects the bad breast, which then heightens its sense of danger and anxiety, because now the persecutory object is both outside and inside the ego. This means that the split object that's characteristic of the paranoid-schizoid position goes hand in hand with a split inside the ego. The result of this splitting is that the ego is disintegrated or incoherent—or, as Klein puts it, "in bits."[12]

The depressive position, which follows the paranoid-schizoid position, and which counters some of the extreme splitting of the latter, is, for Klein, in some sense a developmental achievement because it's marked by a greater integration of both the ego and of the primary object—though we'll have to talk more about what integration means for her because the matter is more complicated than one might assume. Also, as I've already stressed, Klein doesn't believe that it's ever entirely possible to transcend the paranoid-schizoid position, that it's part of the adult's psychic constitution as well. But for our present purposes, let me just say that the key moment in the transition from the paranoid-schizoid to the depressive position occurs when the mother is recognized as a whole object. At one point, Klein dates this transition to the moment when the infant first recognizes its mother, which happens early—at four or five months of age—and it would be interesting to contrast this claim with Lacan's account of the mirror stage, because for Klein this isn't just about recognizing the other but also about self-recognition: the infant's recognition of its mother as a whole object enables it to recognize itself as a coherent ego.

When the infant is able to recognize the mother as a whole object, it realizes that the object that it has been destroying in its phantasies is the same object that it also loves and depends on. This realization leads to what Klein calls depressive anxiety. Whereas persecutory anxiety results from the fear of the ego's annihilation, depressive anxiety is caused by the fear of the loss of the loved object, a fear that results from the way in which the ego has managed its persecutory anxiety by directing its aggression toward this very object. Consequently, Klein's depressive position is closely bound up with guilt, the fear of loss, mourning, and ultimately the drive for reparation, which is the urge to repair the damage that was done, whether in reality or in phantasy, to the object.

Many readers of Klein stop here, with her account of the depressive position as the hallmark of psychological maturity. But Klein actually talks a lot, particularly in her early work, about *working through* or *overcoming* the depressive position, which implies that for her there's something beyond the depressive position.[13] However, as far as I can tell, she never describes this beyond very precisely, nor does she ever give it a name or describe it as a new, third position. As a result, it's unclear what exactly it means for her to work through the depressive position.[14] But the way I've come to understand it is that it's basically an extension or a deepening of the basic features of the depressive position rather than something radically distinct from it. Working through the depressive position seems to involve moving from the initial experience of depressive anxiety to a greater tolerance of ambivalence, a more secure establishment of the whole object, and an increasing capacity for reparation.

All of this is to say that, for Klein, subject formation, if it goes well, enables the working through of the depressive position, which in turn involves both the secure internalization of the good object and the tolerance of the fundamental ambivalence of one's relationship to the object—that is, the acceptance of the fact that the loved object and the hated object are one and the same. One result of this process is that, as much as possible, one's relationship to one's internal objects corresponds more accurately to the actually existing external objects—parents or other primary caregivers—that are the basis for one's internalized introjections.[15] Klein's point in this context is that the superego is frequently much more cruel and aggressive than the parental figures on which it's based,[16] and that this disconnect between the excessively sadistic internalized objects and the actual objects on which they are based is also something to be worked through in the depressive position, with the aim of bringing one's internal and external objects more closely into alignment.

MR: That was extremely helpful. I'm intrigued by the idea that, for Klein, there might be something "beyond" the depressive position—even if this simply means that there must be a continuous working through of this position—because, you're right, critics usually stop at this position, as if reaching it meant that the task of becoming a viable subject had been accomplished. My hunch is that if there's a beyond of the depressive position, it might have something to do with creativity because working through is always a matter of creativity. And what you said about the capacity to tolerate anxiety and ambivalence also seems relevant to the idea that the depressive position might need to be continuously worked through.

Beyond this specific point, my initial impression is that so much of what you said about Klein makes sense from a Lacanian perspective that these two thinkers might not be as antithetical to each other as critics tend to presume. The notion of the psychotic core of the psyche seems extremely Lacanian, as does the primacy of the death drive and aggression, and even the idea that there's a relationship to the object from the very beginning. This last idea—that there's a relationship to the object from the onset of life—isn't something that most Lacanians place emphasis on, but I think that this relationship exists.

I'll return to this theme later. At this point I want to ask you about the idea that you glean from Klein that in adult subjects there's the possibility of reverting to the paranoid-schizoid or the depressive position. Does this mean—and here I'm trying to translate your statement into crudely concrete terms—that a person who is depressed, say, when she is thirty-five, is in some ways reliving the depressive position? Is adult depression a repetition of the depressive position?

AA: Yes, I think that's right. The idea is that any loss that we experience later in life is experienced as a loss only insofar as it reactivates the experience of loss in the depressive position. I also think that Klein's work poses a very real question about whether and to what extent we ever get out of the depressive position, and even about whether we should want to—which is of course just another way of posing the question of the beyond.

MR: That makes perfect sense. And again, it accords well with Lacan, who argues that every adult loss reactivates the originary loss—the loss of *das Ding* (the Thing)—experienced during language acquisition, which for Lacan is a significant part of subject formation. The obvious difference is that Klein's depressive position predates the Lacanian process of being wounded by language (the "loss" of the Thing).

AA: Right. For Klein, it's only to the extent that an adult loss reactivates a primary loss—which in turn is a function of the fact that the object that we have lost has in some way reactivated some aspect of our relationship to the primary object—that it's experienced as a loss in the first place and therefore as something that needs to be worked through. I think you could definitely make connections here to Lacan's account of *das Ding*.

MR: Yes. You lose *das Ding*—or more precisely, you fantasize about having lost *das Ding*—and then every subsequent loss is in some ways a repetition of that primary loss, which means that you're working through that loss with every additional loss you experience. I would in fact go as far as to say that the Lacanian subject is intrinsically melancholic, because it's born from a loss that can never be redeemed for the simple reason that it only exists as a retroactive fantasy. This points to the possibility that subjectivity is a matter of constantly working through melancholia, which doesn't seem very different from positing that being a subject is a matter of a continuous working through of the depressive position.

AA: That's great. But what might drive a wedge between Klein and Lacan are their divergent attitudes toward the ego. Lacan is extremely critical of Klein's position on the ego, and much of that disagreement appears to stem from the fact that Klein maintains that the aim of analysis is to integrate and strengthen the ego. For example, she describes the goal of analysis as follows:

> In analysis we should make our way slowly and gradually towards the painful insight into the divisions in the patient's self. This means that the destructive sides are again and again split off and regained, until greater integration comes about. As a result, the feeling of responsibility becomes stronger, and guilt and depression are more fully experienced. When this happens, the ego is strengthened, omnipotence of destructive impulses is diminished ... and the capacity for love and gratitude, stifled in the course of splitting processes, is released. ... By helping the patient to achieve a better integration of his self, [analysis] aims at a mitigation of hatred by love.[17]

MR: It's true that the last thing Lacan wants is an integrated ego. But the quotation you just read implies that what Klein understands by ego integration is so complicated that it might bypass at least some of Lacan's qualms. Lacan despises the notion of strengthening the ego. But I don't get the sense from Klein's statement that strengthening the ego is, for her, a straightforward procedure. Can you explain the matter more fully?

AA: You're right that it's important to keep in mind what Klein does and does not mean when she talks about strengthening the ego.

Lacan frequently criticizes ego psychologists for believing that the ego needs to strengthen its defenses against the id and, moreover, to enlist the help of the superego to accomplish this task. This type of ego strength isn't what Klein has in mind. For her, strengthening the ego means enhancing its capacity for integration. And crucially, this doesn't mean resolving all intrapsychic tension or diminishing the influence of the unconscious or of the drives. Rather, it means being able to tolerate the existence of conflictual drive impulses without resorting to splitting and manic defenses. In other words, strengthening the ego isn't about establishing rational mastery or internal dominance, but rather about developing a greater tolerance for ambivalence. And as the passage I just pointed to makes clear, it's also about love: love and the drive for reparation as forces that can ameliorate the effects of primary aggression. But here again I want to emphasize that this doesn't mean overcoming primary aggression—Klein doesn't think that this is possible, though she does think that there are better and worse ways of managing aggression. If it were possible to get rid of primary aggression, it would make no sense to talk about the depressive position as a matter of tolerating ambivalence. Ultimately, for Klein, strengthening the ego is about developing a richer, more expansive, more heterogeneous, and more internally differentiated ego, and she also says quite explicitly that this is a process that's never complete, that complete integration is impossible.

Klein's view reminds me of what Whitebook describes as Freud's unofficial position on the ego.[18] For Whitebook, Freud's official position is the rationalist view according to which the ego attempts to become the master of its own house by repressing or controlling the drives. On this picture, which is more or less the view of ego psychology, the goal of the ego is to accomplish what the early Frankfurt School liked (critically) to call the domination of inner nature by enlisting the help of the superego in bringing the id to heel. But, according to Whitebook, Freud's unofficial position measures the ego's strength by its capacity for "expansion, greater integration, and differentiation of its associative web."[19]

Crucially, this approach takes seriously the role of the unconscious in psychoanalysis. As Whitebook explains, this process of integrating the ego involves the preservation of unconscious material and the synthesis of this material into "larger and more differentiated unities."[20] It's a matter of augmenting the subject's whole personality. Although Whitebook doesn't mention Klein as someone who develops this unofficial position—his primary point of reference is Hans Loewald—I would argue that Klein could be seen as the first analyst after Freud to develop it. And more importantly for our conversation, this conception of the ego doesn't sound at all like the imaginary ego that Lacan attacks for its narcissism and inauthenticity. Rather, it sounds like an ego that's able to increasingly incorporate previously split off unconscious content and also to tolerate the ambivalence that inevitably results from this incorporation.

MR: This is helpful because I do think that Lacan criticizes a different version of ego psychology and/or object relations—and I realize that these aren't the same thing—from the Kleinian model you have just explained. In order to explicate his objections to strengthening the ego, I'll need to briefly outline his theory of subject formation.

In the Lacanian narrative, we're obviously dealing with the trinity of the symbolic, the imaginary, and the real. There's a link to Klein in the sense that even though the Lacanian developmental trajectory on some level seems to run from the real (jouissance) through the imaginary (the mirror stage) to the symbolic (language), Lacan emphasizes that all three of these registers remain an important part of the adult subject's psychic constitution. In other words, like the paranoid-schizoid and depressive positions, they are positions that you can slip in and out of. For example, when you have sex—if it's good sex—the real (jouissance) dominates; when you fall in love, you tend to slide into the imaginary, looking in the beloved person for a mirror for your narcissism; when you give a lecture, you're mostly in the symbolic register.

In this narrative you start with an immersion in the real in the sense that you don't have a sense of yourself as a "subject," defined in the technical Lacanian sense: there isn't yet a subject of discourse or a subject of the unconscious; there's just bodily being (jouissance). But this doesn't mean that there's a symbiotic fusion with the primary caretaker, or some kind of an originary "plenitude," as some Lacanians—and plenty of non-Lacanians—claim. It's true that, in Lacanian theory, there's no ego before the mirror stage. But in *Seminar I* Lacan emphasizes that intersubjectivity exists from the very beginning of life, that there's a *rudimentary* recognition of the other as a separate entity even before the mirror stage and the intervention of the signifier.[21]

To be sure, Lacan suggests that the child doesn't have the capacity to clearly distinguish between itself and the world, that in some ways it *is* the world. If this weren't the case, the cut of the signifier that transforms the child into a speaking subject wouldn't be experienced as traumatizing, wouldn't engender the sense of lack that, for Lacan, emerges as a consequence of language acquisition. Nevertheless, I wouldn't characterize the matter in terms of being fused with the caretaker, particularly not in any naturalistic terms, for reasons that I'll explain tomorrow.

For now, acknowledging that, even in the Lacanian model, there's a rudimentary sense of intersubjectivity in the prelinguistic child is important because without this acknowledgment, his theory of the mirror stage doesn't fully cohere. You already alluded to the possibility that there may be a loose parallel between the Lacanian mirror stage and Klein's depiction of the child's early relationship with its primary caretaker. I agree, and here's why: the caretaker—or the object relation (which, for Lacan, is always mediated by the symbolic order, the big Other)—is part of the mirror stage. Yes, the mirror stage has to do with the child's (mis)recognition of its own image: it's when the elementary (still prelinguistic) ego begins to form, which means that it's also when narcissism begins to emerge; in this sense, the mirror stage *is* a stepping stone from the real to the symbolic. But this trajectory can only work if the object relation mediated by the symbolic is in the mix from the beginning.

This is because what's important about the mirror stage isn't just that the infant (mis)recognizes itself in the mirror—that it has the excited, jubilatory realization that the image, the perfect "statue" in the mirror, is "me." What's equally important is the triangulation between the mirror, the emerging "me," and the caretaker who is holding the child up to the mirror. In other words, the mirror stage isn't merely about the child recognizing its image in the mirror; what's equally significant is that the caretaker—through smiles, gestures, cooing sounds, or words—*approves* of the image that the child sees.

In *Seminar X*, Lacan describes how the child tends to turn to whoever is holding it up to the mirror, the implication being that the child is asking this person to recognize its image as desirable. It's worth quoting Lacan on this because it's common for critics to get fixated on Lacan's much more solipsistic-sounding earlier essay on the mirror stage:

> Already, just in the exemplary little image with which the demonstration of the mirror stage begins, the moment that is said to be jubilatory when the child, grasping himself in the inaugural experience of recognition in the mirror, comes to terms with himself as a totality functioning as such in his specular image, haven't I always insisted on the movement that the infant makes? This movement is so frequent, constant I'd say, that each and every one of you may have some recollection of it. Namely, he turns round, I noted, to the one supporting him who's there behind him. If we force ourselves to assume the content of the infant's experience and to reconstruct the sense of this movement, we shall say that, with this nutating movement of the head, which turns towards the adult as if to call upon his assent, and then back to the image, he seems to be asking the one supporting him, and who here represents the big Other, to ratify the value of this image.[22]

The inauguration of the child's fantasmatic, narcissistic relationship to its image is therefore intrinsically tied to the presence of a symbolically mediated object relation: the big Other has already entered the picture. This in turn means that—contra to the idea that there's no intersubjectivity prior to language acquisition in Lacan— there *has* to be some elementary comprehension of the distinction between self and other and perhaps even of communication. After all, the child doesn't need to be able to speak in order to be embedded in the symbolic order; if anything, the child's reality—including its bodily reality—is symbolically mediated from the get-go. This is also a topic I'll talk about more tomorrow.

The dynamic of triangulation in the mirror stage implies that if the other doesn't give the recognition that the child seeks, if the other communicates that the child's image is unacceptable, is a bad image, it's difficult for narcissism to emerge. Indeed, you could jump from this idea that the mirror stage doesn't invariably grant narcissistic satisfaction to Frantz Fanon's analysis of what it means to be a subject in a racist world that doesn't recognize you as a desirable subject. In this scenario, the image that stares at you from the mirror is one that those around you don't view as valuable, and

Fanon is brilliant at expressing what this does to your ego: you're literally shattered.[23] Toni Morrison depicts the same scenario in *The Bluest Eye*, which is a story of how a little black girl is destroyed—to the point of becoming psychotic—in part because the surrounding world doesn't recognize her image as desirable.[24] My point is that social inequalities can impede the development of "healthy" narcissism by signaling to the emerging (or even adult) subject that something is wrong with its image. I'm not here following Lacan faithfully because he tends to be critical of all forms of narcissism. But I think that my commentary is a feasible extension of his theory of the mirror stage.

Another important point about the mirror stage is that it's also an embryonic state of lack: it's already a moment of alienation in the sense that the child doesn't realize that the image in the mirror isn't an accurate representation of its ontological, physical, psychic, and affective reality. I've already signaled this by using the word *misrecognition*, as Lacan also does: the moment of self-recognition is always also a moment of self-misrecognition. As you know, Lacan proposes that the child perceives its image as being more perfect than its reality is, with the result that it's immediately alienated from its "being." I've always read this as the first intimation of lack that emerges in Lacan's theory of subject formation. It's not yet the lack that's introduced by the signifier, by language. But it's nevertheless lack in a nascent sense.

In *Seminar II*, Lacan mentions that in the mirror stage there's a (narcissistic) desire for a pleasing image of the self. Logically, this means that there must already be a sense of lack because, from a Lacanian perspective, there can be no desire without lack. Deleuzians would disagree. But for Lacan desire cannot be dissociated from lack. So in the mirror stage there's an alienation that's already a lack of sorts.

After the mirror stage comes language acquisition, which introduces the notorious Lacanian lack-in-being: the price that all of us pay to enter the symbolic order as socially intelligible (albeit neurotic) creatures. And language—as Žižek likes to remind us—"murders" the Thing, the originary (non)object.[25] The result is full-blown desire: the desire to fill the void left by this originary object, which is always a fantasy object in the sense that it never existed. As I suggested in the context of claiming that the Lacanian subject is intrinsically melancholic, the subject merely retroactively imagines having lost an irreplaceable object. But this doesn't change the fact that the desire to recover this object turns the subject outward, toward things other than the self, including other people, who might be used to plug the hole left by the loss of the Thing. In other words, the fantasy of having lost the Thing generates an attempt to regain the wholeness that the subject (falsely) imagines that the Thing provided. From this viewpoint, one of the tragedies of human life is that we (at least many of us) spend our entire lives striving to regain something that we never in reality had to begin with. We move from one object to the next—or to use Lacan's vocabulary, from one *objet a* to the next—in an attempt to fill the gap within our being, but our quest will never be fulfilled because the Thing is a retroactive fiction.

Let me round up this overview by returning to Lacan's critique of ego psychology and certain versions of object-relations theory: for him, the problem is that these psychoanalytic approaches don't seem to recognize what for him is elementary, namely—and you nailed this issue at the beginning of our conversation today—that the ego is imaginary, a misleading narcissistic illusion. Moreover, he believes that the ego keeps unconscious discourse from making its way into consciousness, thereby impeding the emergence of the subject in the proper psychoanalytic sense. For Lacan, the subject isn't the human being walking around; the subject isn't the individual. Rather, the subject is a creature of the unconscious who speaks the discourse of the unconscious, and for Lacan the ego represents a resistance to this discourse, represents a defense against what he calls the "truth of desire."

We know that Freud said that "where id was, there ego shall be."[26] I think that Lacan recognizes that for the subject to come into being, some of id (jouissance) must be replaced by the ego. But he's also faithful to Freud's recognition that the ego (and particularly the superego, which in some ways is an offshoot of the ego) can become too dictatorial, thereby blocking the unconscious. And for a psychoanalyst, nothing is worse than blocking the unconscious, right? As a consequence, if the excessively strong ego is what, even for Freud, blocks the unconscious, you can understand why Lacan goes after the ego with a vengeance. For him, the ego is the enemy of the subject of the unconscious and therefore of psychoanalysis as a clinical practice: when the analysand's ego gets in the way, the analysis goes nowhere. This is why one of Lacan's objectives as an analyst was to weaken the ego. He thought that this was the only way to get the unconscious to speak.

In *Seminar II*, Lacan maintains that the objective of analysis is to ensure that the analysand no longer relates to the analyst—who can represent the big Other—on the level of the imaginary ego, expecting the analyst's ego to offer it support, to strengthen it, but rather as a subject of discourse; the aim of analysis is to dissolve the resistances of the ego so that this ego—profoundly altered (weakened) by the analytic process—can eventually get "to the point where the subject is."[27] Only in this way can "the fundamental discourse"[28]—the discourse of the unconscious, meaning the "truth" of the subject—find its way into consciousness. So rather than saying where id was, there ego shall be, it's almost like Lacan is saying, where the ego was, *the subject* shall be.

AA: So Freud's dictum "where id was, there ego shall be," on this interpretation, doesn't mean bringing the id under the domination of the ego; it means dethroning the ego to the point where it merges with the id?

MR: It's more like the ego is burned off so that the subject of discourse—the subject of lack, of the unconscious—can come into existence. If you allow me to use Kleinian vocabulary that would probably have driven Lacan nuts, the problem with the ego for Lacan is that it splits the good from the bad. This splitting is just done differently from what Klein is talking about: the ego simply denies the bad by pretending that everything is hunky-dory. To express the matter differently, Lacan believes that the ego is purely libidinal. As he states, "Libido and the ego are on the same side."[29] In other words, the narcissism of the ego disavows the death drive, which means that the subject who leans on its ego for support is deluding itself about the ambivalences of life. Lacan doesn't talk about the integration of the person. Nevertheless, I would suggest that, through his critique of the ego, he's approaching a notion of subjective enrichment that includes the ability to cope with the derailment introduced by the death drive.

I'm the first to admit that Lacan's vehement critique of the ego can come across as extreme, particularly as there are many people who don't have much ego strength to begin with, whose egos have been squashed in the manner that Fanon and Morrison describe.

However, in the background of his critique of the ego hovers a subject who no longer splits the good from the bad but instead accepts that life is composed of both light and shadow. In addition, he believes that the ego intervenes in the analytic process, which is why he believes that the biggest mistake an analyst can make is to strengthen it.

AA: Interestingly, but perhaps not surprisingly, Klein restates Freud's famous dictum as well, but she interprets it as pointing toward the claim that "the ultimate aim of psycho-analysis is the integration of the patient's personality."[30] As I've stressed, for Klein this means incorporating more and more unconscious content into a richer, more internally differentiated, and more expansive ego that can tolerate the ineliminable ambivalence that results from the duality of the drives. Although this is a long way from how Lacan reads Freud's dictum, I think that it's also quite distinct from the approach of ego psychology, which aims to strengthen the ego at the *expense* of the unconscious.

MR: It sounds like one difference between Klein and Lacan on this issue is that, for Klein, the enrichment of personality takes place on the level of the ego whereas, for Lacan, it takes place on the level of the subject of the unconscious. From a Lacanian point of view, subjective enrichment could be thought of as a matter of being able to tolerate the derailment that's introduced by the death drive, by jouissance. In this sense, like Klein, he has a notion of being able to cope with ambiguity, anxiety, and conflict. His vocabulary is different from Klein's, and I think that his emphasis lies more strongly on disintegration than integration. By this I don't mean that his *goal* is disintegration—subjective destitution—but merely that he takes it for granted that the subject is always to some degree disintegrated and needs to find a way to live with this reality.

AA: That's interesting. Can I ask you about the nature of defense in the Lacanian paradigm? You said that for Lacan the ego is a defense against the unconscious, which means that strengthening the ego amounts to strengthening the defense. This leads me to wonder how Lacan understands the idea of defense. Does he conceptualize it primarily in terms of repression? I ask because one of the fascinating features of Klein's account is her rich description of different kinds of defenses that are even more primordial than repression. To be sure, repression plays a role in her account, but it arrives on the scene relatively late, after splitting, manic defenses, idealization, projection, introjection, and projective identification—this whole complicated repertoire of defenses that I think aren't meant to *replace* the notion of repression but rather to supplement it.[31] Of course Klein still believes that repression exists and that it's an important form of defense, but she insists that these other kinds of defenses must be analyzed as well, because they too can be impediments to analysis and to psychological well-being.

One could say that, as the ego is for Lacan, for Klein defenses are an impediment to accessing and understanding the discourse of the unconscious, which Klein clearly states is the main task of psychoanalysis.[32] For Klein, the interpretation of defenses as they present themselves in analysis is part and parcel of analyzing transference. And if they are more primordial than repression, analysis needs to work on them before it can get to something like what Lacan's after.

In this context, it seems pertinent to remember that even though Klein follows the classic Freudian model of psychosexual development, she deviates from this account in one important respect, having to do with the Oedipus complex: Klein argues that the Oedipus complex starts much earlier than Freud thought and that, as a result, there's a rudimentary superego in place in very young children, even as early as the age of two. If one is willing to accept the Freudian account of the superego, Klein's insight seems like a genuine innovation, because it posits that the mental life of young children is much more complicated, and that the complications emerge much earlier, than Freud believed.

MR: I'm impressed that Klein was able to focus on the early developmental phases of young infants. She seemed to get a lot of wonderful material from the child analyses she undertook. This prelinguistic part is much less developed in Lacan. I'm not saying that, for Lacan, there's nothing before language acquisition: as I just explained, there's, for instance, a great deal going on during the mirror stage. It's just that, for Lacan, what comes before the subject of discourse is largely indescribable. We can try to capture something about the prelinguistic child theoretically or speculatively, to talk about the real, the mirror stage, ego formation, and so on, but really, we don't know what went on there; we don't have unmediated access to these early formative experiences. Klein in contrast relied on empirical observation to gain insight into these early developmental stages.

Kristeva has in some ways followed in Klein's footsteps, not in the sense of observing infants but in the sense of listening closely to what exceeds the strictly verbal—for instance, the silences that punctuate speech and the melodies, or distinctive cadences, of discourse—in adult patients. She has always wanted to resurrect the prelinguistic. Furthermore, both Klein and Kristeva privilege the mother-child relationship over Freud's Oedipal story. The dangers of essentialization are obvious in this choice. At the same time, there's something to be said for getting away from the Oedipal father.

AA: I agree. It was a tremendously significant moment in the development of psychoanalysis when female analysts began to focus on the pre-Oedipal mother-infant relationship. Klein was one of the first to make this move. This was important for challenging the phallocentric nature of psychoanalytic theory, and Klein paved the way for theorists like Kristeva, for whom the focus on the maternal body would come to be associated with (a certain version of) feminism.

MR: You're absolutely right. And I love the way that you, a moment ago, explained the possibility of various primordial forms of defense. I think that it would be a mistake to fault Klein for not having the same knee-jerk reaction to the ego as Lacan: you have explained convincingly that for Klein the ego's integration is a matter of being able to cope with ambivalence, anxiety, and conflict rather than an attempt to shore up mastery over the unconscious. From this vantage point, Klein's objective is the same as Lacan's: to dissolve the defenses that get in the way of the discourse of the unconscious. Klein just assumes that some of these defenses are more primordial than repression. I'm willing to accept that.

That said, I think that Lacan's antipathy toward the ego isn't just about repression. It also has to do with the possibility that the subject might be overtaken by self-aggrandizing fantasies. As I've noted, Lacan connects the ego to the mirror stage—the idea being that the inception of the ego takes place during the mirror stage—and the obvious problem, as I've established, is that the mirror stage, at least under certain conditions, can give the subject a narcissistic and overly grandiose self-understanding, a self-understanding that's arrogant and too masterful.

I know that you yourself have written extensively about the problematic of the arrogant subject, particularly in *The End of Progress*.[33] So it might help to remember that Lacan was writing in the post-World War II period when critics, including the early Frankfurt School scholars who have been so central to your thinking, were drawing a link between the subject's quest for mastery and systemic social violence. This was the post–Nazi Germany, postcolonial moment when critics were starting to connect the arrogant, autonomous Enlightenment subject to the havoc that had been wreaked across the globe by Westerners who thought that they were the masters of the universe.

This is to say that I think that it's important to situate Lacan within the philosophical tradition that he was working with. He was going after the metaphysical notion of the sovereign subject, which—and I think we agree on this—was a legitimate target. In France, Lacan was in fact among the first—along with Levinas, whose approach was entirely different—to do so, and then Derrida, Lyotard, Barthes, Irigaray, Kristeva, and the rest of the French thinkers of that generation followed suit.

Klein's notion of the integrated ego—now that I understand it better—sounds entirely different from the autonomous Enlightenment self. It in fact sounds fairly similar to what I have attempted to articulate in my writing for a long time. I've tried to convince scholars in my field that there's a difference between the hubris-filled subject of Western metaphysics on the one hand and a subject who possesses a degree of cohesiveness and the ability to tolerate ambivalence, ambiguity, and conflict on the other; I've tried to say that even if we're critical of excessive autonomy, it's pointless to pretend that any of us can function in the world without a degree of psychic integration.

Many scholars in my field who criticize the autonomous subject seem to want to destroy "the subject" as such. I think that this is a theoretical (and ethical and political) dead end because it renders human subjectivity—including relationality—completely unviable. There's no way that we can live as completely fragmented creatures, unless we're willing to step into psychosis. Equally importantly, few of us, not even the critics who are writing tomes on the destruction of the subject, *want* to live like that. This is why I've proposed that we need to distinguish between the masterful subject that Western metaphysics constructed—and launched into the world—on the one hand and, on the other, an alternative modality of subjectivity that bypasses the sins of the metaphysical construct without thereby getting ground to dust. Unfortunately, many critics seem unwilling to accept that this distinction can be made, with the result that they promote a stark either-or choice between a fully autonomous subject and the complete pulverization of the subject. The latter is usually (theoretically) accomplished through the valorization of the death drive, schizophrenia, or madness: Deleuze, Guattari, Edelman, Huffer[34]—whoever you choose—all advocate the same radical notion of desubjectivation. It sounds like Klein is giving us something to work with in the middle, which I very much appreciate.

AA: I couldn't agree with you more about the problems that arise from the complete rejection of the subject; this is a theme that I've written about in connection with various (in my view, mis-) readings of Foucault.[35] And I agree that Klein offers a conception of subjectivity that occupies a productive middle ground between the rational, autonomous, and transcendental subject of Western metaphysics and the embrace of a radical desubjectivation. I also think that your contextualization of Lacan in terms of his relationship to the Western philosophical tradition is helpful and points to an obvious difference between him and Klein. Although Klein certainly knew her Freud,[36] she wasn't trained in the philosophical tradition—in fact she didn't even have a university degree!—and so she wasn't explicitly attempting to situate herself in relation to it.

MR: That makes perfect sense. I guess the insight to draw from Lacan's immersion in the history of Western philosophy is that his aversion toward the ego can be traced to a political impulse. He connects the masterful metaphysical subject to the imaginary fantasies of the mirror stage, which is one reason—certainly not the only reason but one reason—that he tries to force the subject to admit its lack, its castration. Simply put, he wants to replace the ego-driven, narcissistic subject with a humbled, castrated one.

"Castration," for Lacan, is in many ways synonymous with the subject's lack-in-being, and he universalizes the concept so that it isn't gender-specific: men are just as "castrated" as women are. The ego represents an attempt to deny this fundamental reality. This is why the objective of analysis, for Lacan, is to get the analysand to a point where they can cope with their castration, where they will no longer hide behind grandiose fantasies to deny their lack and vulnerability, including the derailment introduced by the death drive, by jouissance.

Lacan also refers to the subject's "fundamental fantasy," which he claims is unanalyzable. The subject can't access its fundamental fantasy, yet this fantasy constitutes the essence of its being, and particularly the core of its pathology. It has to do with the subject's most deep-seated unconscious understanding of its relationship to the world, including other people, which is why—insofar as it finds expression through the repetition compulsion—it determines the subject's destiny. Another way to express the matter is to say that the fundamental fantasy guides the contours of the subject's jouissance. In *Seminar XXIII*, Lacan calls this enigmatic core of the subject's being the *sinthome*. This is a neologism for the kind of symptom that can't be dissolved by analysis.

In this manner, Lacan acknowledges that there's something on the level of fantasy that the subject *can't* get rid of, but for the most part his goal is to banish fantasy formations because he believes that they feed the subject's grandiose (imaginary) self-understanding. This is why he despises ego psychology's attempts to prop up the ego. Basically, he's saying, "All you're doing is turning the individual into an even more arrogant person—one who thinks that they can master not only themselves but also the rest of the world." However, by now I understand that this isn't what Klein is striving to do when she talks about integrating the ego.

AA: That's helpful and brings up other topics to discuss. One of these concerns Klein's conception of phantasy, which may be significantly different from Lacan's notion of fantasy. For Klein, phantasy—spelled with a "ph" in order to indicate that it's unconscious and thus distinct from our everyday understanding of fantasy—is the psychical representative or mental expression of the drive.[37] So if there are drives operating from the beginning of life, as she maintains, there must also be phantasies from the beginning of life. This means that her account of the infant's experience is an account of the structure of its most basic phantasies—which,

I think, helps make this account sound more plausible than it otherwise might be. For example, her famous concept of the good breast—which can sound ridiculous when you first come across it—doesn't refer simply to the body part that the infant encounters but rather to the crude phantasy of a part-object that arises out of the infant's experience of having its hunger satisfied. In other words, the infant imbues the breast "with qualities going far beyond the actual nourishment it affords."[38]

On Klein's account, phantasy distorts our perception of reality, of the flesh and blood others with whom we interact, yet it isn't possible to get beyond phantasy, to interact with others in a way that isn't filtered through our own phantasy life (or for them to interact with us in a way that isn't also similarly filtered). However, as I've indicated, Klein believes that we can and should strive to bring our unconscious phantasy life, or the way that we relate to our internal objects, more in line with the actual others on whom those internal objects are based. But these two poles can never completely converge because we're always going to experience our relations with others—and with ourselves and even with our own bodies—through the lens of unconscious phantasy.

This point is important because if one reads Klein in too naturalistic or crudely empiricist a way, one can be tempted to react to all her talk about good and bad breasts, devouring and scooping out, and the rest of it by saying, "This is the most wildly outlandish description of infantile experience imaginable; why on earth would anyone ever accept it?" Downplaying the centrality of phantasy in her work makes it too easy to dismiss her ideas as overly speculative—which many people, including some critical theorists, unfortunately do.

MR: I think that Lacan would concur that there's no way to relate to the world or other people (or even oneself) beyond the distortions of fantasy, that fantasy is inevitably going to be in the mix. Partly this is because of the fundamental fantasy, which regulates the subject's entire trajectory in life—regulates, precisely, how it relates to the world and others. This is why I said that it's linked to the subject's "destiny" through the repetition compulsion. But partly there's no beyond of fantasy in Lacan because he's realistic about the impossibility of ever banishing all of the subject's narcissistic fantasies. Nevertheless, he appears to have a degree of faith in the idea that one can loosen narcissistic fantasy formations through analysis.

Lacan's outlook is more drastic than Klein's. When you say that Klein's objective is to ensure that we bring our unconscious phantasy life, or the way we relate to our internal objects, more in line with the real-life others on whom these internal objects are based, Lacan might say, "Accept that there's no cure for your lack-in-being, your self-division, that you're a speck of dust, *nothing*, and stop expecting others to live up to your ridiculous fantasies."

AA: I agree that there's potentially an important difference here, but I would say that it points to one of the things that I find most productive about Klein's work—namely, her attempt to stake out some kind of a middle position between an intersubjective and an intrapsychic conception of the subject's development.

The term *intersubjective* is indicative of Klein's emphasis on the infant's real relations with other people, most importantly its primary caregiver. Klein maintains that the caregiver's love and responsiveness to the infant's needs enable it to internalize the good object and begin the transition to the depressive position. From the intrapsychic side, Klein endorses the basic Freudian idea of the centrality of psychic reality, and her account of phantasy presupposes that our relations with other subjects—going all the way back to the infant's early relationship with its primary object—are inescapably filtered through our internal world.

What makes Klein's work productive for critical theory is her conviction that the intersubjective and the intrapsychic take place simultaneously and interact with each other. From a Kleinian perspective, the subject is intersubjectively and socially constituted—which is also a central tenet of Frankfurt School critical social theory that can be traced to the influence of Hegel and Marx on this tradition—but the intersubjective and social are always mediated through intrapsychic unconscious phantasy and therefore, ultimately, through the drives. This makes Klein's account of intersubjectivity more complex and ambivalent than other social accounts of the self that reject the notion of the drives and consequently tend to view the self as intersubjectively constituted all the way down.

Still, for Klein, the infant's actual relationships with the people who are the basis for its internalized phantasy objects make a difference in whether it's able to move from the paranoid-schizoid position to the depressive position or to work through the depressive position. For example, experiences of having been neglected—or as she might say, frustrated at the breast—impact the infant's psychological development. But even as they *condition* the course of this development, they don't *determine* it. In addition, Klein believes that certain *constitutional* factors, such as the level of innate aggressivity, and therefore anxiety, that the child is born with, play a role. It's a complicated story but one of the things that I find productive about her view is that it brings these two dimensions—the intersubjective and the intrapsychic—together. And the notion of phantasy could be understood as what bridges these dimensions.

MR: That's interesting because my first impulse is to say that, for Lacan, things are the opposite, that it's the social (the symbolic) that mediates the subject's psychic experience and even the jouissance of the body, the drives. But it doesn't sound like you (or Klein) would deny this, given that you just said that the child's ability to move from the paranoid-schizoid position to the depressive position depends on its relationships with others—that is, on sociosymbolic factors.

More importantly, I think that I understand what you're saying: for Klein, phantasy is what connects the intersubjective and the intrapsychic. I don't think that Lacan would deny the importance of either, though instead of intersubjectivity, he might be more likely to talk about the symbolic order or the *objet a* as a partial object. But what's essential to remember is that, for Lacan, at the beginning there's always the word: the signifier. This is why the intrapsychic—or the notion of inborn drives—as a constitutional factor that's beyond the reach of the symbolic order or biopolitical conditioning is a hard concept to integrate into Lacanian theory.

I'll return to this issue tomorrow. For now, I'll simply say that the way you explained the two dimensions—the intersubjective and the intrapsychic—is reassuring. Segal is similarly reassuring in her summary of Kleinian theory. I admit that when I first started reading Klein, I felt that she implied that those who haven't been well mothered will find it impossible to ever form good object relations as adults. Her theory felt deterministic and dispiriting. But the more I read Klein—and understood Klein through Segal—the more I understood that she believes that although early experiences may condition later experiences, they don't determine them, that there may be a way out after all, which analysis is of course supposed to offer.

I also learned that there may be other ways out besides analysis, such as creative activities. For example, Klein suggests that people who have had horrible formative experiences can sometimes end up more or less fine; even extreme traumatization might not impact them irrevocably.[39] I appreciate this idea. But I admit that arguments about constitutional factors, such as innate aggression and anxiety, make the constructivist in me nervous. I guess that the Lacanian rejoinder to such arguments would be that it's impossible to dissociate even the infant's earliest psychic experiences from the larger social context—the symbolic order—that it's born into. This is the case even if we accept the primacy of the mother-child bond (which I personally have trouble with but this is beside the point here), because the mother, as an independent subject in her own right, has been shaped by myriad sociohistorical, cultural, and political factors. So even if the child primarily interacts with its mother, it's also automatically accessing the larger context through her; the mother doesn't care for the child in a social vacuum.

AA: I understand your hesitation about constitutional factors, though I confess that after having parented two children (out of four) who seem to have been born with a tendency for high levels of anxiety, I find myself open to the idea that there are some constitutional factors at play, even as I agree that it would be a mistake to assume that *only* constitutional factors are relevant, or— and this seems to me to be the corollary view—that everything can be solved by psychopharmacology.

But you're right that Klein doesn't believe that how you were parented or "mothered" entirely determines whether or not you will be able to have successful object relations. This is precisely because she adheres to drive theory more faithfully than later object-relations theorists, such as Winnicott. For her, the subject's development depends on a complicated interaction of constitutional, environmental, and relational factors, as well as on how these factors are mediated through or formative of its unconscious. Klein was well aware that some people who have undergone significant traumas do just fine, while others who, as far as we can tell, haven't undergone such trauma, are severely disturbed.

This is also where analysis becomes important: even if you haven't been able to internalize your good object—whether due to early deprivation or neglect or some other reason—all hope is not lost because analysis is supposed to help you to rectify this. The analyst's love and care for the analysand—and, to pick up an idea developed more in post-Kleinian theory, the analyst's ability to contain the analysand's fragmented and conflicted emotions without resorting to splitting[40]—enable the analysand to securely internalize a good object, which in turn can help them to attain and work through the depressive position. This means that for Klein transference is absolutely key to analytic technique.

In this context, let me return to Lacan's critique of the ego: one thing that struck me in reading *Seminar II* is that he talks a lot about how the problem with both ego psychology and object-relations theory—and I agree that he tends to run the two together in a way that's misleading—is that ultimately they just give the ego of the analyst to the analysand. In other words, the problem isn't only that they aim to strengthen the ego—though, as we discussed earlier, Klein doesn't do this in the same way as ego psychology— but also that, in their attempt to do so, they perform a projection of the analyst's narcissism onto the analysand.

This definitely isn't the goal of analysis for Klein. Yes, the analyst is supposed to help the analysand to attain the depressive position through the internalization of the good object. But this can't be the whole story, given that the analyst can't be equated with the good object, which is after all a part-object that's experienced as good through the mechanism of splitting. Recall that one of the aims of analysis is to overcome this type of splitting, that reaching the depressive position is supposed to allow the subject to experience the object as a whole object who contains both good and bad aspects and whom it both loves and hates. As a result, the analyst shouldn't remain a part-object, which in turn means that they can't be all good: the bad must come with the good. In addition, the analyst is a person who has developed the ability to tolerate ambivalence in themselves and others. So what the analyst is giving the analysand isn't themselves but rather a relationship of love and support and gratification that can enable the analysand to tolerate their own ambivalence. This seems different from the analyst narcissistically projecting their ego onto the analysand.

MR: I keep thinking that there's a parallel between Klein's idea that analysis is supposed to enable the analysand to cope with ambivalence, anxiety, and conflict and Lacan's idea—which I've already alluded to—that analysis is supposed to enable the analysand to come to terms with their lack-in-being. The analytic "cure" in the Lacanian scenario consists of the acceptance that there's no cure, that there's no way to claw your way back to a place of wholeness (which you never had in the first place). You'll need to learn to tolerate the fact that you'll always be wounded, which somehow seems akin to Klein's emphasis on needing to tolerate ambivalence.

I've long known that one reason I've been drawn to Lacanian theory is that I find a twisted kind of comfort in the idea that *all of us* are castrated, lacking, out of joint, distorted, pathological, and basically screwed up. I mean, if everyone is fucked up, it's okay for me to be fucked up too, right? This sentiment runs deep in me and I experience it very concretely. In this context, it may be worth noting that although Lacan doesn't talk about the analyst facilitating the analysand's ability to internalize the good object, he does note, in his seminar on transference, that a good analyst "refuses to give his own anxiety to the patient."[41] Drawing the same link between the presence of desire and the absence of anxiety that Freud already did—meaning that where there's desire, there's less anxiety—Lacan maintains that, for the analyst, "it is good to always have within reach a little well-polished desire so as not to be prone to bringing into play in the analysis a quantum of anxiety that would be neither opportune nor welcome."[42] There's certainly no attempt to impart love here. But there's an impulse to protect the analysand from the analyst's anxiety.

What I'm trying to say is that Lacan's insistence that there's no definitive cure is in some ways akin to the idea that no one is ever going to be fully integrated. From having heard you talk about Klein, I get the sense that she might agree with this in the sense that even if the integration of the ego is a goal, an ideal, for her, she acknowledges that there's no way to actually ever fully get there, that integration is never going to be entirely secure, and that people are always going to lapse back into earlier positions—the paranoid-schizoid and the depressive positions—that are derailing. When

Lacan argues in *Seminar II* that the objective of psychoanalysis is to decenter the subject in relation to its ego, he may sound stonier than Klein, but I don't think that their views are entirely incompatible because Klein appears to also admit that the subject is never going to be completely integrated. What are your thoughts on this?

AA: I agree that even though the integrated ego is an ideal for Klein, she doesn't believe that we can ever fully achieve it. I also agree that there's a way in which Klein's emphasis on the toleration of ambivalence—not the resolution but the toleration of ambivalence—can be connected to Lacan's idea that there's no definitive cure. For Klein, because of the centrality and ineliminability of the death drive, there's no getting over or beyond ambivalence, and therefore no possibility of ultimate resolution. In that sense, she might well agree that we all share some baseline level of being screwed up. The best we can do is to learn to tolerate and manage that aspect of the human condition.

MR: Given that the topic of integration has emerged so centrally in today's conversation, it seems fitting to wrap things up by returning to Lacan's claim that what's important isn't the integration of the ego but rather the emergence of the subject on the level of the discourse of the unconscious. The reason I keep fixating on this issue is that it's directly connected to one of my favorite themes in Lacan: his alignment of the repetition compulsion with our ability to accept our destiny, our lot in life.[43] I'm assuming that—and here's the Kleinian resonance I've been flagging—a tolerance for ambivalence, ambiguity, and conflict is a crucial component of this ability to accept our destiny. But I also appreciate this idea because it has to do with a classically Freudian insight about the necessity to "own" our history—including what's difficult about this history—in discourse.

Lacan emphasizes that the repetition compulsion as an expression of the death drive gives rise to the kind of destiny that we have no choice but to embrace, so that instead of trying to suppress whatever it is that the repetition compulsion tells us about who we are, we should strive to metabolize it on the level of discourse. This is why Žižek keeps urging us to "enjoy" our symptom, suggesting that rather than attempting to banish the symptom, we should step fully into it, and even learn to relish it, because ultimately it's what our destiny is made of.⁴⁴ In this sense, Lacanian analysis is about coming to tolerate our repetition compulsion, the pebble in our shoe that can't be analyzed or otherwise conjured away. This is why the objective of Lacanian analysis clashes so strongly with how many other psychoanalytic schools envision their mission: integration, wholeness, balance, healing, and adaptation aren't aims for Lacan; accepting that there's no cure is.

There's almost a Nietzschean *amor fati* type of mentality in Lacan. Recognizing this explains in part why my interpretation of Lacan is more optimistic than that of many other critics in the field. Žižek sometimes—not always but sometimes—goes in the same direction as I do when he talks about enjoying the symptom. This isn't a matter of destroying the subject—which Žižek admittedly also frequently talks about—but rather of learning to live with our *sinthome*, the fundamental fantasy that makes us who we are, that makes us the singular creatures we are, the absolutely irreplaceable creatures we are, even when there's something painful or conflictual about it; it's a matter of accepting tension as the core of our being.

Insofar as the fundamental fantasy—the guiding force of our destiny—has to do with the death drive, it also has to do with jouissance. This idea is particularly prominent in the later Lacan. In the early phase of his theorizing, he's so structuralist that you can get the impression that nothing beyond the signifier matters to him—that the body, the drives, and affect have no place in the Lacanian paradigm. Many critics, particularly Anglo-American nonspecialists who haven't moved beyond a certain point in Lacan's thinking—beyond the handful of essays in the *Écrits* that every theorist is supposed to have read—have interpreted Lacan in these terms, which means that they assume that the structuralist narrative of the early Lacan is the only thing that he offers. But his ideas shifted drastically over the decades, and when you read his later seminars, you realize that it's all about the body, the drives, affect—and yes—jouissance; the real dominates in the later Lacan. This is one reason that accepting your fate, in the later Lacan, has to do with accepting the jouissance of the drive, which can make you incredibly uncomfortable, and which is ultimately always connected to death.

AA: I'm glad you returned to Lacan's notion of integration because I was struck by it: integration is the note on which he ends *Seminar*

II, and I think that the way you link it to the idea of accepting our destiny is compelling. Perhaps in the end the difference between him and Klein on this point is more terminological than anything else. It's true that Klein doesn't seem to regard the ego or the ideal of ego integration as problematic. But when you think about what she means by integration—which involves phantasy and the duality of the drives—perhaps *ego* just isn't the right term anymore, or at any rate, as we have established, she doesn't mean the same thing by the ego as Lacan does. Perhaps when she refers to the ego, she means something closer to what Lacan means by the subject.[45] And if that's correct, what she's talking about is really something more like an integration of the psyche or the self that isn't so different from what Lacan means by integration.

It might be tempting to frame the difference between Klein and Lacan as a contrast between thinking about subject formation in terms of integration versus thinking about it in terms of lack. However, this wouldn't be accurate because Klein's account of subject formation turns not only on integration but also on *loss*: after all, the depressive position is *depressive*, melancholic. It emerges in response to an experience of loss, of losing the idealized good object (or the fear of losing it as a result of one's own aggression). In connection with this emphasis on loss, Klein draws an interesting contrast between manic and genuine forms of reparation. In manic reparation, the subject attempts to put the lost or shattered object back together and pretend that it never attacked or destroyed the object in the first place, whereas genuine reparation involves accepting the harm that one has done to the object in phantasy and in reality, tolerating the fundamental ambivalence of one's relation to the object and to one's self, and *containing* all that complexity and ambiguity. So even if the Kleinian story isn't quite one of fundamental lack, it's a story in which loss plays a crucial role.

MR: Here again it seems that the issue is more terminological than conceptual. Lacan talks about lack; Klein talks about loss. But my intuition is that they are getting at something quite similar. I mentioned earlier that the Lacanian subject is intrinsically melancholic, born out of an originary loss (lack) that it then repeats throughout its life. For Klein, the depressive position is likewise a melancholy strain that the subject can never definitively banish. I see parallels here.

It also makes sense that Kristeva explicitly draws a connection between the Lacanian lack-in-being and loss in the sense that—I think—you're talking about in the context of Klein because she has been influenced by both Lacan and Klein. Later, I would like to talk about the connections between the depressive position, melancholia, and creativity. For now, let me just say that Kristeva states that there's no imagination that isn't secretly melancholy.[46] That is, for Kristeva, creativity is intrinsically linked to loss, including the kind of loss that arises from having hurt someone, from having severed an intimate tie. For Lacan as well, creativity arises from lack. Instead of discussing the loss of real objects, Lacan tends to stick to the constitutive lack-in-being that has to do with the retroactive fantasy of *das Ding* as a lost object, but for me these two levels of lack/loss are connected.

My general point is that even though for both Lacan and Kristeva, lack and loss are frequencies of suffering, they are also the foundation of creativity, of all the things for which life—sometimes at least—feels worth living. It's perhaps also worth noting that this connection between lack/loss and creativity is a Western philosophical story that we have heard in countless versions: there's a connection between nothingness and being, lack and creativity, loss and renewal, negativity and affirmation, that has been in our tradition for a long time. One can go all the way back to Plato, to the splitting of the arrogant creatures with four arms and four legs—

AA: In the *Symposium*.

MR: Exactly. Then desire arises from this splitting—this lack, loss, or desperation. And the ball of yarn starts to unravel.

2

Fusion

MR: We thought that in this second conversation, we should tackle the question of whether, in either Klein or Lacan, one can find the idea that during the first months of life—before the child begins to speak—there exists a symbiotic fusion between it and its primary caretaker, more often than not conceptualized as the mother. The stakes of this inquiry are ideologically high because it raises concerns about the idealization of the child's formative experiences, about essentializing the mother-child bond, and about the possibility of blaming the mother for all manner of developmental failures and adult pathologies.

I've suggested that the standard narrative about Lacanian theory that has for decades circulated within the American academy tends to posit such a prelinguistic state of fusion, implying that there's something blissful about the jouissance of the real. I want to argue that this is a misconception, that—as I've emphasized—for Lacan the signifier intervenes from the get-go, even if the infant itself is incapable of speaking. Furthermore, there's arguably little that's idyllic or reassuring about jouissance. This makes it impossible to speak about a harmonious presymbolic state of fusion. But let's begin with the Kleinian side of things. Is there any debate about this issue? And if so, what's your opinion on the matter?

AA: I'll put my cards on the table right away by saying that I'm deeply skeptical about the notion of primary fusion and that part of the reason for my interest in Klein is that—at least as I read her—she doesn't support this story. I see her work as offering a compelling counterpoint to the version of intersubjective or relational psychoanalysis that has been taken up by some Frankfurt

School critical theorists, such as Axel Honneth. In his theory of recognition, Honneth leans heavily on Winnicott's notion of primary fusion, which suggests that the infant starts out in a state of undifferentiated merger with its primary object, typically its mother (though it's important to emphasize that this needn't be the biological mother or even necessarily a woman). Honneth argues that the break-up of this primary fusion is so painful, traumatic, and anxiety producing that it instills in the subject a drive or motivation to attempt to recover something as close to it as possible.

Honneth believes that primary fusion is a state of seamless and unmediated togetherness with the caretaker that's blissful in the sense that all of the infant's needs are satisfied before they can even be experienced as needs; there's no deprivation, no lack. In addition, Honneth describes this experience of fusion as the "zero point" [*Nullpunkt*] of all relations of love and recognition.[1] In other words, subsequent modes of love and recognition supposedly function as approximations of this undifferentiated fusion. This means that, interestingly, love and recognition are, for Honneth, always a kind of second best because they are by definition *mediated* relationships to another subject, whereas what we're constantly trying—and necessarily failing—to recover through our relations of love and recognition is the original experience of fusion that can never be recaptured because to do so would be to dissolve the boundary between self and other and thus to obliterate the subject. It's an oddly postlapsarian vision of human life, according to which we all start out in a state of paradise that's later lost and that we then spend the rest of our lives striving in vain to recover.[2]

MR: I'm *stunned* by how similar Honneth's account sounds to the standard narrative about Lacanian theory that I just referred to. I outlined some of this narrative yesterday because I agree with much of it, *except*—notably—the part about an unmediated fusion with the primary caretaker. According to this narrative, the subject's loss of the Thing—which results from language acquisition—leads to an interminable quest to fill the void within its being. Lacanians don't use the term *recognition*, but the idea is that the subject pursues various substitutes—*objets a*—for the Thing in an attempt to recapture a lost wholeness. However, these *objets a*—which, due to the fabrications of fantasy, come to be housed in the people the subject desires—are always inferior stand-ins for the Thing that the subject can't regain without annihilating itself (because, as you just said, fusion would obliterate the distinction between self and other). Later in our dialogue, I'll go into greater detail about the relationship between fantasy, the *objet a*, and real-life objects of desire because it's a complicated dynamic where—on my interpretation, which diverges from the interpretations of many other Lacanians—fantasy isn't always a terrible thing. For now, it suffices to translate the Lacanian story into Honneth's vocabulary by saying that the subject's pursuit of the *objet a* is arguably equivalent to a quest for recognition because ultimately what the subject is looking for is a flattering mirror that would fulfill its narcissistic need for an idealized—"whole"—version of itself.

Unfortunately, what frequently gets cut out of this story is the fact that—as I mentioned yesterday—for Lacan the initial fusion with the caretaker (or the Thing, the real) is a retroactive fantasy and that he believes that the child is from the first moments of its life entangled in a network of symbolic meanings, which is why an unmediated, purely biological fusion with the caretaker is logically impossible. I'll return to this central theme in a moment. But I want to flag right away that I'm flabbergasted by the similarities between Honneth's narrative and the Lacanian narrative that circulates within the Anglo-American academy, particularly in undergraduate survey classes.

AA: I'm not sure that I would say that fusion is biological in Honneth's account. It might be more accurate to say that it's ontological, or ontogenetic. But I agree that the similarities are surprising, given that in other respects Honneth's engagement with psychoanalysis is quite far from Lacan's.

When Honneth initially formulated his conception of primary fusion,[3] he claimed that the baby and the mother exist in a prolonged state of fusion—in which not only the baby but also the mother experiences herself as undifferentiated—that persists for several months. This story about maternal fusion or reverie or preoccupation has always seemed to me to be an incredibly ideological and problematic way of presenting what motherhood is or should be like.

Starting in the 1980s, there has been lots of empirical work in infant research that calls into question whether or not it makes sense, even from the point of view of the baby, to characterize early infantile experience in terms of fusion.[4] Although I think that there are good reasons to be a bit skeptical about the methodology of infant research, the basic claim that the infant is intersubjectively or interpersonally related—rather than "fused"—more or less from the time of birth seems intuitively plausible. Interestingly, although Honneth acknowledges the challenge that this empirical research poses for his argument, he isn't willing to give up his belief in primary fusion. Instead, he insists that even if it's a mistake to talk about the infant and the mother existing in a prolonged *state* of fusion, it still makes sense to posit that the infant experiences *moments* of fusion, for example, when it's being nursed. In this vision, the baby at the breast with a blissed-out expression on its face becomes paradigmatic of moments of fusion, and it's then the break-up of these moments that gives rise to the drive to attain recognition.[5]

In connection with this story about the break-up of primary fusion, Honneth draws on Freud's late essay "Inhibitions, Symptoms, and Anxiety" to propose that aggression results from separation anxiety.[6] Honneth maintains that the painful and traumatic experience of losing fusion gives rise to separation anxiety—the primary form of anxiety for Honneth. This in turn is the source of aggression. The point of this story is to deny that there's anything like a primordial aggressive drive, while at the same time acknowledging that aggression is ineliminable because it's the necessary result of the inevitable break-up of fusion.

On this view, aggression can be inexorable without being rooted in the death drive. Essentially, the story about primary fusion not only provides Honneth with a way of explaining what motivates struggles for recognition—namely, the attempt to find a mediated form of the unmediated fusion experience of early infancy—but also gives him a way of accounting for the ineliminability of aggression without having to resort to what might seem like an overly naturalistic language of the drives.

I have a couple of concerns about this picture. First, because it denies primary aggression, it seems to leave little room for ambivalence. It's not exactly that Honneth banishes the drives. In fact, I think that there's an unstated assumption about the *erotic* drive operating in the background of his view in the sense that this version of critical theory assumes a basic prosocial bond that enables individual socialization. In other words, love is important to Honneth's account, even central. But what's missing is an account of the death drive and the deep psychic conflict and ambivalence that arise from the duality of the drives.

Second, Honneth's account of primary fusion as the zero point of all relations of recognition seems not only to idealize the mother-infant bond in a problematic way; it also rests on the assumption that fusion is blissful, that it's a state we would be motivated to attempt to recover, which leaves aside its terrifying and overwhelming aspects. But perhaps more to the point, in his recent work Honneth performs some complicated gymnastics to try to save his account of fusion as the zero point of recognition. From my perspective, this seems weird. After all, why does he have to hang onto this story? What work is it doing for his account of subjectivity? But then I read Whitebook's biography of Freud, and it struck me that this is also in a way Freud's story.

MR: Because of Freud's notion of oceanic feeling?

AA: Well, as I mentioned yesterday, Whitebook argues that there are two strands in Freud: the official and unofficial positions.[7] According to Freud's official position, the child starts out in a state of primary narcissism, governed solely by the pleasure principle and completely cut off from reality, including the needs, desires, and thoughts of other subjects. In this account, the goal is for the self to figure out a way to connect to reality, to accept the reality principle and the limits that this principle inevitably places on the operation of the pleasure principle. The unofficial position, in contrast, is a story about primary fusion, which Whitebook seems to think is preferable to the official position because it's where Freud acknowledges the importance of the maternal object relation—which Whitebook associates with the "archaic mother"—and of the pre-Oedipal in the development of the psyche—ideas that, as we noted yesterday, were famously developed by female analysts working in the wake of Freud, including, in her own way, Klein.

Although I'm all for challenging the idea of primary narcissism—and the problematically individualistic assumption that human beings are basically self-interested and asocial that seems to go along with it—when I was reading Whitebook's account, I was thinking, "Really, the archaic mother? Seriously? Are we really going back to that?" Perhaps this is unfair to Whitebook, but I kept waiting for him to say something like, "Oh, when I talk about the archaic mother what I mean is," and then give an explanation for why he isn't essentializing or idealizing the mother-infant relationship or the maternal body, or at least address the kinds of things that feminist theorists have been worrying about for the last thirty years. But he doesn't do this, which is why it seems to me that there's an unproblematized idealization or phantasy of the archaic mother at work in his account.

One reason I think that Klein is so interesting is that her claim that the infant is object related from the start implies a rejection not only of primary narcissism but also of primary fusion. After all, for the infant to be object related from the beginning, it must have a rudimentary ego. This means that even if the infant has a difficult time distinguishing between its internal and external objects, it would be strange to describe its initial situation as one of merger or fusion.[8] Furthermore, although Klein places great importance on the mother-infant relationship, her emphasis on primary aggression and the ineliminable ambivalence that this aggression generates makes it impossible for her to idealize the archaic mother.

Klein has an image of human beings coming into the world as struggling, striving, and aggressive little creatures. They may have an elementary capacity for love but it has to be developed, whereas the capacity for aggression is expressed from the beginning. To be sure, the infant's attachment to the mother, to the breast, is partly libidinal, so that from the start there's an interplay between the libidinal and the aggressive, between love and hate.[9] But the death drive is what organizes the paranoid-schizoid position as a whole, which is why objects are split into part-objects and the subject experiences itself as disintegrated, fragmented, and in bits. This implies that even though the infant in the paranoid-schizoid position feels love for its primary object, its starting point is one in which the death drive or aggression is primary.

And then what one might characterize as mature, depressive love is what enables the infant to move out of the paranoid-schizoid position and attain some measure of coherence and secure attachment to whole objects in the world. In the Kleinian paradigm, love is therefore a hard-won and fragile achievement. Our starting point isn't a pure state of love, of unmediated being together with another person where subject and object can't be distinguished. Rather, our starting point is ambivalent to the core, and the love that enables us to tolerate and manage this ambivalence is a precarious achievement. This means that although Klein in some sense offers an intersubjective account of subjectivity, hers is a much more complex and ambivalent picture than the one offered by Honneth (and by Habermas, for that matter, though his understanding of individuation through socialization doesn't rest on a psychoanalytic story about primary fusion). Klein's intersubjective theory of the self emphasizes the fundamental ambivalence of the drives and the intrapsychic and phantasmatic aspects of our relations with others.

How would you characterize Lacan's position with respect to primary fusion? Does his position carry the idealizing, problematic implications that I'm worried about in Honneth and Whitebook?

MR: My opening statement today already revealed that I don't think so. There are certainly theoretical reasons for why you could end up with that interpretation because there are moments when Lacan suggests that one needs the mediation of the symbolic order—basically, the phallus (the Name of the Father)—to break up the mother-child dyad in order to bring into existence the subject of discourse (and, by extension, of the unconscious). So there are undeniably aspects of Lacanian theory from which you can get a glimpse of something like a lost paradise. But honestly, I find this paradise more in the interpretations of some post-Lacanian critics than in Lacan himself.

One of the best places to begin to tackle the question of fusion in Lacan is his critique of Michael Balint in *Seminar I*. Lacan accuses Balint of creating a theoretical aporia that's an analytic dead end. And this is precisely because Balint falsely posits a closed circuit of primary fusion where the mother fulfills the child's every need. Lacan mocks Balint's idea that, for the infant, everything good comes from the mother. Lacan is also critical of the notion that the infant doesn't recognize the mother as an independent entity, as a subject in her own right. And he's similarly critical of the assumption that the mother experiences her relationship with the child as entirely harmonious and perfectly satisfying.[10]

Balint presents the same vision of mother-child harmony as Honneth does, and Lacan summarily demolishes it. Lacan asserts that there's an object relation from the start, claiming that "observation shows us that there really is an object relation."[11]

Along closely related lines, and importantly for our purposes, he stresses that the infant possesses the capacity for intersubjectivity from the beginning: "Contrary to Balint's perspective ... we must start off with a radical intersubjectivity"; "there has to be intersubjectivity at the beginning."[12] I emphasize this point because there are Lacanians who make it sound like intersubjectivity is irrelevant to Lacanian theory, that the small-o other doesn't matter to him. *Seminar I* shows otherwise.

Regarding the notion of mother-child fusion, Lacan makes two points that are designed to demonstrate its lunacy. First, he illustrates that if you start with this notion, you have no way of getting to intersubjectivity later. Balint attempts to generate intersubjectivity from fusion love as the child gets older, and this, for Lacan, is the basic contradiction—the theoretical aporia I referred to a moment ago—of Balint's doctrine.[13] Lacan asks how the child is expected to get from fusion love, where supposedly there's no differentiation between self and other, to intersubjectivity and concludes that Balint doesn't have an explanation for this shift. This is why, in relation to the ideal of primary fusion, Lacan states: "I have massive objections to this conception, my objections will show how it literally dissipates everything which analysis has contributed."[14]

Second, Lacan accuses Balint of not having any sense of the child's polymorphous perversity, selfishness, and sadism. According to Lacan, one of the most important discoveries of psychoanalysis is that "the child is a pervert."[15] And because Lacan regards selfishness and sadism as part of the child's perversion, I would connect his comment to Klein's idea that aggression is primary. In addition, for Lacan, the child's perversion is one reason that there's intersubjectivity from the beginning: selfishness and sadism only make sense if there's an other—someone separate from the self— toward whom they can be directed.

For Lacan, the fundamental problem with Balint's approach is that he, like so many other analysts, treats the child like a little animal who doesn't recognize the other. According to Lacan, this is "a complete error" because it naturalizes both the child and the mother-child bond,[16] failing to identify the basic distinction between humans and other animals, which for Lacan is of course the signifier, the fact that at the beginning is the word. I can see why it might be hard to fathom how the child's relationship to the world can be symbolically mediated before it begins to speak. But if you give the matter a moment's thought, it becomes clear that one doesn't yet have to be a speaking being to be enmeshed in a world of symbolic messages. For starters, as I mentioned yesterday, the mother—or whoever the primary caretaker happens to be—is inevitably embedded in a sociosymbolic network of meanings, and therefore so is the child.

I want to stress that the distinction that Lacan draws between humans and other animals doesn't imply that humans are superior to animals; rather, it's a matter of recognizing that the signifier transforms the human subject into a maladapted animal. In *Rupture: On the Emergence of the Political*, Paul Eisenstein and Todd McGowan explain this issue compellingly, linking the primacy of the signifier in human life to the subject's constitutive dislocation. Admittedly, they are talking about the speaking subject. But their argument is relevant to Lacan's critique of Balint's tendency to define the human child as a little animal. They claim that the signifier distorts the subject's natural state, rendering it "damaged in relation to its being."[17] In other words, the distinction between humans and other animals is essential, "not because the human is endowed with a soul that the animal lacks," but because the human subject isn't primarily an instinctual being.[18] Its biology has been interrupted by the signifier, which is why it never fully coincides with itself. And like Lacan, Eisenstein and McGowan argue that psychoanalysis is the first theory to recognize this reality.

What this comes down to is the acknowledgment that humans are more pathological than other animals. As I've stressed, we're all ontologically alienated, derailed, and out of joint; we don't comfortably fit into our environment. Eisenstein and McGowan in fact propose that what's most significant about human beings is that they seek satisfaction by repeating their failures, including their failure to attain wholeness. In other words, what's distinctive about humans—as opposed to other animals—is that they continuously return to the existential, psychological, and emotional tasks that they haven't been able to finish, which is why the repetition compulsion is the status quo of human life. As Eisenstein and McGowan state, "Though we are consciously human and strive to succeed, we are unconsciously inhuman and seek out the repetition of failure."[19] The allusion to the "inhuman" here doesn't refer to animals but to something mechanical, machine-like—language-like, if you prefer—about the unconscious. This is why, on the level of the subject of the unconscious, there's no possibility of adaptation: deformation is inerasable.

In *Seminar X*, Lacan conveys this point emphatically by describing the child's "trauma of birth" as a moment when the child is "literally choked, suffocated."[20] That is, what's traumatic about birth isn't separation from the mother but instead "the inhalation, into oneself, of a fundamentally Other environment."[21] And this "Other environment" is where the signifier lies in wait. As Lacan explains in *Seminar II*, the child is inserted into the symbolic order with its first wail.[22] In other words, with its very first cry, the child becomes entangled in a symbolic network that can't but have an impact on its biological constitution, let alone on its relationships with its caretakers.

Let me put it this way: the signifier waits for the child in the delivery room well before the mother even arrives in that room. For instance, gendering through signifiers often begins before the child is born. And then right after birth the doctor or nurse holds the child up to the mother and says, "It's a girl!" In some cases, there might even be a tinge of disappointment in this exclamation. In the alien environment into which the child is thrust, the big Other—along with its avatars, the small-o others upon whom the child depends for its survival—awaits with its confusing (ambivalent and ambivalence-inducing) messages. After that, forget about simple biology or even about the purity of ontology. And forget about an uncomplicated fusion with the mother.

For Lacan, even the drives are shaped by their encounter with the symbolic order, knocked off their natural course by the signifier. Earlier you alluded to the idea that by denying primary aggression, Honneth is trying to avoid a naturalized understanding of the drives. But from a Lacanian perspective, this is a pointless effort because there's no such thing as a natural drive. This is why Lacan hates the term *instinct*. For him, there's little that's instinctual about humans; rather, we're infused by drives (jouissance) that can no longer be considered as straightforwardly biological because they have always had some contact with the symbolic world. For example, the "drive" to eat isn't just a natural function for humans: it comes with a whole host of social meanings, which is one reason that it's a complicated matter for some people, including some infants; it's not merely about fulfilling an instinctual need for nourishment but a socially mediated act.

In *Seminar II*, Lacan gives an evocative example of how the symbolic intervenes in the reality of the prelinguistic child. He observes that a child reacts differently to a painful blow depending on whether it's accidental or punitive: the child's response to bumping its head against the sharp corner of a table (an accident) isn't the same as its response to a parent slapping it (punishment). Both actions hurt, but the symbolic message is entirely different, and even if the child doesn't yet speak, it grasps something about this message.

In this context, Lacan maintains that "the symbolic relation is constituted as early as possible, even prior to the fixation of the self image of the subject, prior to the structuring image of the ego."[23] In other words, the relationship to the symbolic predates the mirror stage and the emergence of the ego, which means that the prelinguistic child isn't functioning within the realm of "brute reality,"[24] but rather a reality that has been symbolically constituted. Moreover, this constitution is in part at least a function of the child's particular history, including its formative (symbolically mediated) object relations. This is why our repetition compulsion takes a distinctive shape: insofar as our drives have been contorted by the signifiers that greet us when we enter the world, that continue to shape us throughout our lives, and that are tied to specific types of object relations, our repetition compulsion has become singularized. And—to get back to our main theme—there's no space in this model for the notion that there could be some kind of a primordial fusion between mother and child.

AA: There are ways to connect what you have said to Klein because, for her, whatever fusion experience there might be in our past, it would have to be in the womb. For me, this is an indication of how deeply she resists the idea of primary fusion. For example, she writes:

> While the pre-natal state no doubt implies a feeling of unity and security, how far this state is undisturbed must depend on the psychological and physical condition of the mother, and possibly even on certain still unexplored factors in the unborn infant. We might, therefore, consider the universal longing for the pre-natal state also partly as an expression of the urge for idealization. If we investigate this longing in the light of idealization, we find that

one of its sources is the strong persecutory anxiety stirred up by birth. We might speculate that this first form of anxiety possibly extends to the unborn infant's unpleasant experiences which, together with the feeling of security in the womb, foreshadow the double relation to the mother: the good and the bad breast.[25]

What I find fascinating about this passage is that Klein is so skeptical of idealization—and the vision of blissful fusion is perhaps the archetype of idealization—that even as she's entertaining the idea that birth trauma might be what breaks up prenatal fusion with the mother and thus gives rise to persecutory anxiety, she's also suggesting that *even in the womb* the infant's relationship to the mother is ambivalent.

As far as I can see, this is the closest Klein comes to granting the possibility of primary fusion. Unlike Balint's account, her perspective seems to rise to Lacan's challenge that in order for there to be intersubjectivity at the end, it has to be there from the beginning. If there's anything like an experience of primary fusion, it would only exist in the womb—and even then, she's not completely convinced—and it would be broken up at birth. It's as if the experience of being born is one of radical disruption—like the baby emerges and thinks to itself, "What the hell was that?! Why is the universe attacking me?" [laughter]

MR: The monstrous big Other is here! [laughter]

There are certainly times when Lacan links the Thing—the (non) object that the subject yearns for as a site of lost wholeness—to the mother, but the denaturalization of this relationship is central to his thinking. I've already emphasized that he believes that the notion of an originary fusion is a retroactive fantasy—that this fusion never actually existed. For instance, in *Seminar VII* he specifies that even though the subject is driven to find the lost object, "the object indeed has never been lost."[26]

It's also relevant to keep in mind that Lacan ridicules other psychoanalysts for assuming that it's the breast specifically that matters to the child. He stresses that the breast can easily be replaced by a bottle and that the mother can easily be replaced by another person.[27] Furthermore—and this point seems related to Klein—Lacan claims that the breast is part of the child's "inner world and not part of the mother's body"; "during breastfeeding," he continues, "the breast is part of the individual who is being fed. It is merely *stuck onto* the mother."[28]

Lacan proposes that the anxiety that accompanies weaning has less to do with the fact that the breast no longer fulfills the child's needs than with the fact that it reveals itself to be an entity that can come and go independently of the child's wishes; the child is forced to relinquish something that it experiences as a part of itself.[29] Although it might be tempting to read this as proof that Lacan believes in an originary mother-child fusion, his point is instead that the breast, for the child, is a partial object which takes on a disturbing and confusing character. In other words, like Klein, he's talking about the child's relationship to the breast as a partial object—the status of which is unclear and therefore ambivalence inducing for the child—rather than about the child's relationship to the mother as a whole object. Lacan doesn't go to Klein for this idea, but instead uses Winnicott's notion of the transitional object to make his case,[30] positing that the problem for the child isn't that the breast is taken away but rather that it's shown to be what Lacan calls a "yieldable" object[31]—something that, after all, isn't part of the child.

On some level this sounds terribly misogynistic because now even the breast doesn't belong to the mother: she's just a prop for the breast, and it's the child, rather than the mother, who is an active agent. But on another level, it feels like there's something thoroughly Kleinian about this picture: it feels like Lacan is describing a situation akin to the paranoid-schizoid position, where the child experiences itself as being in bits and gets anxious because one important bit is severed from it. And if the breast is merely "stuck onto" the mother, does this mean that the mother is also in bits?

AA: I agree that this sounds Kleinian: the breast is part of the child's inner world, but it's also part of the mother's body. Initially the infant is unable to distinguish clearly between its internal objects and the external objects to which they are connected. This isn't to say that the infant exists in a state of undifferentiated fusion, but rather that its rudimentary ego is fragmented and incoherent, and that it therefore relies heavily on projection and splitting as defenses against the internal operation of the death drive. In this state, phantasy plays an outsized role in the child's relations with its external objects.

MR: You just made a key distinction: being fragmented and incoherent isn't the same thing as being fused with the caretaker. Perhaps it's the inability to see this distinction that leads some critics to cling to the idea of fusion. The Lacanian real is a concept that attempts to convey something about bodily and psychic fragmentation and incoherence.

Fragmentation and incoherence are part of the adult subject's constitution as well, emerging particularly strongly during moments when its symbolic and imaginary supports falter, but for the infant they dominate. So when Lacan posits that the infant begins its life in the real, he's simply getting at the idea that the infant doesn't yet have an organized bodily or psychic life: it's primarily a creature of drive energies that haven't yet been structured into a socially intelligible entity, which, among other things, means that its body isn't under its control. This is why the infant depends on its caretakers to tend to its bodily needs. But this doesn't mean that the child is fused with its mother. If anything, we're here in the vicinity of psychosis, which is why it makes perfect sense that Klein maintains that the paranoid-schizoid position is the starting point of human life. What the paranoid-schizoid position and the Lacanian real as a site of jouissance have in common is an almost psychotic degree of disorder.

Yet, as I keep stressing, the symbolic starts to make inroads into the infant's constitution from the beginning of life. This is why Lacan maintains, in relation to the breast, that what matters isn't the breast itself but rather the social message—a message that's always mediated by the big Other—that arrives with the breast: in this instance, the message is that whoever is offering the child the breast (or the bottle) is expecting it to eat. Lacan proposes that when it comes to the breast, what's important is "not need *of* the other ... but need *in* the Other, at the level of the Other."[32] That is, the significant part isn't that the child needs the (m)other; rather, what matters is that there's a need *in* the (m)other: she wants the child to eat. And even though the child can't yet speak or process verbal messages, it has some sense of this need in the other, this need that's needing it to eat.

Lacan goes through similar explanations for other bodily functions. In the anal phase—during potty training—at issue is the "demand" in the other, the demand arising from the other, the fact that the other wants the child to get down to business, right here and now. In the phallic phase, at issue is what Lacan calls the "*jouissance in the Other*,"[33] which he views as one of the causes of castration anxiety because there's something completely overwhelming not just about the idea that you're supposed to give the other unmitigated jouissance but also about the other's jouissance as such: witnessing the other's jouissance can generate anxiety. Lacan is working with the Freudian erotogenic zones, the body's openings to the outside world, including the eye and the ear, always linking these openings to the social messages that animate them.

The details of all of this don't matter for our purposes. What does is Lacan's conviction that even if the bodily real dominates in infancy, everything is nevertheless symbolically mediated. Equally important is the point I made a moment ago about the confusing nature of symbolic messages because what's indecipherable can be overstimulating. Lacan captures this idea by the concept of the enigmatic signifier—a concept that was later developed by Jean Laplanche[34]—which is why, for Lacan, the hysteric's question (and recall that those of us who aren't psychotic are all hysterics) is a constant *che vuoi?*: What do you want from me? This presumably isn't how other animals relate to each other.

AA: While Klein doesn't have a fully developed account of language that could rival Lacan's theory of the symbolic order—though some Kleinians, most notably Hanna Segal and later Wilfred Bion, have developed a theory of symbolization out of her work[35]—I think that she would agree that the child's relationship to the breast isn't a natural one because for her this relationship is structured by phantasy.

In this context, I want to address what you said about how some readers of Lacan believe that he doesn't offer an account of intersubjectivity. My sense is that it's not that there's *no* relationship to the other in Lacan; instead, it seems that this relationship is a phantasized one all the way down. In other words, it's not a relationship with an actual person, but rather with a phantasized projection, and with a symbolic overlay, of another person. This may be a significant difference between Lacan and Klein because even though Klein emphasizes the importance of phantasy, she doesn't want to *envelop* the relationship to the other—let's call this the *real* other or the *external* other—in phantasmatic constructions; she wants to say that there *is* a relationship to the real external other, and that how this relationship goes matters even though it's also always mediated through the subject's intrapsychic dynamics.

MR: That's probably a fair characterization of Lacan's take on relationality: it's always linguistically (the symbolic) and fantasmatically (the imaginary) mediated, except at moments when the real gains ascendancy, as might be the case in certain types of love relationships. In a later conversation, I'll talk about the manner in which specks of the real can enter relationships in ways that lend them a special weightiness. But it's true that it's hard to envision what "authentic" relating might look like within the Lacanian paradigm. It's not that Lacan (prescriptively) *wants* to impede relationships that aren't symbolically or fantasmatically mediated. He simply believes that these are impossible, whereas it sounds like, for Klein, a degree of authenticity—the kind of relating that eludes fantasy formations—remains an ideal even if it's difficult to attain.

AA: Klein places a greater emphasis than Lacan does on the possibility of relationships with real external others. But I wouldn't want to suggest that she believes that phantasy can ever be completely conjured away: no matter how authentic a relationship is, phantasy always remains a part of it. This is why it would be an oversimplification to say that Klein naturalizes the mother's body: for her as well, the milk itself matters less than what the milk represents. Even though Klein is definitely talking about the infant's actual relationship with its mother or someone who fulfills the caretaking function, there's also a way in which its relationship to this object is still thoroughly phantasmatic, at least while it remains in the paranoid-schizoid position.

In reality, there's no good breast in the way that the infant in the paranoid-schizoid position perceives it: there's no pure source of goodness and creativity and nourishment and gratification, just as there's no bad breast that's wholly persecutory, attacking, or devouring. The lesson of moving to the depressive position is that the child comes to realize that its relationship to its primary object is both gratifying *and* destructive. What's phantasmatic for Klein is the *purity* of the good breast, its complete separation from the bad breast. This idea is a phantasy—maybe even a fundamental phantasy?—that has to be given up. Does this make sense?

MR: It makes perfect sense. I wonder, though, whether the wholly persecutory, attacking, and devouring object—and I'm here thinking about the whole object rather than the breast—might in some instances be a reality. No one can be wholly good; but there could, unfortunately, be a "caretaker" who could be wholly bad. But more to your point, if I understand you correctly, Klein proposes that there can be a powerful fantasy of the good and bad breast as separate—even as warring—entities without there being anything in the real world that corresponds to this fantasy. These notions of goodness and badness have to come from the child's fantasy life, which implies that, as is the case for Lacan, the signifier (in one form or another) is there from the beginning: there's the capacity to represent things, to imagine things, in ways in which they don't exist in reality.

AA: This is why the depressive position is so important for Klein: it allows the child to realize that the idealizing/demonizing phantasy of the good and bad breast is just that: a phantasy. But that's a realization that the subject can only access once it has moved to the depressive position. In this way, the dynamic is similar to the Lacanian idea that once the subject is split by the signifier, it's left with a fantasy of wholeness but also with the realization that this can only be a fantasy.

MR: Except that Lacan doesn't have much faith in people's ability to realize that the ideal of wholeness is a fantasy. For him, one of the tragedies—or comedies, depending on your perspective—of life is that most people never realize this, with the consequence that they spend their lives chasing a wholeness that forever eludes them. In this manner, Lacan grasped the structure of cruel optimism long before Lauren Berlant coined the term.[36]

But do you mind saying more about the idea that Klein has a stronger investment than Lacan does in the child's relationship to a real-life other upon whom it depends and for whom it develops ambivalent feelings? I ask because the literalization of the mother is among Lacan's biggest gripes against Klein. He in fact explicitly accuses her of situating "the mythic body of the mother at the central place of *das Ding*."[37] According to Lacan, Klein makes a tremendous mistake in equating the mother with *das Ding*. For Lacan, in contrast, *das Ding* isn't the mother; it isn't a definable object of any kind, which is why he calls it a nonobject.

AA: This is complicated. Let's consider the line you just quoted. Why does Lacan believe that placing the body of the mother at the place of *das Ding* is a mistake? One pointer to what he believes is mistaken about it emerges when he tells us that, on the level of *Vorstellungen* (representations), "the Thing is not nothing, but literally is not. It is characterized by its absence, its strangeness."[38] And then he goes on to argue something that seems intended as a criticism of Klein, even though he doesn't mention her by name. He states:

> There is not a good and a bad object; there is good and bad, and then there is the Thing. The good and the bad already belong to the order of the *Vorstellung;* they exist there as clues to that which orients the position of the subject, according to the pleasure principle, in connection with that which will never be more than representation.[39]

I take this to mean that Lacan believes that by situating the body of the mother in the place of *das Ding*, Klein offers a conception of the Thing that's too concrete and also too internally differentiated. As we have discussed, one of Klein's key ideas is that the child's relationship to its primary object is deeply ambivalent, and Lacan seems to be saying that there can be no ambivalence in the relation to the Thing because this relation precedes the distinction between good and bad.

MR: You're right that this is complicated. We're back at Lacan's insistence on the significance of the signifier: he's asserting that the object itself isn't good or bad, that the notions (or fantasies) of goodness and badness belong to the order of representation. In addition, he's commenting on what I fixated on yesterday, namely how the Thing functions as the destiny-defining fulcrum around which the subject, through the pleasure principle—frequently contorted into the repetition compulsion—pivots for its entire life. It's for this reason that Lacan refers to the Thing as what "orients the position of the subject": the Thing, or more precisely, the subject's unconscious quest for the Thing, determines the subject's psychic trajectory, and therefore, ultimately its entire fate.

All of this is to say that you're right about what Lacan's critique of Klein amounts to: he believes that as soon as the notions of goodness and badness emerge in relation to the breast, the child has already entered the realm of signification. The good and the bad exist on the level of representation, whereas the Thing—which, despite its destiny-defining power, only functions as an absence, a gap in the subject's psychic life—belongs in the real. This renders it unrepresentable. We can—and do—try to represent it: among other concepts, we use the notions of goodness and badness to circle the Thing, but ultimately it eludes our attempts to fix its meaning, which is why, although it's "not nothing," it also "literally is not." It's "something" in the sense that it orients the subject's psychic destiny. Yet it's not a concrete object in the world, it "literally is not." According to this logic, Klein's mistake is to think that she can materialize the Thing as the mother's body. I have to admit that, given what you have said about the centrality of phantasy in Klein's theory—about how phantasy structures the infant's relationship to the breast/mother—Lacan may here be oversimplifying her line of thinking.

AA: What's more, Lacan is willing to go so far as to talk about "the maternal thing ... the mother, insofar as she occupies the place of that thing, of *das Ding*."[40] So at the same time that he criticizes Klein's account of the maternal body, he's incorporating a version of her idea, and even associating one of his central concepts, *das Ding*, with this idea. So what exactly is it about her view that he's rejecting?

MR: Admittedly, this is at times my question as well because, in the context of *das Ding*, Lacan sometimes sounds quite Kleinian, yet he's also clearly—even vehemently—striving to distance himself from her. I think that one reason that it's so difficult to cut through this theme cleanly is that it's hard to explain why the mother isn't the mother—the immediacy of the concrete mother—for Lacan. It may help to remember that he's a structuralist (or a budding poststructuralist). As I've explained, from Lacan's perspective, the subject doesn't have a relationship to anything—the self, the psyche, the world, concepts, objects, or even its own body—except through the signifier; there isn't an unmediated relationship to anything. This is why there's no good or bad object, but merely representations (*Vorstellungen*) of goodness and badness.

For Lacan, anatomy truly isn't destiny. Rather, it's how the symbolic order codes anatomy, along with the subject's unconscious relationship to the Thing, that becomes destiny. The concepts of good and bad guide the subject in relation to objects, including the nonobject, the Thing. But these concepts aren't intrinsic qualities of any objects. They are human inventions that mediate the subject's relationship to objects. Yes, the mother can come to mythologically occupy the place of the Thing. But this is just a fantasy. The Thing is "not nothing" in the sense that it can be filled with content. But it itself doesn't exist as a concrete entity (it "is not"). It's merely a container for fantasies.

Nevertheless, I concede that Lacan, especially in *Seminar VII*, where he goes into detail about *das Ding*, isn't always nearly as far from Klein's account as he would like us to believe.

AA: I agree. I think that this comes back to a point I've emphasized before, which has to do with the relationship between the intersubjective and intrapsychic. On the one hand, regardless of how phantasmatically mediated the child's relationship to the breast is, it nevertheless has to do with the material, physical presence of the primary caregiver. On the other hand, much like in Lacan, the breast is in some ways a part of the child, of the child's inner world, meaning that it's a phantasy object.

To be sure, Klein frequently talks about the breast and the milk and the feed in terms that seem extremely—even absurdly—literal. This manner of talking may seem naïve in the face of the Lacanian conviction that everything is symbolically mediated. It appears to naturalize a particular, gendered understanding of parenting and mothering. I've already noted that one can read Klein in this concrete way. This may even be the most straightforward interpretation of her work. However, strictly speaking, even for Klein, the dynamic between the mother and the child can't *just* be about the breast and the milk and the feed: as you suggested a moment ago, it's always also about the child's unconscious phantasies about what the breast represents. And what the good breast, for example, represents is love, care, goodness, support, etc.

Winnicott's idea of the maternal function might be helpful here: whereas Klein herself tends to talk about the mother and the breast in literal terms, I don't think that we need to interpret her in that manner. Her argument could be read to mean that there has to be something that *functions* like what she calls the good breast: it could be a bottle held by a father, a non-biological parent, or a caregiver. We could even imagine a maternal function distributed across a number of different individuals. Although there are aspects of Winnicott's work that I find problematic—particularly his emphasis on primary fusion and his rejection of the death drive— his notion of the maternal function seems helpful for illustrating how the Kleinian maternal body or breast can be understood in denaturalized terms.

But—and here I'm circling back to a point that I've already made because it's important—it's crucial for Klein's argument that there *be* a relationship to a primary object on whom the infant is radically dependent for love, care, support, nourishment, and gratification. That's a concrete, perhaps even an empirical claim, but it doesn't seem to me to be for that reason objectionable. It's simply to say that love, care, support, and so on are things that infants need in order to survive and thrive, given certain features of the human condition, such as the fact that—unlike some other animals—we're born radically helpless and dependent on caregivers to meet our basic needs. Indeed, what makes the child's relationship to the object fundamentally ambivalent is precisely its radical dependence on this object, the object's tendency to frustrate its desires, and its innate aggression. I think that something like this is all that Klein's account of subject formation needs in order to get off the ground.

This means that one could adopt a denaturalized version of Klein's position that would be less vulnerable to the kinds of criticisms that Lacan makes. There are in fact moments in Klein's work where she comes close to expressing this kind of a denaturalized view. For example, even though in *Envy and Gratitude* she argues that the breast is instinctively felt to be a source not merely of nourishment but also of life itself, and that the gratifying breast grants the infant a sense of security, she also maintains that this "depends on the infant's capacity to cathect sufficiently the breast *or its symbolic representative, the bottle*."[41]

MR: Nice! Against the backdrop of everything you have said, I want to note that one reason Honneth's idealization of the mother-child bond is so suspicious is that it leads to the—perhaps unintended but nevertheless pronounced—assumption that if something goes wrong with the child, it's the mother's fault because she didn't provide a good enough holding environment, was too preoccupied with her own life to allow for complete merger, and so on. I can see why this disturbs you.

What I've learned from you is that there's *nothing* in Klein that could be used to support Honneth's theory of fusion. He assumes the kind of mutual attunement in object relations that you have shown Klein to resist: there's too much aggression, too much of the death drive, in Klein to support Honneth's model. This is an eye-opening insight because it's all too easy to group all object-relations analysts together and presume that they all advocate perfect object relations and that if the first one with the mother misfires, the rest will be ruined too. I've learned from you that, for Klein, the first object relation is *bound* to misfire; it's always going to be full of ambivalence.

AA: Absolutely! There's a passage at the beginning of *Psycho-Analysis of Children* where Klein claims that psychoanalysis undermines the illusion of the paradise of childhood by revealing childhood to be a conflict-ridden, complicated, and ambivalent experience.[42] And it's interesting to think about Klein as radicalizing this insight and undermining the illusion of the paradise of *infancy*. For her it's not just the four- or five-year-old child who is experiencing Oedipal conflicts; it's also the two-month-old who is having these complex, ambivalent phantasies.[43] By contrast, the story of blissful primary fusion seems to be a textbook case of the illusion of the paradise of infancy that Klein challenges.

MR: On this theme, again, Lacan isn't far from Klein's position. In *Seminar VII*, he mentions that *das Ding* is connected to what Freud calls *die Not des Lebens*: "Something that *wishes*. 'Need' and not 'needs.' Pressure, urgency. The state of *Not* is the state of emergency in life."[44] The "*Not*"—the need—at issue here is a state of emergency in life, an immense pressure. This can be linked to the unruly, chaotic aspects of jouissance, to a too-muchness of drive energy that courses through the body from the very beginning of life.[45] That is, Lacan characterizes *das Ding* as being connected to an emergency-inducing jouissance that would be impossible to read in terms of a peaceful mother-child union.

AA: Which is different from Honneth's view that fusion means being completely at home with another person.

MR: [laughter] Whereas the Lacanian child is screaming, "This is an emergency. This is terrifying! Get me out of here!"

To recap: the Thing introduces an emergency into life because even though it orients our relationship to the world, thereby guiding our destiny, attaining it would be deadly. As Lacan explains, to satisfy our "need" for the Thing would be to reach "the terminal point."[46] It would be the ultimate triumph of the death drive. This is why we can only approach the Thing through the mediation of *objets a*.

Referring to the Thing, Lacan maintains that "it is in its nature that the object as such is lost. It will never be found again."[47] This means that the Thing can "be found at the most as something missed"; more specifically, it can only be approached through "its pleasurable associations."[48] The *objets a* are these pleasurable associations. They give us a little taste of what we're looking for. They offer dim reverberations of the Thing, thereby functioning as points of reference for our desire while making sure that this desire doesn't overwhelm us; they allow us to experience a manageable amount of jouissance. One of the tasks of the pleasure principle is to orchestrate this dynamic.

I realize how contradictory this sounds: *das Ding* was never lost because it never existed, yet it nevertheless gives direction to our destiny by generating the kind of desire that causes each of us to take an idiosyncratic route in our search for it. And what makes the matter even more complicated is that even though our search won't succeed, it can't be said to be futile because—potentially at least—it creates a trail of worthwhile ideals, artifacts, inventions, beloved people, and works of artistic, spiritual, or intellectual beauty. Although these things aren't equivalent to the *objet a*, there's a connection between them and the *a* in the sense that they can fantasmatically come to house this *a*. This is how they gain the power to stir us.

I'll return to this idea when we discuss love. At the present juncture, the relevant point is that one reason that the objective of Lacanian analysis is to enable the analysand to understand that there's no ultimate cure is that, like Klein, Lacan doesn't believe in a paradise that can be regained. You can imagine why this is difficult for many people to accept because the fantasy of a lost paradise replicates the foundational Christian notion of an Eden that has been lost but that will one day be recovered. Even though there are

Catholic elements in Lacanian theory, he has no patience with this story. Thus: no cure, no salvation, no object that can heal us.

AA: It seems true that Klein and Lacan aren't too far apart on this issue. For Klein, there's no good object that can cure you because the good object can only be wholly good by being split from the bad object. The internalization of the good object goes together with the acceptance of ambivalence and thus with the recognition that there's no purely good object; instead, there are whole objects with good and bad parts which are both loving and frustrating at the same time. For this reason it wouldn't be fair to say that, for Klein, the goal of analysis is to make the analysand feel whole. Her goal is to enable them to tolerate ambivalence, ambiguity, and conflict without resorting to splitting.

MR: It seems that both Klein and Lacan reject the ideal of wholeness in a holistic sense that would imply balance and stability. Lacan categorically rejects wholeness by claiming that the subject is fundamentally lacking. Klein may *appear* to be an advocate of wholeness because she wishes to transcend the splitting that characterizes the paranoid-schizoid position, yet her vision of what a relationship to the other as a whole person means demands a recognition of ambivalence, ambiguity, and conflict. Furthermore, the partial object seems important to both thinkers. In the Lacanian paradigm, the *objet a*, in being merely a partial substitute, a faint echo, of the Thing, is tolerable, whereas the Thing itself would be devastating. I realize that the *objet a* isn't equivalent to the splitting that characterizes the paranoid-schizoid position, yet some conceptual similarity lingers.

AA: Your way of describing the *objet a* certainly brings Lacan closer to Klein, at least in terms of the question of the relationship between the intersubjective and the intrapsychic. I suppose that, once again, the differences between them might be mainly of emphasis. Even if one interprets the *objet a* in the way that you suggest and makes space for something like an object relation in Lacan's work, the intrapsychic still appears to take priority for him, and he appears more suspicious about the intersubjective. In contrast, although Klein would agree that our intersubjective relations are filtered through intrapsychic dynamics, those relations can also play a beneficial role in helping us to stabilize our internal world, assuming they go well enough.

MR: You're right that, instead of thinking in terms of object relations, Lacan tends to remain on the (arguably mostly intrapsychic) level of the partial object, the *objet a*, though—as I've shown—he doesn't entirely ignore the intersubjective. It's more like he believes that the *objet a* as the cause of the subject's desire is ultimately more fascinating and powerful than the subject's relationships with whole objects. Or perhaps it would be more accurate to say that, for Lacan, relationships with whole objects are always fantasmatically mediated by the *objet a*. This seems akin to the idea that, for Klein, relationships with whole objects are mediated by phantasy. So, yes, I agree that this divergence of approaches seems more like a matter of emphasis than of utterly incompatible views.

AA: It's thought provoking to arrive at this conceptual convergence. But can I ask you for a clarification on something you said earlier? When I asked you about fusion in Lacan, you responded by indicating that scholars often mistakenly read him as being committed to a claim about fusion because of the idea that the father, representing the symbolic order, breaks up the primary relationship with *das Ding*, the maternal object, thereby founding the subject of lack. Yet on your reading, *das Ding* is a retroactive fantasy. So I want to ask again, thinking about the importance of the death drive in Lacan, which seems to be an ontological version of Freud's speculative, biological Nirvana principle: isn't there some residue in Lacan of the notion of fusion in his conception of the death drive and the real in the sense that these are connected at least to a fantasy of an early state of complete plenitude, pleasure, wholeness, and absence of all tension, that's akin to death?

MR: Okay, so, yes, the subject's retroactive fantasy of plenitude, pleasure, wholeness, and absence of tension exists, which means that in Lacanian theory a *fantasy* of fusion is unquestionably a part of the subject's psychic life. But at no point do I see Lacan as suggesting that this fantasy is anything other than a fantasy.

Moreover, if I cut through the complexity of Lacan's thinking about the death drive, I would say that it's the opposite of the Freudian notion of reducing tension, of getting back to a place of quietude (or Nirvana). It's much closer to the emergency of life—*die Not des Lebens*—that I described earlier: it has to do with the destructiveness of the drive, which, again, I would link to Klein's emphasis on primary aggression. This is why Lacanians such as Žižek and Edelman have gotten so much political mileage from the death drive: they theorize it as a force that can demolish both the subject and the social/symbolic establishment.[49] The Kleinian connotations are obvious in the fact that this manner of theorizing—and within queer theory, Edelman is notorious for this—is explicitly labeled as "paranoid." In their most extreme manifestation, theories that valorize the Lacanian death drive can be thought of as literalizations of the paranoid-schizoid position: they aim at the shattering of the self and the symbolic order into bits. We can come back to this in a later conversation.

In Lacanian theory, the death drive can't be uncoupled from jouissance, from the unmanageable overagitation of our being, from the real that overflows the symbolic and imaginary edifices that sustain us as socially viable entities. As I've explained, in the usual course of life, we're contained by collective symbolic structures as well as by our imaginary fantasies (our narcissistic, overly coherent sense of ourselves). When the jouissance of the real erupts within this symbolic-imaginary system—seeps through the cracks and keeps us from maintaining our composure—it's the death drive that gains ascendency. In this sense, the death drive has to do with the ways in which jouissance can overwhelm our symbolic and imaginary persona. And of course there's also the more gradual self-destructiveness that the repetition compulsion—as one face of the death drive—inflicts on the self. For all these reasons, I believe that the death drive, for Lacan, is more or less the antithesis of quietude.

For the same reasons, I would say that, in the context of Lacan, it might make more sense to talk about an anti-ontology than an ontology. This would accord with the robust critique of the sovereign self that Lacan staged—a critique that made him an important precursor to French poststructuralism. However, in the present context, my point is that the death drive prevents the subject's closure as an ontologically coherent being. Overagitation, anxiety, and being saturated by an uncontrollable excess of energy would all be manifestations of this dynamic. Some of this restlessness is socially generated because we live in a culture that places so much pressure on our minds and bodies that we can't always handle all the stimulation that surrounds us. But some of it seems constitutive of human life—so I guess ontological in that sense—and this makes it hard to link the Lacanian death drive to primordial fusion because it's a force that undermines our every attempt at quietude.

AA: That makes sense, but it seems to me that there are two aspects of the death drive in the Freudian paradigm: there's the aim of the death drive, which is the release of all tension; and then there's the way in which this aim is achieved, namely by dissolving the boundaries of the self. Much of what you have just described corresponds to the latter aspect—the dissolution of the boundaries of the self through self-shattering, which is both terrifying and promises ecstatic pleasure—but I'm wondering if Lacan thinks that the ultimate goal of this dissolution is the absence of tension. In other words, if tension arises from the attempt to hold the self together, and if you undergo a process of self-shattering that allows you to merge with the real, wouldn't that mean, ultimately, the absence of all tension? Tension seems to result from trying to harness the death drive or the drive energies of the real without letting them destroy you, but being destroyed seems to be the same thing as quietude or the absence of all tension.

This is the sense in which it seems to me that Lacan works with a more classically Freudian conception of the death drive than Klein does. Because for Klein the death drive isn't about merger, quiescence, or lack of tension but rather simply about hatred, aggression, and destructiveness. In some ways this could be seen as a creative misreading—or at least a highly selective reading—of Freud because Freud thought of aggression as only one manifestation of the death drive, whereas Klein tends to equate the two.

Another place where Lacan and Klein might diverge concerns the origin of the death drive. I believe that Lacan claims in *Seminar VII* that the death drive emerges with the cut of the signifier, that it's the result of symbolic castration. For Klein, in contrast, the death drive seems organic or constitutional. As I've mentioned, unlike Lacan, she doesn't shy away from using the term *instinct*. In some ways, this is a misleading term for her to use because she thinks that the drives are always object related and in that sense best understood not as biologically rooted forces that well up from inside the individual but rather as modes of relating to others, whether lovingly or destructively. But in another sense the term *instinct* is perhaps appropriate because there's no ultimate answer for her to the question of where the death drive comes from. Rather, her view seems to be: "At the beginning was the death drive" [laughter]. That's just the kind of creatures we are.

MR: Interesting! I see what you're getting at. I understand what you mean about self-dissolution leading to quiescence. This would obviously happen if the subject died. Yet it feels that, like Klein, Lacan conceptualizes the death drive as part of the living subject, as a force that the living subject has to contend with. In this context, I'm again tempted to draw a parallel between the paranoid-schizoid position and jouissance as manifestations of the death drive: both are destructive yet neither can be definitively banished from the living subject's experience. As a result, even if technically the loss of tension would be the consequence of self-dissolution, I'm not sure what it would mean to talk about the death drive in this manner unless one is referring to suicide. Suicide might be the most extreme expression of the death drive, but even critics who use Lacanian theory to fetishize the death drive, desubjectivation, and the pulverization of the subject—such as Žižek and Edelman—aren't usually talking about actual death; rather, they are talking about social death, social unintelligibility, or about a kind of asocial monstrosity.

As to where the death drive comes from, you're right that for Lacan it can't be dissociated from the signifier. Yes, human beings, like other animals, are born with drives (with what Klein calls instincts), but as I've stressed, for Lacan these drives don't have a way of staying natural. You said that, for Klein, it's almost like "at the beginning was the death drive." For Lacan—as I've emphasized repeatedly—"at the beginning was the word." I guess this is a biblical moment. On the one hand, the drives, the real, and jouissance exist from the beginning: the child is born with drives, so it's not like the death drive *only* emerges due to the signifier's meddling. On the other hand, the signifier meets the drives so immediately that if there's going to be a drive of any kind, it's going to be one that has always already been modified by the signifier. The best way to grasp this idea may be to return to the repetition compulsion as one face of the death drive. My sense is that, for Lacan, the repetition compulsion is inextricable from the always unique ways in which the signifier has cut into the subject's biological constitution. So in *that* sense, there's no death drive—in this case, no repetition compulsion—without that cut.

AA: I see, that's helpful. I would like to go back to the link you made a moment ago between the paranoid-schizoid position and jouissance because I find it interesting. It's true that, for Klein, given that splitting and fragmentation are expressions of the death drive, whenever we fall back into the paranoid-schizoid position, we succumb to the force of the death drive. However, unlike with Lacan's understanding of jouissance, for Klein there's little that's positive or valuable about this type of experience—it's basically akin to psychosis. That said—and we can discuss this in greater detail later—there are Kleinians who have argued that the destructiveness of the paranoid-schizoid position can be valuable for creativity by enabling us to break up ossified, static patterns of being and thought in order to create space for something new. In this sense there might be a way of thinking about harnessing the energy of the paranoid-schizoid position much like Lacan talks about tapping into the drive energies of the real. But the question, in both instances, is how to do so without being destroyed in the process.

MR: I agree. I see a parallel between the paranoid-schizoid position and jouissance in part precisely because I believe that in both cases, one can go either in the direction of psychosis—which is one component of Lacan's theorization of jouissance[50]—or in the direction of creativity. The challenge is to manage to stay on the side of creativity without falling into psychosis. Let's definitely come back to this topic.

3

Anxiety

MR: The topic of our third conversation is anxiety. Would you be willing to get us started by elaborating on Klein's distinction between persecutory and depressive anxiety?

AA: Well, first of all, Klein repeatedly emphasizes that the concept of anxiety is central to her. For example, she distinguishes her work from that of Ronald Fairbairn, another object-relations theorist, by saying that while his approach is "largely from the angle of ego-development in relation to objects," her own is "predominantly from the angle of anxieties and their vicissitudes."[1] For Klein, successfully working through anxiety is a precondition not only for subject formation but also for psychoanalysis.

MR: Before you go on, can you explain why Klein believes that the working through of anxiety is necessary for subject formation?

AA: This has to do with the relationship between aggression and anxiety. As I've already stressed, for Klein, aggression is primary in the sense that it's there from the beginning of life. Aggression, in turn, gives rise to anxiety. In order to achieve the kind of integration that we talked about in our first session, which entails a greater incorporation of unconscious content, the subject has to work through its anxiety so that love can take precedence over aggression.

We already know that, for Klein, there are distinctive types of anxiety that correspond to each of her two positions. The paranoid-schizoid position is accompanied by persecutory anxiety, which takes the form of fearing the annihilation of the ego or self. This fear is simultaneously internal and external. Initially, persecutory anxiety emerges internally, as a consequence of the fear of obliteration that the death drive arouses; later, this fear is projected onto the bad breast, which emerges as a persecutory figure that threatens to withhold love, creativity, nourishment, gratification, and so forth.

For Klein, splitting and idealization are among the defenses that correspond to persecutory anxiety. Splitting enables idealization: it's by splitting the breast into good and bad—by relating to it as a part-object—that the child can idealize the good breast as a benevolent source of love, creativity, nourishment, and gratification. And although Klein doesn't talk as much about demonization as she does about idealization, these are obviously two sides of the same coin: it's only by demonizing the bad breast that the good breast can be purified of all badness. Projection and introjection are also defenses against persecutory anxiety: the child projects its aggressive tendencies outward onto the bad breast in part to try to rid itself of these tendencies. As a result, it experiences the aggression as coming from the external persecutory object. The solution, then, is to introject—internalize—the good object, or the good breast, which provides internal stability that can counteract the operation of the death drive.

This dynamic of projection and introjection, in turn, gives rise to depressive anxiety: the form of anxiety that corresponds to the depressive position. Depressive anxiety emerges once the child starts to experience the primary object as a whole object—that is, as a single object that's both good and bad at the same time. The child realizes that the bad breast that it has attempted to destroy—primarily in phantasy, but also in reality by biting and kicking at the breast—is the same as the good breast that it has idealized and upon which it depends for love, nourishment, and gratification. This realization generates depressive anxiety, which is anxiety about the harm that has been done to both the internal and the external object by the child's own destructiveness. Depressive anxiety then gives rise to guilt and the attempt to repair the damage that has been inflicted.

Although Klein has a great deal to say about the characteristic defenses against persecutory anxiety, she has less to say about defenses against depressive anxiety. One that she does discuss is the manic reparation that I briefly referred to at the end of our first conversation, where the subject acts as if the object can be easily put together again in a way that denies the destructiveness of its own aggression.

MR: Can I ask a question that has to do with adult subjects? I know that in the clinical picture, anxiety and depression can coexist, which is why so many people are prescribed medications that target both. SSRIs, I think, fall into this category. Nevertheless, I'm used to envisioning anxiety and depression as having different empirical manifestations in the sense that when someone is anxious, they are agitated, restless, or overanimated, whereas when someone is depressed, they are desolate, listless, and catatonic, unable to get out of bed. How does this work in Klein?

AA: Thinking of anxiety in terms of agitation, restlessness, and overanimation probably corresponds more to Klein's understanding of persecutory anxiety. Depressive anxiety is more complicated, and perhaps encompasses both anxiety and depression in the sense that you have just used those terms. It's a form of anxiety based on the fear that, in attempting to destroy its persecutory object, the subject has also destroyed its good or idealized object. But it's also depressive in that the depressive position is founded on an experience of loss—namely, the loss of the idealized version of the good object. This loss has to do with the fact that when the subject enters the depressive position, it accepts the ambivalence of both the object and its attachment to this object. In other words, the depressive position is marked by the realization that the object that one loves is also the object that one hates, and that the object is both good and bad, gratifying and frustrating, at the same time. This realization entails a gain in complexity and internal differentiation. But it also results in the loss of the idealized good object, which the subject previously experienced as perfectly benevolent, all-nourishing, and all-gratifying. Does this clarify things?

MR: Yes, it does. But it intrigues me—and I would love to hear your thoughts on this—that on the topic of anxiety Klein arguably sounds more brutal than Lacan does. Lacan talks about anxiety in a few different ways, some of which I'll get to in a moment, but what's relevant for my point is that the Kleinian notion of persecutory anxiety can also be found in Lacan, who describes how the subject can become overwhelmed by anxiety because it fantasizes that the other is persecuting it, is essentially threatening to annihilate it. But in Lacan, I don't get the sense that there's any implication that the child's (or the subject's) persecutory fantasy arises from its realization that it has harmed the other (who is now coming after it to exact revenge). When I read Klein, I sometimes can't help but feel that she's saying something like, "Your anxiety is your own fault because you have destroyed your object, and now the object (in your phantasy) has turned against you."

AA: I'm not sure that it would be fair to say that Klein *blames* the child for its anxiety. It's true that the primary cause of anxiety for Klein is the child's own aggression, so in that sense, perhaps you could say that it's the *cause* of its own anxiety—but not because of anything that it has done, which means that the notion of blame is probably a bit out of place. In the final analysis, the cause of anxiety is the internal operation of the death drive. To be sure, the child's radical dependence on its mother and its realization that the mother won't always immediately gratify its needs and wishes can result in aggression, which then gives rise to anxiety, but the ultimate source of anxiety for Klein is innate aggression or the death drive. So, yes, it may sound like a harsh view, but not because it blames individuals for their predicament; rather, it arises from Klein's negative assessment of human nature.[2]

MR: Your point about Klein's negative assessment of human nature makes me think of your claim that she believes that the ambivalence of the drives is ineradicable, which in turn means that aggression can never be definitively banished. At the same time, your commentary on the depressive position implies that the impulse to split—and therefore maybe also the death drive?—can be tempered. Is this what you mean when you say that, in the Kleinian model, the more the ego gets integrated, the less distance there is between good and bad objects?

AA: Yes. In a paper on transference from the 1950s, Klein gets at exactly this point. She explains the goal of analyzing transference as follows: "When anxiety and guilt diminish and love and hate can be better synthesized, splitting processes—a fundamental defence against anxiety—as well as repressions lessen while the ego gains in strength and coherence; the cleavage between idealized and persecutory objects diminishes"—meaning that, as you just said, good and bad objects come closer together—and "the phantastic aspects of objects lose in strength."[3] She then continues with a statement that seems crucial for our discussion of Lacan's critique of the ego: "All of which implies that unconscious phantasy life ... can be better utilized in ego activities, with a consequent general enrichment of the personality."[4]

As we have determined, Klein's use of the term *ego* appears to correspond more closely to the Lacanian subject than the Lacanian ego. For her, integrating the ego isn't about denying anxiety or deluding oneself with regard to the death drive; it's about working through anxiety and learning to tolerate the internal and external manifestations of the death drive and the ambivalence that results from its ineliminability. And it's also an attempt to mitigate the force of the death drive through reparative or even—to preview something we'll discuss later—creative activity.

MR: Speaking of the death drive, I was fascinated over dinner last night when you mentioned that when you observe little children, you sometimes *see* the death drive in action. You have much more experience with children than I do, so can you say more about this? I'm curious in part because even though I have a deep awareness of death as something that awaits me, that awaits everyone I love—so that I grasp, maybe all too immediately, why Heidegger talks about *Dasein* as a matter of being-toward-death—the death drive has always remained enigmatic to me. I don't mean that I don't understand the theory. But I don't have a good sense of what the death drive entails, *practically speaking*. Is it a matter of aggression directed toward the self? Is it self-destructive behavior? Or is it aggressive behavior aimed at others (who might then retaliate)? Or is it all of these?

AA: I guess I would say what Klein herself says in a well-known passage, which is that in her clinical work with children she saw the struggle between the life and death instincts playing itself out all over the place.[5] Anyone who has spent a lot of time with toddlers would most likely find it conceivable to say that aggression is one of our primary ways of relating to the world. I mean, there's just a tremendous amount of screaming, biting, kicking ...

MR: Stubborn refusal?

AA: Yes, that too, flat-out refusal. The best example of the death drive that I can think of is the moment when I would say to my three-year-old, "It's time to go to daycare, let's put on your boots!" and she would scream "No!" at the top of her lungs, as if the request to put on her boots was absolutely trying to destroy her.

As I've explained, Klein believes that the aggression that arises from the death drive can be directed inward or outward. Also, as we have discussed, Klein's account of the death drive is distinct from Freud's because she doesn't base it in the drive to return to quiescence. The Kleinian death drive could almost be equated with hate. In addition, not only are we born with it, but it also comes *first*. This is what I find really interesting. Why is that?

One way to approach this question is to articulate the distinction between Klein's two positions in terms of the duality of the drives. The animating force of the depressive position is love or eros in the sense that Freud uses the latter term in his late work: the depressive position is an erotic stance in that it binds the self together into a richer, more integrated unity. The animating force of the paranoid-schizoid position, in contrast, is the death drive, which is why the experience of that position is fragmented, fractured, and in bits. And it's the paranoid-schizoid position that comes first.

Of course, as I've mentioned, there also has to be love in the paranoid-schizoid position insofar as Klein's story is about how the child relates to its primary object—where the object is understood as a libidinal one. In the paranoid-schizoid position, the infant relates lovingly to the part-object which is the good breast while simultaneously relating destructively to the bad breast part-object. So love is possible in the paranoid-schizoid position but the position *itself* isn't characterized by love or eros but rather by splitting and fragmentation—that is, by aggression and destructiveness.

The achievement of the depressive position, then, is to utilize the binding power of eros to mitigate hatred, aggression, and destructiveness. For Klein, the strength of the ego—including its ability to tolerate anxiety so as to soften the force of the death drive—is a function of its capacity for love.[6] Nonetheless, the love or eros that's manifest in the depressive position is fundamentally ambivalent in the sense that it has aggression, loss, and guilt built into it.

MR: In her book on Klein,[7] Segal gives some examples of both the death drive and the drive for reparation from her own—clearly Klein-influenced—clinical practice. At one point, she talks about her sessions with a little girl. In the first session the girl destroys a box of paints that she's supposed to use to draw a picture. She arrives at the session and goes after the paints with a vengeance for no apparent reason. Segal interprets this as an aggressive, destructive, and death-driven moment. Then in the next two sessions, the girl makes tentative attempts at reparation: she tries to put the paints back together, but can't, so she gets frustrated and starts screaming, but eventually she asks for help. Segal reads the girl's act of asking for help as a move toward the depressive position: the girl realizes that she has destroyed something and displeased the adult who was trying to help her and that it's time for her to try to make things better.

It seems that in this example it's possible to see both persecutory and depressive anxiety at work. It shows how anxiety can give rise to aggression, but it also shows how it can lead to—or even be part of—the attempt to repair. For me, it's intuitively easy to grasp a scenario where anxiety generates the wish to make things right. But it sounds like Klein places a great deal of emphasis on the connection between anxiety and aggression.

AA: Yes, she does. And in my experience, the claim that anxiety and aggression are closely linked seems entirely plausible. This could mean that people who experience a high degree of anxiety lash out aggressively at others because they can't manage their inner turmoil. But Klein suggests that the reverse is also true, that anxiety is a feeling of inner turmoil that results from a heightened level of aggressivity. I have no idea how one would establish which comes first, anxiety or aggression, but they definitely seem to be connected. This is why, although I don't know exactly how to assess the truth of Klein's claim that aggression comes first, I think that it's a provocative extension of Freud's understanding of the death drive.

MR: What jumps to mind in this context is what some Lacanians describe as the "undeadness" of the death drive, of the repetition compulsion.[8] On the most basic level, this means that, for Lacanians, as for Klein, the death drive is ineradicable. But what I also find interesting about this undeadness is that it can be linked to the idea that even though the death drive is pushing the subject toward destruction, toward an injuring repetition, it's also on some level trying to master a trauma that hasn't been properly worked through. The death drive is undead, repeatedly awakens in order to push the subject into the same traumatizing position. It's almost like its logic is that if it keeps putting the subject in the same tormenting situation, *eventually* the subject will figure out how to manage the situation and thereby stop the damage that the situation is causing (or has caused). But of course in most instances, this strategy just drives the subject further and further into the lacerating place of traumatization. This dynamic must generate a tremendous degree of anxiety, which I can see translating into frustrated aggression directed against others. This would be one Lacanian way to understand the connection between anxiety and aggression.

AA: Klein describes how anxiety and aggression interact with one another in a vicious circle, and how important this is for thinking about social change. On this, it's worth quoting her at length:

> The repeated attempts that have been made to improve humanity—in particular to make it more peaceable—have failed, because nobody has understood the full depth and vigor of the instincts of aggression innate in each individual. Such efforts do not seek to do more than encourage the positive, well-wishing impulses of the person while denying or suppressing his aggressive ones. And so they have been doomed to failure from the beginning. But psycho-analysis has different means at its disposal for a task of this kind. It cannot, it is true, altogether do away with man's aggressive instinct as such; but it can, by diminishing the anxiety which accentuates those instincts, break up the mutual reinforcement that is going on all the time between his hatred and his fear.[9]

Just as an aside, several years ago I used this quote as an epigraph for a paper on Klein and critical theory. I placed it as a block quote at the top of the first page of the paper, with a footnote indicating that Klein was the source. When I got the reviews back for that article, one of the reviewers said that although the paper itself was perfectly fine, I really needed to rewrite the abstract because it was the most arrogant, pompous, and outrageous abstract that they had ever seen [laughter].

MR: [laughter] That's hilarious.

AA: My reaction was to think: "I *wish* I had the nerve to write an abstract like that!" But more to the point, Klein's elaboration of the mutual reinforcement between aggression and anxiety, between hatred and fear, and the way that she attempts to give us resources for breaking up this vicious cycle—all of this seems potentially productive for thinking about politics. It seems straightforwardly applicable to thinking about our contemporary political situation, for example, about the reinforcement between hatred and fear that's being mobilized by the alt right against the figure of the immigrant, the refugee, and the Muslim. I hope that we can discuss this more in a later conversation.

MR: I find Klein's statement incredibly provocative in its sheer simplicity: she's saying that, collectively, we haven't been able to solve the problem of violence because we have underestimated the degree to which human beings are driven by aggression born out of fear (or anxiety). And she offers psychoanalysis as an (always imperfect) solution. Lacan says something related about the impossibility of progress in human life and the role that psychoanalysis has played in discovering this impossibility in *Seminar II*. This goes back to the idea that humans are deformed and incapable of adapting to their environment. He states:

> What does analysis uncover—if it isn't the fundamental, radical discordance of forms of conduct essential to man in relation to everything which he experiences? The dimension discovered by analysis is the opposite of anything which progresses through adaptation, through approximation, through being perfected. ... In man, it is the wrong form which prevails. In so far as a task is not completed the subject returns to it. The more abject the failure, the better the subject remembers it.[10]

Psychoanalysis discovered that humans don't progress through adaptation, through being perfected. In the subject, it's the "wrong form which prevails." And the more this wrong form prevails—the more impossible you find it to complete the task of righting this wrong—the more insistently you return to it; the more abject your failure, the better you remember it, even if just unconsciously, and the more you return to it. This is related to what I said about the undeadness—the persistence—of the death drive a moment ago. The repetition compulsion as your "destiny" drives you back to the "wrong form which prevails," inducing you to reenact it. As Lacan continues, "That's what the need for repetition is, as we see it emerge beyond the pleasure principle. ... The human being himself is in part outside life, he partakes of the death instinct. Only from there can he engage in the register of life."[11] The subject is always in part outside life, in the claws of the death drive, which is undead in the sense of being inhuman, mechanical, and which is the only place from where the subject can approach any kind of a life. This is why progress is difficult.

In a recent essay of yours, you address the complexity of the ideal of progress in a manner that I find arresting. On the one hand, you emphasize the necessity of adopting the negative—or realistic—view of human beings that Klein (and I would add, Lacan, in his own way) advances. On the other, you propose that, from a Kleinian viewpoint, even though the notion of progress as a forward-looking aspiration or moral imperative "is predicated upon a kind of wishful thinking,"[12] we aren't entirely doomed because even if we can't completely eliminate aggression, we may be able to learn to better manage it. In addition, like Klein, you hypothesize that if we can alleviate anxiety, we may also be able to alleviate aggression. Once again, the matter comes down to being able to tolerate ambivalence, ambiguity, conflict, and tension, which would reduce the need to split the world into the good (the idealized me) and the bad (the demonized other).

In this context, you connect Klein to Adorno, which I think is brilliant—I mean, who mentions Klein and Adorno in the same paragraph? You posit that progress, for Klein, amounts to something quite cautious that's conceptually close to Adorno's "negativistic conception of progress as the avoidance of catastrophe."[13] You point out that, for Klein, catastrophe results from an unrestrained process of splitting, projection, and introjection—from a full-blown materialization of the paranoid-schizoid position. And then you suggest that her account of the depressive position as the ability to tolerate, without any hope of reconciliation, the ambivalence of the self and of its relationships to objects can be compared to Adorno's notion of negative dialectics, "understood as a kind of non-repressive togetherness of difference."[14]

I can't help but think about the Lacanian claim that the only cure is to recognize that there's no cure as a version of Adorno's "negativistic conception of progress." Can you say more about your argument about Klein and Adorno?

AA: The basic idea I have is that the subject in Klein's depressive position—which is characterized by the drive for integration—is doing something akin to what Adorno conceptualizes as an alternative to what he calls identity thinking.[15] To be sure, Adorno would have been allergic to any talk of integration. On his view, integration is central to identity thinking, which is the kind of subsumptive logic that subordinates all particulars and differences to universals, thereby doing great violence to particularity and difference. For him, this logic is characteristic of both modern philosophy—he's primarily thinking of the idealist tradition of German neo-Kantianism and Hegelianism—and of capitalist modernity and it culminates in the violence of the Holocaust. This idea is central to his critique of late capitalist modernity. As he states with his characteristic bluntness: "Genocide is the absolute integration."[16] It therefore makes sense that Adorno was critical of psychoanalytic approaches that focus on integration. For him, saying that the goal of analysis was the achievement of a well-integrated personality meant asking the subject to reconcile itself to a world that's riven by internal conflict and contradiction. Integration for him meant a problematic form of normalization, what he called a "false reconciliation with an unreconciled world."[17]

MR: Adorno's objections to integration sound more or less identical to those of Lacan, which isn't surprising given that both were critical of the history of Western metaphysics. Both despise the idea that psychoanalysis can be turned into a tool of normalization that asks the subject to reconcile itself to the existing—hegemonic and oppressive—social order.

AA: Indeed. However, for reasons that we have discussed, I don't think that what Klein means by the integration of the ego in the depressive position is the same as what Adorno means by integration. She's not talking about a false harmony that's achieved through the subsumption of the drives under the mastery of the rational ego. This isn't to say that she goes as far as Adorno does in claiming that internal psychic conflicts can be resolved only through a radical change in the social world. She's a psychoanalyst rather than a social theorist. Nevertheless, her idea of tolerating without any hope of reconciliation the indissoluble ambivalence between the life and death drives strikes me as similar to how Adorno describes negative dialectics as the *non*identity of identity and nonidentity.[18] This negative dialectics is his alternative to tyrannical identity thinking, which seeks to merge identity and nonidentity into a higher order of identity (or unity).

Although Adorno was famously reluctant to spell out in any detail a conception of utopia or the good society, he does occasionally suggest what the alternative to identity thinking would be like, and central to this alternative is that it involves a non-totalizing and open-ended "togetherness of diversity" that's "above identity and above contradiction."[19] To me, this sounds very much like the Kleinian depressive position which is above identity—in the sense that the fundamental ambivalence of the drives is retained without either drive being subsumed into the other—and also above contradiction in the sense that the splitting characteristic of the paranoid-schizoid position has been overcome. The subject in Klein's depressive position is able to contain diverse and contradictory drives in a coherent way without either subsuming these drives under the rational mastery of the ego or splitting them into clashing poles. This is why I think that Klein can be seen as offering a psychoanalytic model of subjectivity that corresponds to Adorno's conception of negative dialectics.

With respect to progress, Klein and Adorno are allied in rejecting any and all positive utopian visions, even if not for the same reasons. Adorno thought that it was impossible to produce a vision of the good society from within a society as fundamentally wrong as ours. Having witnessed the descent of Europe into fascism and the Holocaust, which for him gave the lie to the idea that history can be read as a story of progress, he believed that the most we can hope for is a faint glimmer of possibility that things could be otherwise, a glimmer that would allow a weak messianic light to shine through the cracks and fissures in the present social order.[20] Although he didn't completely discard all hope for the future because doing so would have been to wallow in conservative despair, his understanding of progress is negativistic, meaning—as you said when you quoted my essay—that progress entails the avoidance of catastrophe.[21] Klein arrives at a comparable view in the psychoanalytic context. Whitebook suggests that psychoanalysis "considers utopianism to be undesirable in principle."[22] This is partly because psychoanalysis teaches us to be suspicious of the idealizing assumptions—about human nature, rationality, and so forth—on which visions of utopia are based. But it's also because psychoanalysis provides a reflection on the dangerous degree of narcissism and infantile omnipotence embedded in such idealizing assumptions, including the idea that we have the power to realize our utopian aspirations, to make them come to life in the real world.[23] Whitebook's perspective seems to sum up Klein's position perfectly.

Yet Klein doesn't think that there's *nothing* we can do: even if strong conceptions of utopia are problematic, and even dangerous, because they deny the ubiquity and persistence of primary aggression, there are still better and worse ways of managing aggression (including sublimating it) and of breaking up the vicious circle of anxiety and aggression that leads to perilous forms of splitting. In a way, Klein suggests that we will never be able to make progress—in the sense of figuring out better ways of managing the risks associated with the death drive—until we face the death drive's ineliminability. However, I think that Klein would agree with Lacan that the recognition that there's no cure—no possibility of completely eradicating the negative effects of the death drive—doesn't mean that there's nothing for us to do. Indeed, accepting that there's no cure is the key to enabling whatever positive work psychoanalysis can do.

MR: I agree that the recognition that there's no cure isn't a matter of nihilistic capitulation. It's more like this recognition allows you to start living in a richer, more present way: instead of squandering your energies in a futile quest for wholeness, you learn to live with the brokenness of your being while simultaneously looking for ways to repair some of it (without falling into the illusion that it could ever be entirely fixed). This may sound like a dreadful strategy for tackling social problems because it implies that you're simply going to give up in the face of their complexity. Yet in *Capitalism and Desire*, Todd McGowan posits that the mistake that many progressive social movements make is that by pursuing progress narratives—utopian visions of an immaculate future—they replicate the logic of capitalism, which tells us that effort will be rewarded, that if we just try hard enough, eventually everything will be perfect.[24] And you're right that psychoanalysis—at least the genre of psychoanalysis associated with Freud, Klein, and Lacan—teaches us to be skeptical of such idealizing progress narratives.

Psychoanalysis also teaches us that anxiety is an inescapable component of human life, which brings me to what Lacan has to say about it, which is so much that I can only scratch the surface of his interpretation. From *Seminar X*—Lacan's seminar on anxiety—I want to extract three ways of thinking about the topic that all have to do with Lacan's understanding of why the subject frequently experiences the other as menacing. In this instance, I'm referring to the interpersonal other rather than the big Other, though obviously it's impossible to seamlessly separate the two, given that every subject has been formed by and lives under the auspices of the big Other. Still, I want to focus on the interpersonal other because I, once again, hope to counter the common misconception that Lacan operates with a solipsistic, asocial model of subjectivity.

In yesterday's conversation, I already stressed that this assumption about the asociality of Lacan's model of subjectivity is misleading when I pointed out that Lacan believes that intersubjectivity exists from the beginning of life. His seminar on anxiety, in turn, showcases the importance of intersubjectivity in the experience of the adult subject by focusing on the ways in which anxiety arises in response to the (fantasized or actual) desires, demands, or threats originating from the other. I'll get to the relevant details of Lacan's argument in a moment, but let me start with a condensed outline to illustrate right away why I believe that my point about intersubjectivity is warranted.

First, Lacan suggests that I might get anxious because I fear that the other might deepen my lack: I'm already a creature of lack, but the other might wound me and heighten my sense of being castrated and deficient. Second, I might worry that the other might suffocate me. This is in many ways the opposite of being afraid that the other might intensify my lack: the problem here is my distress about the possibility that the other might *deprive* me of my lack—essentially, steal my lack—and because lack is what makes me a subject, this is *really* threatening. Third, I might feel anxious because there's something overagitating and overwhelming about the enigmatic signifiers emanating from the other. Lacan is here arguably more object related than Klein, for whom anxiety appears to be inborn insofar as it's linked to aggression, which, as you have argued, is primary. Lacan's account of anxiety as an effect of the subject's encounters with the outside world in fact makes it surprisingly compatible with recent critical theoretical models—such as affect theory, which we'll discuss tomorrow—that insist that bad feelings such as anxiety are at least partially socially generated. For instance, being persecuted by the other (let alone the big Other) isn't always a fantasy but a vicious reality. Although Lacan analyzes anxiety in interpersonal—rather than large-scale social—contexts, his formulations may be useful for grasping why the contemporary era feels like an age of anxiety.

It does feel like there's something about our cultural moment that's saturated with anxiety, right? Of course I'm not a historian, so I don't know if it's empirically true that there's more anxiety now than there was, say, a hundred years ago, but many critics in my field are implying that this is the case: they are suggesting that there's something about our information-saturated neoliberal late capitalist era that makes anxiety impossible to avoid because it mandates incessant performance and productivity, insists on constant self-improvement, and asks us to maintain a positive attitude even as it piles one demand after another on us. And it doesn't help that we're urged to achieve balance in our lives because the very fact that we can't achieve it—that the frenzied pace of life that we're expected to maintain makes it impossible for us to achieve it—only heightens our anxiety: we're failing at the very thing that's supposed to free us from anxiety and this makes us even more anxious.

Here's the Cliff Notes version of Lacan's theorization of anxiety. First, Lacan renders concrete the subject's terror of the other deepening its lack by (mockingly) describing the straight man's sexual performance anxiety. Lacan's point is that for a man the height of sexual release—meaning orgasm (jouissance)—is also always a moment of metaphorical castration: he loses his erection. So much for phallic might. Lacan describes the phallus as evanescent, specifying that detumescence is the logical outcome of every attempt at phallic mastery. This is one of my favorite passages from *Seminar X*:

> The … organ can be said to yield, each and every time, prematurely. When the time comes at which it could be the sacrificial object, so to speak, well, let's say that, in the ordinary case, it had ducked out a long while before. It's no more than a scrap, it is no longer there for the partner save as a keepsake, a souvenir of tenderness. This is what the castration complex is all about.[25]

The phallus can be erected temporarily, but then it collapses, becomes a mere "scrap." Moreover, in the man's anxious fantasy life—and maybe sometimes, from the woman's perspective, also in reality [laughter]—it often deflates prematurely. Recall that Lacan argues, not just in this seminar but also in *Seminar XX*, that women have access to a surplus of jouissance. You can spin this idea in a variety of ways—we could go all the way to Saint Teresa and mysticism with it—but in the present context, the most literal reading might be the most useful: women are multi-orgasmic, which means that sometimes the guy just can't keep up. And sometimes he fails to deliver the goods even once.

Lacan argues—and this is why anyone who believes that Lacan is phallocentric should read this seminar—that once the man "has made love like everyone else does and lies uncocked,"[26] and especially if the woman hasn't derived any tangible profit from the encounter, hasn't had an orgasm, she knows exactly what her role is supposed to be: she realizes that her assignment in heterosexual relationships is to prop up the man's ego, "to offer man's desire the object behind the phallic claims, the non-detumescent object to sustain his desire, namely, to make her feminine attributes the signs of man's almightiness."[27] In other words, the woman's tiresome task is to ensure that the man doesn't have to face his lack of might, his vulnerability. This isn't a pretty picture of heterosexuality, but I wouldn't characterize it as phallocentric or antifeminist.

Lacan's point is that the deflated penis isn't of much use to the woman. Love can compensate for this irrelevance. But this doesn't alter the fact that the dynamic that Lacan depicts has to do with the failure of the phallus as a signifier of power. This is why it becomes "the common-place of anxiety."[28] Furthermore, this evanescence of the phallus is why, according to Lacan, some men "foment almightiness,"[29] put on excessive displays of power in order to conceal their fundamental anxiety about their lack.

Lacan implies that the phallus is only of interest to psychoanalysis insofar as it fails, insofar as it signifies the reality of castration. In other words, if Lacan goes on and on about the phallus, it's not—and this is what many non-Lacanian critics don't grasp—because he wants to valorize it but, quite the contrary, because he wants to dethrone it by revealing how completely illusory its power ultimately is. Moreover, recall that Lacan believes that women can also lay claim to phallic power. Due to gender discrimination, women might find it more difficult than men to wield this power. But—because for Lacan anatomy isn't destiny—in principle women can aspire to possess this power. This means that the anxiety that Lacan in *Seminar X* aligns with men's sexual performance anxiety can also impact women who choose to "foment almightiness." Any situation where you're afraid of being shown lacking or losing mastery is, from this point of view, intrinsically anxiety inducing.

During all of my years of teaching Lacan, I've found it difficult to explain to undergraduates what he means by castration because they tend to fixate on the idea of losing one's penis, when in fact castration is a much more capacious concept in Lacan, not only (sometimes at least) more or less synonymous with the subject's constitutive lack-in-being, but also connected to the anxiety of potentially having to involuntarily "yield" a part of oneself. Last year, I finally came up with an example that created a genuine aha-moment for my students. Many of them are into pop culture, so I mentioned a scene in the television show *Gotham*, which is a DC comics show based on a cartoon, which in turn means that pretty horrific things can happen. There's this one scene where the queen of the underworld, Fish Mooney—played brilliantly by Jada Pinkett Smith—is completely cornered by the bad guys, has no way out, and she takes a spoon and yanks one of her eyes out of its socket—

AA: [reacts with shock]

MR: Yup. You're watching the scene and asking yourself what the hell Fish is going to do to save herself, and suddenly her eye is on the floor, and you ... well, you understand what Lacan means by castration. In fact, in his seminar on anxiety, there are reprints of two paintings from the 1630s by Francisco de Zurbarán, and in the first of these a woman is holding two eyes on a platter. In the second, a woman is holding two cut-off breasts—nipples facing upward—on a platter.[30]

AA: Fascinating—this sounds very much like what Klein would call persecutory anxiety, anxiety about being broken up into bits.

MR: Right. And the breasts? Did Zurbarán understand something about the good and bad breast? Why not two dicks on a platter? [laughter]

The second way Lacan portrays anxiety might also have resonances with the Kleinian model. He refers to the praying mantis, who decapitates her partner after copulation. This is obviously also an image of castration. But in this part of the text Lacan is more interested in the idea that an other person—like the praying mantis—can come too close, can become persecutory, suffocating. Here the problem is less that you're rendered lacking than that the other's overproximity robs you of your lack. Lacan states:

> Don't you know that it's not longing for the maternal breast that provokes anxiety, but its imminence? What provokes anxiety is everything that announces to us, that lets us glimpse, that we're going to be taken back onto the lap. It is not, contrary to what is said, the rhythm of the mother's alternating presence and absence. The proof of this is that the infant revels in repeating this game of presence and absence. The security of presence is the possibility of absence. The most anguishing thing for the infant is precisely the moment when the relationship upon which he's established himself, of the lack that turns him into desire, is disrupted, and this relationship is most disrupted when there's no possibility of any lack, when the mother is on his back all the while, and especially when she's wiping his backside. This is one model of demand, of the demand that will never let up. ... Anxiety isn't about the loss of the object, but its presence. The objects aren't missing. ... Once more, *there's no lack*.[31]

There's a lot going on here: The breast is too close (imminent, looming). Fort-da is impossible because the mother doesn't leave. You aren't allowed to experience your lack, which, for the Lacanian subject, equals the death of subjectivity. In this scenario of the other being too close, what you're lacking is your lack. Or at least you're being threatened with the loss of your lack. Yikes!

Finally, the third way of thinking about anxiety from a Lacanian viewpoint has to do with the enigmatic signifier, which is related to what I just said about the overproximity of the other: when the other is too close, it's also quite possibly emitting messages that the child (or even the adult) can't decipher. In the long passage I quoted from Lacan, he mentions a "demand that will never let up." The enigmatic message could be interpreted as such a demand. The anxiety that such a message—an enigmatic but insistent demand—can produce is easy to understand on the level of the big Other: when Homeland Security or the University Administration wants something, the motivation of the demand isn't always clear. I don't know about you, but this is a huge anxiety factor for me. Likewise, enigmatic messages arising from small-o others, especially loved ones, can be equally rattling.

Another way to express the matter is to say that when you don't know what people want from you, you no longer know what you are to these people, who you are in relation to these people. Lacan maintains that this dynamic is at the core of the hysteric's *che vuoi?*, which I've already called attention to as the hysteric's characteristic stance in relation to others. The hysteric's question is: What is the other's desire with regard to me? What does the other want from me? Who am I in the eyes of the other?

These explanations of anxiety are one reason I believe that it's easy to apply Lacan's thinking to collective situations of social inequality, even though he himself doesn't do so. The guy who comments on your appearance on the street when you're trying to focus on your own concerns, or the person who stares at you on the subway because your gender isn't easily readable, or the policeman who does a "stop and frisk" on a black man for no clear reason—these are all instances of the other being too close, too demanding, and also too enigmatic, and you're like, "What the fuck do you want from me?" But sadly, usually your anger is laced with anxiety.

AA: This all sounds incredibly productive. In terms of connecting it to Klein's account, it seems that the first two kinds of anxiety that you draw from Lacan are about the dialectic of fusion versus individuation that we discussed yesterday. So even if they don't exactly map onto Klein's vision, they are very much at issue in her work. Perhaps the first form of anxiety you outlined is closer to Klein's notion of persecutory anxiety because it's about the fear that the other is going to destroy me violently by castrating me. I don't think that Klein would talk about the matter in terms of castration, but persecutory anxiety is definitely about a fear of annihilation at the hands of the other, even if this fear is in part rooted in projective identification, by means of which the infant has projected its bad feelings onto the object, which it subsequently perceives as persecutory.

The second type of anxiety, the fear of being suffocated or deprived of lack—I wonder if there's an analogue for it in Klein. As we determined yesterday, I don't think that Klein accepts the standard psychoanalytic story of fusion, though she does talk about the infant's fears of being devoured (which, for her, are rooted in the infant's own attempts to destroy the libidinal object by biting or devouring it).[32] But one thing that interests me about this kind of anxiety is that it might offer yet another reason for being suspicious of the idealization of the mother-infant fusion. In Honneth's work, for example, fusion is presented as a wholly wonderful experience, whereas on the Lacanian view, insofar as it involves an elimination of lack that's tantamount to an annihilation of subjectivity, it's also terrifying.

Lacan's account reminds me of one of my favorite passages from *Dialectic of Enlightenment*, where Horkheimer and Adorno describe the tremendous effort and internal structure of domination that's required to hold the modern, bourgeois subject together: "Humanity had to inflict terrible injuries on itself before the self—the identical, purpose-directed, masculine character of human beings—was created, and something of this process is repeated in every childhood."[33] As a result of this sacrificial structure of modern subjectivity, they continue, "The fear of losing the self, and suspending with it the boundary between oneself and other life, the aversion to death and destruction, is twinned with a promise of joy which has threatened civilization at every moment."[34] In other words, the dissolution of the boundary between the self and the other—whether you think of it in terms of fusion or plunging into the jouissance of the real—may promise unmediated joy yet it's also terrifying. And it's precisely the terrifying, overwhelming, and deeply threatening aspects of fusion that seem to be missing from Honneth's theory.

MR: Lacan's idea that one face of anxiety has to do with the fear of self-annihilation as a consequence of fusion certainly presents a direct challenge to Honneth's idealization of the mother-child relationship. However, perhaps even more fundamentally, it presents a challenge to the very notion of fusion itself because you can't possibly be anxious about fusion unless you have a sense of the other as someone who can challenge the boundary between itself and you, unless—as we discussed yesterday—there's a rudimentary sense of intersubjectivity from the beginning. I suppose my assumption is that if you're already fully fused, you're not anxious about fusion; you can only be anxious about it when it's something that you can imagine happening but that hasn't yet happened. Maybe this isn't the right analogy, but I'll use it anyway: you can be anxious about death before it happens but presumably not when you're actually dead.

In the second form of anxiety that I extracted from Lacan, you're not anxious because you're fused with the other but because the other won't leave you alone; the other is too present. The guy who stares at you on the subway because your gender isn't readable, or because he's trying to objectify you sexually, isn't attempting to fuse with you; he's just uncomfortably close. This is related to Hannah Arendt's argument about how we live in a society where the overproximity of others is ubiquitous.[35]

AA: Yes, but for Klein, the other is both an external and an internal object. Insofar as the other is part of you, part of your internal world, it will never leave you alone!

MR: *Je suis un Autre* (Rimbaud). Klein gives us a foretaste of the poststructuralist deconstruction of subjectivity. But I'm wondering if we might be speaking on two different levels here. For the infant, the other is both external and internal. And for adult subjects, intimate others—including colleagues—are both external and internal. But the random guy on the subway seems primarily external. Yes, he's *trying* to get under your skin, and may even succeed, thereby becoming internal. But he's not internal to you when he enters the subway car, except as a potential personification of the omnipresent social problems of heteropatriarchy, homophobia, and misogyny that have indeed most likely already infiltrated your psychic life in damaging ways.

AA: You're right that Klein is talking about what you're calling intimate others, such as the primary caretaker. In that context, the fact that the other is both external and internal may be a source of anxiety, but it can also be a source of strength, provided that you have been able to internalize a good object that has formed the core of your ego.

As far as the anxiety generated by the other's enigmatic messages goes, as I've said before, since Klein doesn't have a fully developed account of language, I'm not sure that she has an analog for this conception of anxiety. For her, symbolization results from the move to the depressive position, and in that sense it might be better understood as a response to anxiety than as one of its causes.

MR: Here I should add, though, that the enigmatic signifier can be unspoken, that it's not necessarily linked to language.

AA: Right, but it would still be linked to the symbolic order or to symbolization broadly understood, wouldn't it? I think that Klein sees this as a mature, depressive response to anxiety.

MR: I don't think that this is incompatible with Lacan. While he believes that the enigmatic signifiers of the other can generate anxiety, he views the subject's *own* processes of signification—narrativization, sublimation, creativity, free association, "full" (meaningful) speech, and so on—as an antidote to anxiety. At least this is how I interpret him, for reasons that I'll explain when we go into greater detail about creativity. In addition, because the capacity to (verbally) signify arises from lack—because the symbolic order gives you the gift of discourse at the same time as it castrates you—it's intrinsically linked to the melancholy structure of subjectivity that I've referred to before. In this sense, we might be close to the Kleinian depressive position, even if the Lacanian subject (or child) reaches the place of sadness later in its developmental trajectory.

It seems to me that many of us write or speak—even babble—as a way to alleviate anxiety. We even go to analysis in order to be able to speak to the empty space in front of us. And I don't think that the other's signifiers are always menacing: certainly they can comfort, soothe, and calm us. Between friends, the exchange of discourse is an invaluable resource for basic sanity. My point is merely that there are times when the other's signifiers remain so mysterious that they become a source of anxiety.

AA: That's an important clarification.

With respect to Klein and Lacan's overall conceptions of anxiety, I'm interested in an opaque comment that Lacan makes in *Seminar XI* that sounds like it might resonate with Klein's account. Someone from the audience asks Lacan to explain why—during his previous year's seminar on anxiety—he claimed that anxiety doesn't deceive. Lacan responds that it's true, anxiety doesn't deceive.[36] And then he continues with a statement that sounds similar to what Klein says about anxiety: "In experience, it is necessary to canalize it"—

MR: Canalize?

AA: I think this means to give it direction or to channel it. Lacan goes on to say: "to take it in small doses, so that one is not overcome by it. This is a difficulty similar to that of bringing the subject into contact with the real."[37] The notion of processing anxiety in small doses so that one isn't overcome by it but instead can work through it, metabolize it, sounds close to Klein's understanding of the working through of anxiety.

MR: Absolutely. The reference that Lacan makes to the real at the end of his statement makes it clear that he's getting at exactly what you just expressed. He's gesturing toward the fact that none of us can survive a full-blown encounter with the real for long. Imagine an eight-hour orgasm: it would be intolerable. This is why we need to circle the Thing, the heart—or the black hole at the heart—of the real, by cathecting to *objets a* that give us a little taste of it rather than hurling us headlong into its sphere. What he's saying about anxiety is similar, namely that in order to survive or work through it, we have to be able to metabolize it gradually, bit by bit.

The idea that anxiety doesn't deceive is a refrain that runs through the anxiety seminar. I take it to mean (at least) that anxiety is one of the few things about human life that never lies. You may be able to pretend to have it. But you can't pretend *not* to have it. And then the question becomes, what happens if you can't metabolize it? Do you fall into the position of the schizophrenic, the psychotic, or the manic side of the bipolar? Do you fall outside the symbolic?

AA: Into Klein's paranoid-schizoid position, in other words.

MR: Ah, brilliant!

AA: Speaking of the ability to metabolize anxiety, it seems important to return to the question of what might constitute an antidote to it. A moment ago, you suggested that for Lacan, this antidote might be sublimation, creativity, or discourse. I think that for Klein it might be love. But I want to be careful in making this argument because I don't want to idealize her conception of love by making it seem like a happy-happy thing, by turning Klein into a Pollyanna. As I've stressed, given Klein's commitment to the primacy of aggression, she believes that there's no love—no primary object love or any other kind of love relationship, analytic transference, or social bond held together by eros—without guilt, anxiety, aggression, and ambivalence. At the same time, as complicated as love is for Klein, it's clear that she nevertheless regards it as a potential antidote to hatred, aggression, and destructiveness. Love (in the form of reparation) not only helps us to mitigate or undo the damage done by aggression; it's also crucial for the achievement of the depressive position and the development of an integrated personality that won't collapse back into the persecutory anxieties and defenses of the paranoid-schizoid position.

Love thus plays two roles. First, it allows the child to move from the paranoid-schizoid to the depressive position. In other words, part of the story about this transition is that the child needs a secure enough attachment to its good object—which just means enough experiences of love, support, gratification, and nourishment—to enable it to gradually moderate its aggressive impulses. Later in life, in situations where aggression (inevitably) comes to the fore and splitting, projection, and other primitive defenses are at work, love serves as a corrective to these defenses in the form of the drive for reparation.

Second—and I'll return to this theme in a later conversation—love, understood in Klein's complicated and ambivalent sense, could be connected to discussions of reparative as opposed to retributive justice as a way of thinking about how reparation can play an important political role in response to experiences of large-scale social conflict.

MR: I can see how Klein's notion of reparation can be useful for thinking about how it might be possible to mitigate social and political conflicts. In this context, I'm thinking about the passage from Klein that you read earlier regarding the connection between fear and hatred, where the implication was that the only way to decrease hatred is to decrease fear. So the challenge is to figure out how to decrease fear.

But can I ask for a clarification about Klein's model? I can see how the depressive position, and the impulse to repair that goes with it, functions as an antidote to the paranoid-schizoid one, which—as you explained earlier—contains the worse of the two kinds of Kleinian anxiety, the persecutory anxiety that leads to aggression toward the other, whereas depressive anxiety leads to self-beratement and aggression toward the self. Does this mean that, for Klein, aggression toward the self is always more acceptable than aggression toward the other? Is she Levinasian in this way?

AA: I'm not sure that that's quite right because both types of anxiety are directed both outward and inward. That is, persecutory anxiety leads not only to aggression toward the object but also to aggression pointed inward in the form of internal fragmentation. Depressive anxiety in turn generates the drive to repair not only one's object—to experience it as a whole object with both good and bad aspects—but also oneself by integrating (in the sense of expanding and enriching) one's ego. In addition, although depressive anxiety is related to guilt—to the harm done by one's destructiveness— the Kleinian model is different from the classical Nietzschean or Freudian model of guilt as internalized aggression in the form of self-beratement or self-laceration. For Klein, guilt generates the impulse to reverse the damaging effects of destructiveness and to preserve the life of the other.[38] Ultimately, the depressive position is held together not by aggression but rather by love.

MR: That's well articulated. The contrast with Nietzsche and Freud helps to clarify the matter for me.

AA: There's one more aspect of Klein's account of anxiety that I want to put on the table, which relates to a differentiation that she makes between two sources of anxiety. In her paper on the theory of anxiety and guilt,[39] she distinguishes between what she calls external or objective anxiety and internal or neurotic anxiety. External anxiety stems from an actual experience in the world, such as the child's radical dependence on the mother. Internal anxiety, by contrast, arises from the fear of having destroyed the good object, which means that it's ultimately rooted in one's own aggression. This distinction maps on pretty neatly to the distinction between external reality and psychic reality, or between the intersubjective and the intrapsychic. Klein's claim is that these two sources of anxiety—and, by extension, these two realities—can never be fully pulled apart:

> There is from the beginning a constant interaction between these two sources of anxiety, that is to say, between objective and neurotic anxiety or in other words, anxiety from external and internal sources. Furthermore, if external danger is from the beginning linked with internal danger from the death instinct, no danger-situation arising from external sources could ever be experienced by the young child as a purely external and known danger.[40]

Klein is saying that the reason the child experiences the deprivation of the breast, and thus its relationship to the external object, as anxiety producing is that this deprivation plays into the child's fear of annihilation at the hands of its own death instinct. Internal or neurotic anxiety is the primordial experience of anxiety.

Klein goes on to say: "But it is not only the infant who cannot make such a clear differentiation: to some extent the interaction between external and internal danger-situations persists throughout life."[41] And then she offers an interesting example: "This was clearly shown in the analysis carried out in war-time. ... even with normal adults anxiety stirred up by air-raids, bombs, fire, etc.—*i.e.* by an 'objective' danger-situation—could only be reduced by analysing, over and above the impact of the actual situation, the various early anxieties which were aroused by it."[42] In other words, the reason that people found air-raids, bombs, and fires so anxiety producing was that these dangers reignited or rearoused their early anxieties, and thus the only way to calm their anxiety was to address these early anxieties (rather than simply to address the objective situation).

This suggests that one person might be extremely anxious even in a situation that isn't objectively dangerous, whereas another person might not be at all anxious even in an objectively dangerous situation, perhaps because they have such high levels of internal anxiety that they defend against the objective danger by denying it.[43] So the two types of anxiety are constantly interacting in complicated ways. This is yet another moment where the relationship between the intersubjective and the intrapsychic is prominent in Klein.

MR: Klein's claim regarding air-raids, bombs, fire, etc. is provocative. It's difficult to process the idea that the anxiety aroused by these objective dangers can only be reduced by analyzing preexisting (presumably much more enigmatic) internal anxieties. It's like saying that people with PTSD—say, from war or rape—can only ever be helped by digging into their childhoods, which, frankly, sounds far-fetched.

Klein's argument makes me think of two earlier moments in today's conversation: first, when I admitted that I sometimes feel like Klein is suggesting that the subject is wholly responsible for its own anxiety, and second, my example of the guy on the subway. I understand what you meant when you said that the subject can be the cause of its anxiety without having done anything wrong, so that blame isn't a relevant notion in this context. Nevertheless, the idea that the intersubjective can never be dissociated from the intrapsychic makes me balk because it implies that if the guy on the subway manages to get under my skin, it's because there's something in my intrapsychic constitution that matches his aggression. I'm not saying that Klein is wrong. I'm merely acknowledging that this is an uncomfortable idea, and an important theme in the context of critical theory because this theory—both your Frankfurt School version and my more general version—has tended to focus on external causes of anxiety, violence, and aggression. So what do we do with Klein's assertion?

The only way I can begin to think through this question is obliquely, by referring to an idea that I've developed in the context of Lacanian theory but that only partially comes from him, namely that I believe that it's essential to analyze lack, dispossession, deprivation, and other forms of wounding—and here I need to explicitly add anxiety and aggression to the list—on two different levels: the constitutive and the circumstantial. In Lacan, constitutive (ontological) lack is a given. But I've always thought that this lack should be considered in relation to more context-specific, circumstantially generated lacks. Yes, there's your foundational lack-in-being, the nothingness or emptiness at the core of your being. But there are also countless ways in which people are—unevenly—rendered lacking: they are dispossessed, deprived, wounded, made anxious, and made the targets of aggression by context-specific factors that are sometimes entirely predictable (poverty, racism, sexism, homophobia, and other social inequalities) and other times entirely unpredictable (you happen to be born into a vicious family).

It might be possible to align my account of the constitutive and the circumstantial with your account of the intrapsychic and the intersubjective. Moreover, the potential link between them that you have introduced through Klein has long interested me, even if I'm more reluctant than Klein appears to be to insist that the two can never be pried apart and even if I'm more reluctant than she appears to be to assign primacy to the constitutive (or the intrapsychic). That is, I wouldn't necessarily argue that beneath the circumstantial one always finds the constitutive. Rather, I would suggest that the interaction between them can cut in both directions. For instance, regarding anxiety one could hypothesize that if you're grappling with a lot of constitutive anxiety, perhaps circumstantial factors have a greater impact on you. Alternatively, if there are too many circumstantial sources of anxiety that pile up, perhaps this deepens your constitutive anxiety, making you anxious even in situations where there's no obvious cause for it. The same reasoning could be applied to other mental states, such as melancholia: if you're dealing with a lot of foundational melancholia, you might be more vulnerable to external causes of melancholia. On the flipside, if there are too many external causes of melancholia, they might deepen your foundational melancholia, lending your entire character a melancholy tone.

All of this amounts to acknowledging that, on some level, I agree with Klein's assessment that the intrapsychic and the intersubjective are connected. At the same time, a significant part of me—the critical theorist in me who has been trained in ideology critique and is cognizant of biopolitical and necropolitical forces—recoils from the notion that external sources of anxiety can't get to me, even destroy me, without some input from my intrapsychic constitution. I guess I'm having a hard time imagining even the calmest person staying perfectly serene in the face of sexual assault, racist attack, refugee status, war trauma, or a cancer diagnosis. This is why my impulse is to retain a degree of distance between the internal (intrapsychic, constitutive) and the external (intersubjective, circumstantial). I honestly don't know if this is psychoanalytically possible. But it feels essential to me as a critical theorist.

That said, it sounds like anxiety, for Klein, is constitutive of subjectivity in the same way that lack is constitutive of subjectivity for Lacan. I'm willing to agree with this assessment even if I still want to insist on the damaging impact of circumstantial sources of anxiety. In the same way that I don't think that analyzing circumstantial forms of lack negates Lacan's notion of constitutive lack, I don't think that analyzing external sources of anxiety negates Klein's notion of anxiety as foundational to subjectivity.

AA: I agree that what Klein is getting at with her analysis of the intrapsychic and the intersubjective is related to the distinction that you articulate throughout your work between constitutive and circumstantial forms of lack. Whether or not the intrapsychic and the intersubjective can be dissociated from each other in Klein's model is a complicated question.

MR: A related question that I have about this issue—and I realize that we can't resolve it today—is how Klein envisions the intrapsychic. For Lacan, constitutive lack results from the encounter with the signifier. But the signifier/the symbolic/the social doesn't seem to figure into Klein's account of anxiety as an intrapsychic phenomenon. Does she view it as constitutional in the sense that it's linked to a baseline biological response? Earlier you gestured in this direction when you mentioned that Klein believes that some people are born with a higher level of anxiety than others. Although I'm willing to follow this line of reasoning to a point, I'm ultimately too constructivist to believe that this is the whole story. This is where Lacan and Klein seem quite far apart, given that from Lacan (and Foucault) we get the idea that external networks of power can infiltrate our being, can in fact turn us into the kinds of individuals we are.

AA: This is a complex issue in Klein's work, but my sense is that although she's much more comfortable than you or I are with the idea of innate instincts, and although it's true that she sees anxiety as being ultimately grounded in the internal operations of an instinct (the death drive), I believe—and here I'm repeating a point that I've already made—that it would be a mistake to interpret her work in crudely biologistic terms. Lacan accused her of instinctual reductionism,[44] so he may be partly to blame for this misinterpretation.

For Klein, the drive is always mediated through unconscious phantasy, which is its psychical representation or manifestation. So although she claims that the death drive is innate or constitutional (and that the force of the drives can vary in strength from one individual to the next), the emphasis she places on phantasy suggests that we can't have any unmediated access to this aspect of our experience. For this reason, I don't think that she envisions the drives or the body in biologically reductionist terms.[45] Whatever innate or constitutional forces may be at work, they will always and necessarily be filtered through unconscious phantasy. This model may not be quite the same as Lacanian constructivism, but it isn't crude biologism either.

MR: We're back at the idea that what language is for Lacan, phantasy is for Klein: the entity that mediates the relationship of human beings to their environment, to others, and to themselves.

I would like to add that, despite Lacan's obvious attention to external power structures, he seems to believe that there's a layer of anxiety that's just as impossible to get rid of as constitutive lack. As a consequence, the same question that I asked about Klein applies to him equally: if you assert that it's impossible to banish (all) anxiety, where does it come from? The Lacanian answer might be that once the cut of the signifier has constituted you as a specific kind of (anxious?) person, that's what you'll be stuck with for the rest of your life: the fact that something is socially constructed rather than biologically determined doesn't make it any easier to change; for all practical purposes, it might as well be innate.

Interestingly, some versions of Western philosophy, most prominently phenomenology and existentialism, have valorized this type of intractable anxiety: in Heidegger, it's anxiety that individualizes *Dasein*; in Sartre, freedom is linked to anxiety; in de Beauvoir, similarly, anxiety and freedom are associated. It's as if anxiety is the price of subjectivity, like lack is in Lacan. So in some versions of Western philosophy—and I'm also thinking of Kierkegaard here—there's a deep admiration for anxiety as a generative, creative force.

This is notably different from how contemporary progressive theory—and particularly affect theory, which we'll talk about tomorrow—responds to anxiety. Because progressive critical theorists regard anxiety primarily as socially generated—and politically and ideologically motivated—rather than ontological, they don't see anything redeeming about it. I'm not saying that they are necessarily hostile to the philosophies of, say, Kierkegaard or de Beauvoir. Nevertheless, their emphasis falls on the kind of anxiety that should in principle be fixable. Their argument—which I agree with—is that we're living in a society that generates unnecessarily high levels of anxiety.

This explains why there's a fundamental tension between the existentialist notion of anxiety as the price of human freedom—which is linked to the Lacanian notion that there's no cure for constitutive lack—and the progressive critical theoretical notion that anxiety and other bad feelings result from oppressive social relations. It's because I can see both sides of the argument that I have a hard time situating myself in relation to it. At the same time, as I tried to explain earlier today, it's not that difficult to connect Lacan's analysis of anxiety to unequal social relations because his account focuses so strongly on how the other might deepen my lack, or alternatively, steal my lack (that is, my humanity), or how the messages emanating from the other can be so enigmatic (confusing) that they make me anxious.

AA: Maybe we need a concept like "surplus anxiety."

MR: Exactly! A nice twist on Marcuse.

4

Affect

MR: The topic of today's conversation, broadly speaking, is affect. This is because of the rapid ascendancy of affect theory during the twenty-first century, and especially because of the ways in which affect theory, either explicitly or implicitly, questions the relevance of the Freudian-Lacanian line of psychoanalysis for critical theory while appropriating a very particular version of Klein.

Personally, I'm sympathetic to affect theory and don't see it as incompatible with Lacanian psychoanalysis, but there are affect theorists who do. More specifically, some affect theorists, such as Sara Ahmed, have distanced themselves from the ways in which Lacanian theory has been developed by critics such as Žižek and Alain Badiou.[1] Klein, in contrast, has been a significant resource for affect theory through queer theory, with which affect theory is closely affiliated. Some queer theorists—along with some literary critics—have fixated on the Kleinian depressive position as a corrective to the limitations of paranoid critical theory, understood here in the broad sense that I use the term in my work, as a mixture of the early Frankfurt School (Benjamin, Horkheimer, Adorno, and Marcuse), continental philosophy, French poststructuralism, psychoanalysis—usually of the Freudian-Lacanian kind—and deconstructive feminist and queer theory.

In part because of Eve Sedgwick's ground-breaking distinction between paranoid and reparative reading practices, which she borrows from Klein's distinction between the paranoid-schizoid position and the depressive position,[2] critics have mobilized behind the reparative impulse, so that the battle lines now seem to be drawn between those who want to repair and those who believe that a degree of paranoia is intrinsic to critical theory. The latter—and Lee

Edelman is among those who have proudly adopted the mantle of paranoid criticism[3]—continue to do the kind of ideology critique that's always looking for the root of evil: neoliberalism, capitalism, biopolitics, reproductive futurism, and so on. And they unleash their aggression—like the Kleinian baby unleashes its aggression against the mother—against every conventional form of subjectivity, relationality, normativity, morality, meaning, and social structure. On the other side of the divide are critics who use Sedgwick's version of the Kleinian depressive position to suggest that because we already know that the system is corrupt, racist, sexist, homophobic, imperialist, economically greedy, overly individualistic, and so on, ideology critique has become futile and that it might be time for some reparation. Some critics, such as Rita Felski, have taken this idea toward "postcritique," whereas others, such as Heather Love, have moved toward "close but not deep" reading practices.[4] Affect theory, broadly speaking, has asked for a redefinition of what it means to be epistemologically, ethically, or politically radical.

As I admitted at the end of yesterday's conversation, I have some trouble positioning myself in relation to this debate because I appreciate components of both perspectives. On the one hand, it feels to me that some paranoia is probably necessary for critique, for critical theory. Even Sedgwick—on my reading at least—didn't argue that we should *replace* paranoid criticism with reparative criticism.[5] She merely suggested that it would be constructive to create space for reparative interpretative practices. In addition, at times I suspect that the postcritical turn within the literary humanities might partly at least be a manifestation of the antitheoretical (or theory-phobic) impulse of the neoliberal academic establishment, a way to marginalize theoretical scholarship even further than it has already been marginalized.

On the other hand, I know that those who advocate the postcritical approach aren't necessarily *opposed* to critique, that they are merely disillusioned with the kind of paranoid critique that's usually associated with French poststructuralism and Lacanian psychoanalysis because decades of this critique haven't gotten us very far: knowing how the oppressive system works hasn't changed the fact that it works all too well. For this reason, it seems clear that critique isn't enough, that we can't merely keep attacking what we don't like without offering viable alternatives. The concept of reparation has arisen as a palliative to this state of affairs.

Within queer theory—where affect theory has been incredibly productive and influential—critics such as Ahmed, Love, Lauren Berlant, Ann Cvetkovich, and Sianne Ngai have pioneered the shift toward reparative approaches.[6] I don't mean to suggest that all of their work—particularly that of Ngai—can be categorized as reparative. But this work is foundational to affect theory, which, generally speaking, has taken theory in a reparative direction. There are also critics whose work doesn't fall under the rubric of affect theory but who have nevertheless positioned themselves in interesting ways in relation to the paranoid-reparative debate. For instance, David Eng has taken up Kleinian theory in an innovative manner while retaining psychoanalysis, rather than affect theory, as his main reference point.[7] And if you reach further down the genealogy of American progressive theory, before the rise of queer theory, and certainly before the rise of what we now understand as queer affect theory, you find many feminist critics of color, such as Angela Davis, Audre Lorde, Gloria Anzaldúa, and bell hooks, for whom the paranoid and the reparative seemed to commingle in generative ways, even if they didn't use that vocabulary.[8]

All of this is to say that, on the one hand, I'm wary of making hard and fast distinctions but, on the other, I'm aware that affect theory has carved out a persuasive space within contemporary theory and that at least some of its adherents see themselves as offering an alternative to the Freudian-Lacanian line of critique. For me, one question today is whether Lacanian theory and affect theory truly are as incompatible as they have been made out to be. I'm also interested in hearing your thoughts, Amy, on whether the version of Kleinian theory that queer affect theory has adopted represents an accurate interpretation of this theory's complexities. I admit that, based on what you have said about aggression being primary for Klein, and about how it's inerasable, it feels that affect theory's version of reparation might have a more benign inflection than what's available from Klein.

As I just mentioned, affect theory has latched onto Klein's notion of reparation as a remedy for the paranoid tenor of critical theory. But do you think that Klein actually leads us in that direction? Your account of her negative, realistic understanding of human nature implies otherwise. Although I've certainly gotten the sense that, for Klein, reparation is a corrective to the paranoid-schizoid position, it also feels that you have been saying that a repeated sliding back to the latter position is more or less unavoidable, and that reparation is always an incomplete, compromised process at best. What are your thoughts on this?

AA: I agree with you that a degree of paranoia, as this term is being used here, seems necessary for critique and thus for critical theory. As I understand and try to practice it, critique is grounded in the existing social world—which is just another way of saying that it's always immanent. Insofar as our existing social world is structured by relations of power, domination, oppression, and injustice, the task of critique is first and foremost to unmask or reflectively uncover these power relations in order to identify some sort of a critical foothold within the present. If you want to call this a paranoid mode of doing critique, that's fine with me, and I can't imagine critical theory without the critique of power and domination.

That said, I also agree with those affect theorists who argue that critical theory shouldn't stop there and that endlessly exposing relations of power and domination doesn't necessarily change anything. It may even, as Sedgwick suggested, prove too easy and comfortable for critics to inhabit the paranoid mode: if power is endemic and critique is nothing but the relentless unmasking of power, we can never be surprised because we always know how the story is going to end.[9] Engaging in reparative or reconstructive modes of theorizing may be more difficult than the paranoid mode because they require greater imagination and tolerance for risk on the part of the theorist. I know that I have that sense in my own work, that it's easier and in some ways more comfortable to argue against something, to take down someone else's argument or theory, than it is to construct one's own.

All that said, it sounds like what the reparative camp may be missing or at least under-emphasizing is what I've stressed throughout our conversations, namely that Klein's account of reparation is immensely complex and ambivalent, which is one of the things that makes it so great. As I've explained, for Klein, there's no reparation without guilt, remorse, anxiety, aggression, and the fear of persecution. Love is always tinged with the death drive and, as you just said, the danger of sliding back to the paranoid-schizoid position is ever-present. Furthermore—and I've already alluded to this in passing—some Kleinians such as Segal and Thomas Ogden emphasize the value of the paranoid-schizoid position, its ability to break fixed patterns and hegemonies and thus to make space for something new. So, even if it's true that reparation, for Klein, has the potential to mitigate destructiveness, she believes that both destruction and repair are ineliminable features of human subjectivity and of human social relationships. For these reasons, I think that it would be fair to say that from the Kleinian perspective both paranoid and reparative modes are essential for critical theory.

MR: Sedgwick specified that sometimes it's the most paranoid critics who produce the most reparative theories, which implies that she recognized that the line between destruction and reparation can be blurry. I should also acknowledge that affect theory is unquestionably interested in unearthing oppressive relations of power. It just—and you articulated this beautifully—doesn't think that this is enough. However, what most interests me in the present context is that, for affect theory, reparation usually appears to be associated with sentiments of defeat.

At first glance, this attitude may seem aligned with what we have concluded about psychoanalysis, namely that it's incompatible with straightforward progress narratives. I'm thinking back to the passage from Klein that you quoted where she proposes that the repeated attempts to improve humanity have failed because we have underestimated the centrality of aggression in human nature. Yet it feels like both of us would still like to hold onto some hope about the possibility of progress, even if it's just Adorno's "negativistic conception of progress as the avoidance of catastrophe."

In affect theory, in contrast, the catastrophe appears to have always already happened and every attempt to undo it amounts to cruel optimism. This is admittedly an oversimplified rendition of the field, and in a moment I'll try to fill in some of the details that lead me to this interpretation. For now, I want to say that, for me, one of the things that distinguishes psychoanalysis from affect theory—and that makes psychoanalysis productive for the social and political goals of critical theory—is that psychoanalysis retains the ideal of working through: even if there's no cure, even if there's no way to definitively break the repetition compulsion, and even if there's no way to avoid sliding back to the paranoid-schizoid position, there *is* still the notion of being able to change, to develop a different relationship to oneself and to the world.

AA: Can you explain how reparation can be affiliated with defeatism? Doesn't the attempt to repair automatically imply that you're trying to make things better?

MR: You're right: this is a weird contradiction. As I've explained, the reparative impulse of affect theory arises from its exasperation with the ways in which my version of critical theory has wasted energy in its paranoid efforts to dig up social problems that are visible right on the surface of things. At the same time, affect theory is skeptical of Lacanian (and Marxist) attempts to correct social wrongs with grandiose revolutionary gestures. This is what I was getting at earlier when I said that affect theorists want to redefine the meaning of the term *radical*: for them, revolution isn't a convincing solution. As a result, even though there's an inclination toward repair, there's also a deep cynicism about the possibility of overarching social change.

Let me try to approach the divide between Lacanian theory and affect theory by highlighting the point of greatest tension between them: the celebration of the death drive and the so-called ethical "act" in Lacanian political theory. Lacanian interpretations of the act can be traced back to Lacan's reading of Antigone as an ethical heroine because of her uncompromising defiance of Creon's order against burying her brother Polyneces.[10] In the act, the subject commits an action that seems completely insane or outrageous to the rest of the world, and that may result in the destruction of the subject or of its social context. Žižek, Badiou, and Edelman, among others, have developed different versions of the act, but what their theories have in common is a revolutionary radicalness that's supposed to bring about the collapse of the reigning symbolic order. In addition, they—as Lacan already did in relation to Antigone—presuppose that the subject who commits the act possesses a considerable degree of agency: not agency understood in the Enlightenment, rationalist, or liberal sense but rather the seemingly senseless (completely irrational) agency of a subject who is willing to annihilate itself for the sake of its cause, as Antigone does. This is why Lacan states that, through her act, Antigone comes into being as an "absolute individual."[11]

The ethical act represents a materialization of the death drive: you're willing to do something completely self-destructive and you don't give a damn about what your act might cost you.

This type of an act isn't premeditated, but there's something in you—something that has to do with the real, with jouissance—that compels you to commit it. Often the result is merely a symbolic self-annihilation in the sense that you lose your social coordinates: because of the apparent lunacy of your act, you become (temporarily or permanently) unintelligible to the symbolic order; you become a cultural pariah or outcast. But sometimes you literally die.

In some of the theorizing about the act—particularly in Badiou's account of the "event" as a force that creates a swerve in the status quo of life—there's a strong sense that you can bounce back, that you can return to the symbolic order as a *transformed* entity. It's almost like you have to destroy yourself—commit an insane act—in order to be born as a subject. In fact, for Badiou, before the act there's no subject; there's just a creature that's pathetically caught up in the meshes of the symbolic order. In this sense, becoming a subject presupposes the willingness to leap into the unknown. So there's a kind of backhanded heroism to Badiou's version of the ethical act. It's supposed to be about the death drive—about a suicidal plunge into the jouissance of the real—but really it's about the courageous birth of the subject. This may not be the most generous reading of Badiou's theory. But that's how it feels to me, even though I admit that I like Badiou's work.

The crux of the ethical act is that the injunctions of the reigning symbolic order—collective norms of behavior—are powerless against it; insofar as it causes the jouissance of the real to erupt into the symbolic, the symbolic is (at least momentarily) neutralized. This is why Lacanians think of the act as "ethical." They are working with an unusual definition of ethics: the ethical is whatever counters the hegemonic symbolic. In other words, the ethical is intrinsically antinormative. This is why many Lacanians want to respond to structural violence by destroying the structure: they call for revenge along the lines of Benjaminian divine violence. There should be no mourning, remorse, mercy—or reparation.

Sometimes this type of violence is fleeting, so that it doesn't leave a permanent mark. But other times it makes an enduring mark, makes a real dent in the symbolic and leads to genuine change, forcing the symbolic to shift irrevocably. You could think of social movements in these terms. For instance, feminism cracked the façade of the heteropatriarchal symbolic order in powerful ways in the

1960s and 1970s (and obviously since then). There was a collective reconfiguration of the symbolic that made a lasting difference.

That's the valuable part. But there are also problems that affect theory has been deft at pointing out. I'll get to these in a moment. At this juncture, let me just say that, despite my Lacanianism, I'm aware that building an ethics on the idea that anything that's antinormative is automatically ethical is questionable. I realize that turning antinormativity into the new norm isn't the answer to our ethical dilemmas.

AA: I find the Lacanian way of reading the death drive persuasive as a descriptive account. But as you just suggested, its ethical significance is a separate question. Certainly, there are many historical and contemporary instances where it's ethical to challenge the existing symbolic order and its conception of the normative—what's appropriate, expected, routine. In such instances, two conceptions of normativity compete: de facto normativity—what the existing social order takes to be correct—and genuine ethical normativity, which makes, for example, feminism's challenge to the existing social order an ethical one. I can see that there are situations where slaying de facto normativity is ethical. But I'm not sure I would go as far as to valorize the death drive.

For what it's worth, Klein was far from valorizing the death drive. Her understanding of the death drive is more *diagnostic* than ethical. Although she recognizes that all productive and especially all creative activities involve some sublimation of the death drive, she still takes a pretty grim view of it overall. For her, it's important to acknowledge the pervasiveness and ineliminability of our tendency to fall back into persecutory anxieties and defenses such as splitting, idealization, projection, and introjection. As we have already seen, this acknowledgment has important social and political implications inasmuch as it puts constraints on what kind of progress might be possible for us, how much peace and justice we might be able to hope for. This means that the death drive isn't for her something to be celebrated even if it can't be eliminated. Rather, it's something we should strive to mitigate.

MR: I agree with that. I'm beginning to think that on this issue I'm more Kleinian than Lacanian. Furthermore—and here's the affect theoretical side of the divide that I set up earlier—from an affect theoretical viewpoint, which is usually also a feminist viewpoint, the Lacanian vision of the ethical act privileges a deeply masculinist vision of politics. As I say this, I realize that the fact that a moment ago I presented Antigone and feminist social movements as examples of Lacanian antinormative ethics was an attempt to illustrate that Lacanian antinormativity isn't intrinsically antifeminist. Nevertheless, I understand the affect theoretical frustration regarding the Lacanian rhetoric of robust revolutionary acts, which are unquestionably coded as masculine in our society.

In addition, such acts seem alien to the lived realities of most people, particularly the socially marginalized. Affect theory—for example the work of Kathleen Stewart, Berlant, and Cvetkovich[12]— reminds us that the deprivileged are too exhausted to undertake these types of drastic acts. They are doing their best to survive, to get through the day. This is where affect theory's defeatism comes in. It speaks a language of bruised, obstructed, and compromised agency, focusing on the inability of subjects to break the circuits of cruel optimism that attach them to modes of life, scenes of desire, intimate relationships, or ideological commitments that harm them.

For this reason, affect theory tends to be more descriptive than prescriptive, shying away from concrete recommendations for social change, except maybe in an incremental, arguably Foucauldian-Butlerian sense, where you're trying to negotiate with power in order to render your unbearable life just a little bit more bearable. As long as this defeatism doesn't veer into simply accepting the status quo, I'm not sure I can fault affect theorists for it because I understand where they are coming from: I know that it's their focus on deprivileged subjects that creates the sense that there's no way out (maybe because there really is no way out). But it also feels like something is missing. I can't quite put my finger on it—it just feels like there's something that psychoanalysis has that affect theory lacks. Maybe you can help me with this ...

AA: Perhaps what's missing in affect theory is a conception of what we in our last conversation described as the constitutive dimension of subjectivity. My sense is that we're both turning to Klein and Lacan—and psychoanalysis more generally speaking—for similar reasons: to develop a theory of the subject that takes seriously both the psychic and the social dimensions of subjectivity and that enables us to think through how these two dimensions are intertwined in complicated ways. You have spoken of the ways in which both the constitutive and circumstantial components of subjectivity impact the subject's destiny. I, in turn, have repeatedly brought up the relationship between the intrapsychic and the intersubjective.

This seems different from the approach of affect theory, which appears to focus on the circumstantial and intersubjective to the exclusion of the constitutive and intrapsychic. This isn't to say that there aren't valuable insights to be gleaned from affect theory; it's just to say that I think that there's something distinctive and important for critical theory that's worth preserving in the more psychoanalytic approach. Whether critical theory is construed broadly or narrowly, I think that it needs a theory of the subject. As Carl Schmitt once said, every political theory presupposes a philosophical anthropology, or a basic account of the subject, whether acknowledged or not.[13] This doesn't mean that in order to do political theory one has to be committed to a strongly metaphysical or ahistorical conception of universal human nature. Rather, it means that every political theory makes some presuppositions about what kinds of creatures inhabit collective political institutions and structures or engage in the practices that they imagine or critique.

For example, if you believe that people are capable of a high degree of autonomy, communication, and rational agreement, so that they are likely to be motivated by the unforced force of the better argument in political deliberations, Habermasian political theory might look pretty appealing to you. But if you don't think that any of these things are true of people, or that they aren't true enough, you're going to be pretty unsatisfied with it. This is what I mean by saying that critical theory always rests on some claim—whether explicit or implicit—about the kinds of creatures we are because this claim dictates the types of political possibilities that are or aren't real options for us. As I've stressed, for me the value of psychoanalysis—at least of the Kleinian and Lacanian variety—is that it offers a realistic theory of the subject, a theory that shows subjectivity to be more complicated and ambivalent than the essentially rationalist or at least deeply prosocial account that's presupposed in a lot of current work in the Frankfurt School tradition.

MR: I can't believe how well you managed to articulate what I simply couldn't see in the context of affect theory. And your intervention is all the more important because you're a Foucauldian and, as I mentioned, affect theorists are usually working with a loosely Foucauldian model of negotiating with power. For them, this translates into a strong resistance to any theory of "the subject." This is because they associate such a theory with a universalizing notion of subjectivity, which goes against the grain of Foucault's historicist orientation.

Most affect theorists can't get over the assumption that the Lacanian theory of the subject is a universalizing one, and of course, in *some* ways this is true: if you're working with notions such as the symbolic, imaginary, and the real, you're automatically positing something universal (or structural). But I don't think that Lacan would ever deny that the subject is formed in historically specific ways because—contrary to what his critics presume—he doesn't propose a static conception of the symbolic order: the symbolic is simply the reigning sociocultural order, the reigning reality principle, the one that you happen to be born into. It changes over time, though some of its components, such as racism and heteropatriarchy, seem to have a lot of staying power. Moreover, I think that Lacan makes it fairly clear that his commentary is limited to Western contexts.

I agree that we need a theory of the subject, and that this is one of the things that psychoanalysis can offer critical theory. You're right that every social theory presumes—explicitly or implicitly—something about the kinds of creatures we are, so that we might as well attempt to theorize the matter. In the course of our conversations, the two of us have tried to do this, with our thoughts about the ineradicability of the death drive, the intractability of aggression, the persistence of the repetition compulsion as the guiding hand of the subject's destiny, the evanescence of the phallus, the interplay between the intrapsychic and the intersubjective, and many of the other ideas that have cropped up. And we haven't even gotten to desire, love, creativity, sublimation, and politics yet. I don't want to make any general claims, but for me personally, psychoanalysis offers a rich vocabulary for analyzing aspects of subjectivity that aren't readily available to other theoretical approaches.

I also think that what you said about every social theory presuming a basic account of the subject applies to antinormativity as well: every antinormative stance contains a clandestine assumption about normativity—about the just, fair, and right—so that, again, we might as well admit this. My version of critical theory finds this insight difficult to acknowledge—even if it in practice relies on it—because any mention of normativity is automatically linked to the Enlightenment or neoliberalism. For this reason, my version of critical theory doesn't usually make the distinction between de facto (oppressive) and genuine (liberatory) normativity that you brought up a moment ago. Instead, it goes to great lengths to dissociate ethics from normativity, which is how we end up with the idea that ethics equals antinormativity. I tend to think that this is a theoretical and political misstep.

The other important detail about the Foucauldian inflection of affect theory is that this inflection makes it hard to conceptualize agency. If—and here I'm oversimplifying Foucault, but this is more or less the story that gets circulated—the subject is formed at the nexus of power and discourse, then, as I said earlier, the only way to work toward a new social reality is to negotiate with the existing one. There isn't the same emphasis on being able to break with one's social context as exists in Lacanian theory. There's no equivalent of the Lacanian real, which by definition, however momentarily, ushers the subject beyond the symbolic order. This in turn means that there's nothing akin to the Lacanian act or Badiouian event in affect theory. I would love to hear your thoughts on this. Do you think that it's true that the Foucauldian approach implies that breaking free of the chains of power is absolutely impossible?

AA: I think that there exists the possibility of a radical break—of radical change—in Foucault, at least in his early work. I'll come back to this in a minute. But first I would like to say more about the question of historicism in relation to the theory of the subject. I admit that the Foucauldian in me is suspicious of the strong declarations about human nature that one sometimes finds in psychoanalysis, including Klein. I myself have a tendency to resort to this way of talking—about what's possible for "creatures like us"—when I'm explaining Klein, and I confess that such talk makes me nervous. At the same time, I find it hard to disagree, for example, when Freud claims that "men are not gentle creatures who want to be loved, and who at the most can defend themselves if they are attacked; they are, on the contrary, creatures among whose instinctual endowments is to be reckoned a powerful share of aggressiveness," and then defends this claim by asking, rhetorically, "Who, in the face of all his experience of life and of history, will have the courage to dispute this assertion?"[14]

I've been struggling to think about how to reconcile these seemingly incompatible theoretical inclinations in my recent work on psychoanalysis and critical theory. This was already a complicated issue in the early Frankfurt School's reception of psychoanalysis. The early Frankfurt School theorists were deeply committed historicists who nonetheless found psychoanalysis indispensable for developing a compelling diagnosis of their moment in time. Thinkers such as Adorno and Marcuse strove to resolve this apparent contradiction by historicizing psychoanalysis itself: they understood it as providing an account of the specific form of bourgeois subjectivity that emerges under conditions of modern capitalism. This strikes me as very much along the lines of what you just said about Lacan. That said, it may still seem difficult to reconcile the theory of the drives with a Foucauldian commitment to historicism.

Yet it's also important to note that Foucault's position on this question is a bit more complicated than some Foucauldians make it out to be. Foucault doesn't reject all assertions about anthropological universals. For instance, in an encyclopedia article about Foucault's work that's commonly accepted to have been written by Foucault himself, but published under the pseudonym Maurice Florence, Foucault describes his method, not surprisingly, as involving "a systematic skepticism toward all anthropological universals."[15] However, he immediately clarifies that this "does not mean rejecting them all from the start, outright and once and for all," only that "nothing of that order must be accepted that is not strictly indispensable."[16] This leads Foucault to formulate his "first rule of method" as follows: "Insofar as possible, circumvent the anthropological universals ... in order to examine them as historical constructs."[17]

What Foucault is saying is that a commitment to historicism doesn't require that we reject all anthropological universals out of hand, but rather that we only accept those that are "strictly indispensable." What's more, it seems to me that Foucault himself is committed to at least one anthropological universal, namely the claim that there's no outside to power. This claim seems to rest on the presupposition that human beings are the types of creatures who—whenever, wherever, and in whatever way they interact with one another—always exercise power. Although Foucault doesn't—at least as far as I'm aware—acknowledge that he treats this claim as an anthropological universal, it seems clear to me that he does. Perhaps he does so because he finds it strictly indispensable for his work.

This is to say that I'm not convinced that a commitment to Foucauldian historicism necessarily rules out a belief in something like the death drive or the resulting psychoanalytic theory of the subject, though it probably puts some constraints on how this theory is articulated. Envisioning anthropological universals not as unchangeable features of human nature but rather as historically malleable aspects of the human condition would be a way of articulating these universals that fits better with Foucault's commitment to historicism. Thinking along these lines, we could understand the drives as modes of relating to others that emerge in the context of, and in part as a result of, certain features of the human condition—for example, the fact that we're born helpless and radically dependent on caregivers without whom we can neither survive nor develop.[18]

Let me now get back to your question: does Foucault help us to think about the possibility of a radical break from the existing social order, or does his claim that there's no outside to power imply that the best we can hope for is internal resignification or redeployment of power? To be sure, Foucault thinks that modern power works through subjection—that is, through the formation of individuals who emerge as subjects by being subjected to existing relations of disciplinary power. One way to think about agency in the context of this conception of power is to understand it as the subversive reiteration of power from within. Judith Butler's early work offers some compelling versions of this idea and her massive influence on contemporary critical theory (in the broad sense of the term) may be part of the reason that this interpretation of Foucault's theory of power has become standard.

But there's another, more radical conception of transformation that can be found in Foucault's early work, specifically in his account of the discontinuous shifts between one *episteme* or historical a priori—basically, one set of historically, socially, and culturally specific conditions of possibility for thought and action—and another. The term *rupture*, which you discussed the other day in connection with Eisenstein and McGowan's theory, is appropriate here. For the early Foucault, the shift from one historical a priori to another isn't the result of a process of evolution or of a rational learning process; rather, it's the result of a rupture that radically reconfigures our entire way of ordering things. As a consequence, you might say that even if subversive reiteration of existing relations of power is what's possible for Foucault within a particular historical a priori—or perhaps just within the historical a priori of modernity—there's also the possibility of a radical break or shift that would dismantle the existing historical a priori and replace it with a new one.

What's difficult in the early Foucault is to figure out when such shifts are taking place. As I read him, the early Foucault thought that the modern historical a priori was crumbling all around him and that a new *episteme* was already coming into being, one that was connected to his famous heralding of the death of man. Later, it seems that he realized that things hadn't shifted nearly as dramatically as he had thought, that the modern historical a priori hadn't completely broken apart. At that point, he started to situate his work *within* the very modern historical a priori that he was also criticizing.

Foucault's idea of a radical historical rupture obviously isn't the same as the Lacanian ethical act: it's operating on a much broader scale than acts of individual defiance. Still, I think that there's an interesting connection to be made between Foucault and Lacan on this point, and that one could go even further and explore the relationship between unreason in Foucault—which is the untimely outside of history that's the force that emerges during these discontinuous shifts—and the Lacanian real.

MR: You're confirming my long-standing conviction that Lacan and Foucault aren't nearly as incompatible as some critics make them out to be.[19] What you say about the potential link between Foucault's conceptualization of unreason and Lacan's conceptualization of the real makes perfect sense. Moreover, although the Lacanian act is frequently depicted as a matter of individual resistance, Badiou's theorization of the event takes it in the direction of collective uprisings, such as the Russian revolution, that force a shift from one historical a priori to another. This is what I was also getting at with the example of the enduring impact of feminism as a social movement. In addition, when Eisenstein and McGowan talk about ruptures, they are often referring to large-scale social shifts that dramatically transform the collective landscape. In other words, even if Lacan himself focused on the individual subject's ability to resist the symbolic order, his contemporary followers have been interested in overarching social change. As I said earlier, they tend to speak a language of revolution, and the way they conceptualize revolution is supposed to have global implications.

But can I ask for a clarification? For Foucault, what's the lever that makes that shift from one historical a priori to another possible? Is it unreason in the same way as the real is for Lacan?

AA: I'm not sure that Foucault has a consistent answer to that question. In some of his later work, he disavowed the emphasis on unreason in his early *History of Madness*. I suspect that this was an unnecessary overreaction to Derrida's critique of this book: Derrida accused Foucault of doing metaphysics, which was a serious accusation at that moment in French philosophy![20] But in general, in Foucault's work there appears to be a move away from an earlier focus on transgressive freedom to a later emphasis on freedom as a practice of rearticulating existing power relations.

Still, it seems to me that Foucault never completely lets go of the idea that more radical shifts from one historical a priori to another are possible, and that the whole point of critique is to strive to make sense of that possibility. In one of his late interviews, he describes critique as the work of tracing "lines of fragility" and "virtual fracture" within the present historical a priori, a work that allows us to see "how that-which-is might no longer be that-which-is."[21] This imagery suggests that critique might force open the cracks in the present, which could then lead to more radical ruptures. But ultimately I believe that Foucault's methodological challenge to the progress-oriented, teleological notion of history that's so central to the modern historical a priori requires that we bracket the attempt to explain why and how these shifts occur. The goal of Foucault's historical a priori is to radically rethink the notion of history in a way that breaks with all conceptions of progress, cumulative development, and historical learning. And in a way, bracketing the desire to explain the shift from one historical a priori to another, viewing history as just one damn thing after another, is the way to bring about that break.

MR: It's funny: I asked if Foucault allows for the possibility of breaking with one's sociocultural context, and you have just described how Foucault *himself* did precisely this epistemologically, by inventing a new methodology. Your commentary is also compatible with Badiou's understanding of the event: there's no way to explain why or how the event comes about. And what you said about the historical a priori makes me realize that the reason I've never understood why critics get so worked up about the structuralist versus historicist issue—which is often translated into an artificial divide between Lacan and Foucault—is that it's completely obvious to me that every structure is historically conditioned.

You said that "envisioning anthropological universals not as unchangeable features of human nature but rather as historically malleable aspects of the human condition would be a way of articulating these universals that fits better with Foucault's commitment to historicism." I feel very strongly that this is what Lacan does. I've already emphasized that, for Lacan, the symbolic order is historically specific. I've also stressed that, for him, the drives are molded by their encounter with the symbolic order, which implies that they can also be historicized: if the symbolic is historically specific, the same must be true of the drives. Here one could, for instance, pose the question of how the drives have been shaped by the rise of an overstimulating online culture that demands constant connectedness to the world and others. I can't tell you how many people I've heard complain about this as a visceral—in my opinion, drive-related—phenomenon, as something that takes place on the level of the bodily real. If we combine Foucault and Lacan, we could say that we're living in a historically specific *episteme* where technology is sculpting the drives to suit its purposes.

Furthermore, how you're fashioned as a subject is also idiosyncratically conditioned, dependent on your *personal* history. Let's assume, sticking to the Western subject, that we all have a death drive. Well, it's self-evident to me that your death drive doesn't work the same way as mine. Ditto for other psychoanalytic universals, such as the unconscious and desire. Obviously your unconscious doesn't function the same way as mine, nor is your desire the same as mine. There are even people who have the desire to have no desire. This is still a desire, but it has a completely different configuration from the desires of people who desire other things than the annihilation of desire.

There are many countries that have a president as their head of state. This is a structural issue. But who that president happens to be makes a big difference in how the office is run. The same applies to individual subjects: we could all have a death drive, libido, desire, aggression, ambivalence, the unconscious, the capacity to communicate—and a whole host of other "structural" factors—but this in no way determines who we are because all of these structural factors have come into contact with a historically specific collective and an equally historically specific intimate (often familial) world that has forged us into the subjects we are. This is what I was trying to convey when I mentioned that the big Other—along with some small-o others—waits for the child in the delivery room: the child's subjective "structure" will from that moment on be historically specific. Simply put, on my interpretation, psychoanalytic universals always have a historically specific content.

In *Seminar II*—an early seminar which falls within his so-called "structuralist" phase—Lacan responds to Fairbairn's claim that penis envy isn't natural in women by basically screaming: "Who told him it was natural? Of course it's symbolic. It is in so far as the woman is in a symbolic order with an androcentric perspective that the penis takes on this value."[22] That is, it's only because we live in a phallocentric society—a society that grants the possessor of the penis all kinds of social, political, and economic benefits—that penis envy makes any sense. That some people are born with a penis might be a structural (universal) matter; but what we, as a society, make of this structural matter is historically conditioned. This really is the end of the debate for me, the reason I find the structuralist-historicist dispute so thoroughly absurd.

Many contemporary progressive critics insist that everything is historical. For me, this is a given. But—and here I'm again getting at what might be uniquely valuable about psychoanalysis to social critique—something arguably gets lost when the definition of the historical completely excludes psychoanalytic "universals," such as the unconscious, aggression, or the death drive. Something is also lost when the definition of the historical is confined to collective dynamics at the expense of individual histories. Much of critical theory seeks to trace the malaise of Western subjectivity to large-scale forces such as racism, heterosexism, capitalism, and neoliberalism. This interrogation of social forces—such as biopolitics and necropolitics—is urgently important. I've myself undertaken some of it. Nevertheless, I recognize that this approach can render more idiosyncratic factors, such as your family history, invisible; it can render certain forms of damage, suffering, and traumatization indiscernible.

I've mentioned that affect theory strives to understand how bad feelings emerge in response to collective situations of oppression. The field has been incredibly insightful about this. Yet this approach can downplay the fact that not all bad feelings arise from cultural situations: some of them materialize as a consequence of the kinds of difficult family histories or other intimate scenarios of traumatization that psychoanalysis has always been excellent at analyzing. I'm not at all saying that we should replace affect theory or other forms of cultural critique with psychoanalysis. Rather, I'm hoping that in the future there will be more dialogue between these obviously related modes of thinking about the human condition.

In this context, I'm wondering whether one way to think productively about the connections between psychoanalysis and affect theory is to go back to what you said about critical theory needing a theory of the subject. Even though affect theory doesn't explicitly deal with the intrapsychic, and even though it doesn't posit a theory of the subject, I would speculate that its implicit understanding of the subject nevertheless accords with the psychoanalytic characterization of the subject as irrational and affect infused. I know that you have a long history of challenging the rationalist model of subjectivity developed by Habermas and some of his Frankfurt School followers. And I'm assuming that you and others working on Klein in the Frankfurt School tradition are interested in envisioning the subject in a way that emphasizes the affective more than the rational. Your vocabulary may not be the same as that of affect theory, but my sense is that you're getting at some of the same issues about the importance of paying attention to the affective. I'm curious to hear your thoughts on this.

AA: It's true that there has been an extensive discussion within Frankfurt School critical theory about the limits of rationalist models of subjectivity that parallels some of the concerns of affect theory, even if it uses a different theoretical archive and vocabulary. In part for historical reasons, the discussion within the Frankfurt School has mostly taken place via an engagement *with* psychoanalysis. Theorists such as Whitebook, Jessica Benjamin,

Johanna Meehan, Noëlle McAfee, and myself have been arguing for some time that the Habermasian conception of the subject is too rationalist and linguistic, and that we need a more complicated account of the person that considers the irrational and affective dimensions of subjective experience.

This is also a prominent theme in some of Honneth's work. As you know, I'm not entirely convinced that his approach offers the kind of realistic conception of the person that he himself calls for. Still, it should be noted that he engages much more extensively than Habermas does with the irrational and affective features of social life. For instance, at the core of Honneth's philosophical anthropology is a psychoanalytically articulated account of love. For him, love as it's experienced in the family serves as the first and most primordial form of recognition, which is then imperfectly approximated in more abstract forms of social esteem and legal rights.[23] We have discussed the reasons for which I find his understanding of primary fusion problematic. But whatever the flaws of his theory may be, at least it isn't a rationalistic one!

Inasmuch as they place an emphasis on the irrational and affective, Honneth and others could be seen as following in the footsteps of the first generation of the Frankfurt School. For example, Adorno's critique of bourgeois capitalism centers on what he considers to be its principal affect: coldness. Coldness is a side effect of the instrumental, means-as-an-end rationality that predominates in modern societies as a result of the rise of science and technology and of the bourgeois exchange principle that governs capitalist economic relations and that compels us to treat everything, including human beings, as fungible commodities. For him, coldness, understood as the withering of the capacity for love, inures us to the suffering of others and thus makes something like the Holocaust possible. In that sense, Adorno could be understood as an affect theorist *avant la lettre*.[24]

MR: Your commentary on Adorno's conviction that coldness is the primary affect that governs quotidian relations in bourgeois capitalism makes me think of something that I truly appreciate about affect theory, which is its emphasis on the ordinary as opposed to the extraordinary. This is an issue that pits it against Lacanian political theory insofar as the latter agitates for revolutionary change. Again, this doesn't mean that affect theory isn't interested in large-scale social forces. As I just said, sometimes it feels like it focuses on such forces to the exclusion of the personal and idiosyncratic. However, what's genuinely interesting about it is that it keys on how these forces impact individuals on the level of the kinds of concrete everyday pressures that threaten to break them. Frequently the disagreement between Lacanians and affect theorists appears to come down to the question of the level on which traumatization (lack, negation, or dispossession) "really matters." If Lacanians are mostly interested in the subject's constitutive deformation and dislocation, affect theorists interrogate the various ways in which deprivileged subjects are wounded—rendered lacking—by unequal social arrangements. This is yet another debate that I find futile. As I noted yesterday, I don't see these two levels of analysis as being incompatible. In fact I don't think that we can make much headway in understanding subjectivity, ethics, or politics without taking into account both constitutive and circumstantial elements.

AA: Your attempt to think through both constitutive and circumstantial forms of negation, dislocation, alienation, and wounding is a component of your work that I've always found productive because it pushes Lacanian theory—which tends to focus so single-mindedly on the constitutive dimension—into exciting new directions. It also seems to me that, if I may put it this way, yours is a very reparative reading of Lacan insofar as you're always pointing to the positive flipsides of our constitutive lack: the fact that being cut by the signifier not only forms us as subjects of lack but also gives us access to the signifier; that although the ongoing circuit of desire is a never-ending experience of lack, this isn't wholly negative because we can access fragments of the Thing through our *objets a*; and that we can tap into the drive energies of the real to fuel creativity within the symbolic order without embracing psychosis.

Perhaps this explains why you're more inclined than other Lacanians might be to see the value in the Kleinian approach: you're already interested in sociality and intersubjectivity and inclined to be suspicious of starkly antisocial or antirelational views. In other words, I suspect that your distinction between constitutive and circumstantial forms of lack may be more Rutian than strictly Lacanian. Given that this distinction seems to map onto the distinction that I've been drawing in Klein's work between the intrapsychic and the intersubjective, perhaps we could see this as a Kleinian moment in your work?

MR: Thank you for your generous and accurate summary. During my entire career, I've been interested in the affirmative side of Lacanian theory, which has always been obvious to me but which I know is fairly alien to most non-Lacanians (as well as many Lacanians).

AA: In light of your attempts to find the generative side of Lacanian concepts such as lack and the real, I'm wondering if we might also think of anxiety—which I'm assuming affect theorists view negatively—as a potentially productive force that can be harnessed for creative purposes.

MR: That's fascinating and in some ways brings us back to what I said at the end of yesterday's conversation about existentialism valorizing anxiety as the precondition of freedom. As I explained then, this approach clashes with that of affect theorists, who view anxiety negatively because they postulate that, like many other negative feelings, it's largely socially—and therefore unnecessarily—generated. At the same time, there may nevertheless be an unacknowledged connection between existentialism and affect theory on this issue because for affect theory, anxiety, along with other bad feelings such as depression, also connotes a certain kind of freedom: a liberation from the neoliberal performance principle. We're here dealing with two different conceptualizations of freedom, yet both have *something* to do with not being a mere cog in the collective machine.

I realize that what I've just said about affect theory's take on bad feelings may seem completely contradictory: on the one hand, affect theory regards bad feelings negatively because it posits that these feelings result from oppressive social conditions; on the other, it tends to weaponize—and in some ways celebrate—bad feelings insofar as they prevent us from participating in the system that oppresses us. On some level, I appreciate this attempt to turn the system against itself. If the performance principle makes me anxious, I use my anxiety to resist the performance principle: instead of going to work, I agoraphobically order a pizza and watch daytime television. There's a certain beauty to this "solution." But I'm not sure that it can be thought of as a manifestation of creativity. Existentialism might be better at connecting anxiety to creativity. I assume that there's a reason you brought up the potentially productive valences of anxiety. What are your thoughts on the matter?

AA: I was thinking about some of your earlier work. In *The Call of Character*,[25] you make a compelling case for what you call the upside of anxiety by proposing that a tranquil life isn't necessarily a good life, since tranquility is frequently purchased at the price of social conformity. You argue that heeding the call of your character—following the singularity of your desire in an authentic way—is destabilizing, and that while this is anxiety provoking, it shouldn't always be thought of as a bad thing. Perhaps this is something we can discuss further when we talk about creativity, since, based on what I know about your earlier work, I sense that, for you, enhanced creativity is one of the upsides of anxiety.

This seems different from Klein's conception of anxiety, which is mostly negative. Although Klein believes that anxiety can never be fully overcome because it's linked with primary aggression, she tends to view it as something that should and can be mitigated or worked through. At the very least, there are for her better and worse ways to *manage* anxiety and perhaps even better and worse *forms* of anxiety: as I've indicated, she sees depressive anxiety as being more productive than persecutory anxiety because it motivates us to engage in acts of reparation that can help to heal the hatred, violence, and destructiveness that are bound up with persecutory defenses such as splitting and projection. Breaking up the vicious circle of anxiety and aggression is, for Klein, key to working through the depressive position. For her, it's only through the allaying of anxiety that the subject can engage in the process of developing a more expansive and more fully integrated ego— one that incorporates more of its previously split-off unconscious content and that brings its internal phantasy world into closer alignment with the intersubjective world.

MR: You're right that, for me, creativity is one of the upsides of anxiety. Perhaps more than most people, I routinely turn to daytime television as an antidote to the performance principle. But I certainly feel better when I manage to turn to writing instead. It may be hard to imagine how writing—which is obviously a performance of sorts—can allay the pressures of the performance principle, but it definitely does for me, in large part because it enables me to escape external stressors, such as the relentlessness of email (which I exclude from my writing space). This may ultimately not be that different from Klein's perspective: it's a matter of managing, mitigating, and working through anxiety. I have no desire to valorize anxiety itself as a positive force. I merely believe that something positive can sometimes come out of it. Perhaps this is my way of conceptualizing what it might mean to move to—or even work through—the depressive position: writing as a form of reparation.

But given that we're planning to discuss creativity later, let me shift our conversation to another affect: envy. One affect theoretical argument that I like—developed brilliantly by Ngai—is that, due to various social inequalities, envy is in many instances a completely legitimate bad feeling.[26] This is related to what I said earlier about penis envy: it makes sense for women to envy the privilege that the penis bestows upon its possessor (I'm not talking about envying the penis itself but rather the prestige that surrounds it). And it seems to me that there are many other genres of envy that are socially generated, such as envying the absurdly rich, so that a little Nietzschean *ressentiment* might be quite reasonable.

But if I remember correctly, Klein views envy as constitutional. This point remains opaque to me. Where does envy come from for Klein?

AA: For Klein, envy ultimately comes from primary aggression. Envy is a term that emerges in her late work for a specific aspect of the early paranoid-schizoid relationship to the primary object, the breast. She defines envy by distinguishing it, on the one hand, from jealousy, and on the other, greed. She hypothesizes that jealousy involves a three-way relationship in which you feel that someone else deprives you of a loved person or object. The paradigmatic case of this dynamic is to be jealous of your primary object's attachment to another person. For an infant, I suppose jealousy would emerge most often over the caregiver's attachment to their partner or another child.

In contrast, greed and envy are both dyadic. Greed involves wanting to keep all of the good things that are provided by the good breast—life, love, support, and nourishment, all of which are symbolized by milk—for yourself. Klein associates greed with the desire to devour, scoop out, or suck the breast dry. It's an insatiable demand that exceeds both what the child needs and what the object can give. Envy in turn seeks not only to rob the contents of the breast but also to project badness onto the breast in order to spoil or destroy it (and, by extension, the mother). Thus, greed is a kind of introjection and envy is a kind of projection.[27]

Moreover, envy entails anger for, or hatred of, the good breast *because it's good*. The infant experiences the good breast as the source of all life, love, support, and nourishment—that is, as an all-powerful life-giving and life-sustaining force. Moreover, it experiences itself as utterly helpless and radically dependent on the good breast for its survival. Consequently, the good breast has the power to give or withhold life, love, support, nourishment, and so forth, and this is what gives rise to envy. As Klein notes, "The capacity to give and to preserve life is felt as the greatest gift and therefore creativeness becomes the deepest cause for envy."[28] Envy then takes the form of a destructive urge to *spoil* the breast, to ruin its goodness and power, so that one doesn't have to depend on it any longer.

MR: How does this play out in adult relationships? I'm thinking of professional situations where, for example, someone can be envious of another person's success, so that it's like the other person is "too good" and thus needs to be taken down a peg.

AA: Klein defines envy as "the angry feeling that another person possesses and enjoys something desirable—the envious impulse being to take it away or to spoil it."[29] On that definition, it seems that envy is common in adult relationships. Whenever you perceive someone else as being exceptionally good, creative, or even loving, envy emerges and you have to take them down somehow, whether in reality or in phantasy.

MR: It's maddeningly irrational because it's not like another person's success is going to diminish your success, is going to rob you of anything, unless, of course, we're talking about a situation of direct competition, say, for a promotion. But what I see happening so often is that even when there's no direct competition, even when someone's success has no bearing on how their colleagues will fare, the successful one is envied—resented and even hated—by these colleagues.

AA: Yes, exactly. However, I think that the kind of envy that Klein is mostly concerned about emerges in asymmetrical relations of dependence that mirror the relationship between the primary caregiver and the infant. In those kinds of contexts—as in early childhood—envy, greed, and persecutory anxiety can feed on each other in a vicious circle.[30] On my reading of Klein, envy is rooted in the infant's inferior power and asymmetrical dependence on the good breast. Unlike in Honneth's story about the breakup of primary fusion, in the Kleinian paradigm it isn't so much that the mother inevitably disappoints the infant by failing to satisfy its every need, thus causing great pain and anxiety. Rather, on Klein's view, the baby experiences the breast/mother as all-powerful and itself as helpless and radically dependent. As a result, the breast/mother can choose whether or not to satisfy the infant's needs, and this is the source of envy.

Since envy emerges in situations of extreme dependence, probably the clearest example of how it plays out in adult relationships arises in the context of Klein's discussions of how it functions in analysis: envy manifests itself when the analysand comes to resent their dependence on the analyst and consequently attempts to spoil the analyst's interpretations by rejecting them. For the infant, excessive envy stands in the way of building up a good internal object that, in turn, can help the infant to work through the depressive position, to learn to tolerate ambivalence, and to withstand temporary experiences of envy, greed, and hatred. Similarly, for the adult analysand, excessive envy is an obstacle to the work of the transference through which the analyst helps the analysand to establish their good internal object more securely. In this way, envy is central to Klein's understanding of therapeutic resistance. The antidote to both types of envy is gratitude, which, for Klein, is essential for building up the internal good object and therefore underlies one's appreciation of goodness in others and in oneself.[31]

MR: It sounds like envy for Klein is both intrapsychic and intersubjective: based on phantasy as much as on the object relation. Affect theorists in turn read envy primarily as socioculturally generated. Which interpretation more accurately captures a given situation probably depends largely on the context. Interestingly, at the beginning of his seminar on anxiety, Lacan—after having specified that anxiety is an affect—reasons along fairly affect theoretical lines, claiming that what's distinctive about affect is that it's not repressed: "It's unfastened, it drifts about. It can be found displaced, maddened, inverted, or metabolized, but it isn't repressed. What are repressed are the signifiers that moor it."[32] Affects aren't repressed. They float around. We sense them. They are all around us. We're keenly aware of them. We just can't name them. We don't have signifiers for them, meaning that it's the signifiers that we might use to name them that are repressed, inaccessible. This is one reason that affects are so disconcerting: what can't be named is more perturbing than what can. This is close to how affect theorists think about affects as invisible yet palpable currents of energy that are transmitted between individuals.

Teresa Brennan—who was an innovative Lacanian—was among the first to analyze affects as enigmatic flows of energy that drift between people.[33] She was also among the first to connect such enigmatic affects to bad feelings, speaking, for example, about how some people are energy vampires who suck the vitality out of others. More generally speaking, affect theory analyzes the transmission of affects, which is often more visceral than cognitive, felt on the gut level, by the body as much as by the mind. This transmission is frequently done nonverbally.

AA: That reminds me of Klein's account of projective identification, which also involves a transmission of affect. Klein defines projective identification as "splitting off parts of the self and projecting them onto another person."[34] For instance, the child splits off its aggression, projects it onto the mother, and then experiences her as aggressive and persecuting. In such instances, the bad parts of itself that the child wants to expel are its own, which means that it also *identifies* with the object onto which they are projected. But this identification isn't consciously avowed, so that the object is felt to possess these bad features in its own right. Projective identification as Klein understood it is an omnipotent phantasy and, as such, can be a one-way process, where the subject's projective identification doesn't necessarily impact the object's experience or perception.

However, as later Kleinian analysts have explored, it can also, as Michael Feldman maintains, be "an active and dynamic process whereby the mental state of the object is *affected* by the projection."[35] Feldman gives the example of an analysand who had an overly critical, violent, and abusive mother and who continually projected all of her aggression onto the analyst, perceiving him to be a similarly critical and punishing figure. At times, this dynamic made the analyst feel impatient and critical, and therefore, tempted to enact the very aggression that the analysand projected onto him.[36]

What Feldman describes in the context of the analytic situation seems to me to be a common dynamic that we all experience in our daily lives: I'm feeling anxious or upset and, in an effort to manage that feeling, I project it onto my partner or my friend or whomever. I then experience them as being anxious or upset with me, which, in turn, actually makes them anxious and upset. Although Klein doesn't discuss this in terms of the transmission of affects, affect theory's way of depicting the process seems like a good way to understand what's going on in these types of experiences.

MR: That's a great connection to draw.

Speaking of projecting negative affects onto others, I wonder if we could round up today's conversation by addressing the strong—often extremely hostile—responses that Klein and Lacan elicit among critics who aren't familiar with the nuances of their work. On the Lacanian side, there are accusations of obscurity, arrogance, and ahistorical structuralism. On the side of Klein, as far as I understand, the issues revolve around the dangers of biologism, essentialism, and naturalization. Both lines of critique may on some level be accurate, but I hope that our conversations have shown that things are usually more complicated than they seem. Lacan may be obscure and arrogant but I don't think that he's stuck in ahistorical structuralism. He's also extremely funny, which for me mitigates his arrogance, particularly as he knows how to mock this very arrogance. In Klein's case, in turn, the centrality of phantasy undercuts some of the concerns about naturalization.

As we have determined, Lacan may in some ways be responsible for the fact that Klein has become associated with the perils of naturalization. Recall, for instance, our discussion of the moment in *Seminar VII* when Lacan accuses Klein of placing the body of the mother in the place of *das Ding*. What I find particularly interesting about this accusation is that it takes place in the context of a complaint about how the Kleinians have taken over psychoanalysis: "The analysts are so preoccupied with the field of *das Ding* ... that the development of analytic theory is dominated by the existence of the so-called Kleinian school."[37] This is amusing given that much of *Seminar VII* is devoted to a close examination of *das Ding*. Lacan in fact grumpily admits that the Kleinian school is the one that "orients the whole development of analytic thought, including the contribution of our group."[38] So ... I don't know ... there might be a smidgen of envy in the mix here. [laughter]

AA: That might explain why Lacan spends so much time positioning himself against Klein in some of his early seminars. That said, regarding Klein's biologism, I confess that although I find Klein's theoretical model of subject formation and of the relationship between drive and object productive, I often get the willies when I read her presentations of case material. This is part of the reason that we haven't discussed Klein's account of sexuality and the Oedipus complex: this is an aspect of Klein's work that I'm not interested in taking up, not only because it's overly concrete, but also because it's frankly heteronormative. She works with a flat-footed Freudian model of sexuality, with the consequence that in her presentations of case material you frequently find her talking to two- and three-year-old kids about how, when they are playing by running trains into each other, what they are really doing is phantasizing about Daddy bumping into Mommy's dark place, and how frightening that is. [laughter]

In such instances, Klein's concretion seems *too* concrete—and falsely so. She seems to be overinterpreting children's play in light of Freud's theory of psychosexual development and even, in the course of analytic work, attempting to impose this theory on them. In *Seminar I*, Lacan criticizes Klein for precisely this tendency, focusing on her interpretation of the case of little Dick.

MR: Yes, this is what Lacan says: "She slams the symbolism on him with complete brutality, does Melanie Klein, on little Dick!"[39] According to Lacan, Klein imposes on little Dick her pedestrian interpretation, hitting him with "a brutal verbalization of the Oedipal myth, almost as revolting to us as for any reader—*You are the little train, you want to fuck your mother.*"[40]

Lacan moreover accuses Klein of fabricating an unconscious for Dick. He retorts to her claim that she has gained access to Dick's unconscious by proclaiming that she doesn't understand the first thing about the unconscious but instead "accepts it ... out of habit": on Lacan's interpretation, there isn't anything "remotely like an unconscious" in Dick, with the result that it's Klein's discourse which "grafts the primary symbolizations of the Oedipal situation on to the initial ego-related ... inertia of the child."[41]

This is a strongly worded critique, which accuses Klein of imposing habitual (banal) interpretations on her analysands instead of allowing material to emerge from the analysis. And Lacan believes that she does this with all of her analysands, "more or less arbitrarily."[42] That said, Lacan admits that something productive may have come out of her technique with Dick, for it jolted Dick out of his solipsistic bubble to a rudimentary form of symbolization: he called for his nurse.

AA: It's true, it's a strongly worded critique, and in many ways justifiably so. But it's worth emphasizing that Lacan's reading of Klein in that section of *Seminar I* isn't wholly negative. As you suggest, he seems to think that she manages to achieve something with little Dick, almost despite herself, because at the end of the session Dick enters the symbolic by calling for his nurse. Thus, despite his reservations, Lacan has to admit that "as a result of this interpretation something happens."[43]

Furthermore, there are other aspects of Klein's interpretations of children's play that strike me as plausible. Perhaps this has to do with my experience with toddlers: I find her explanations regarding how destructiveness and the drive for reparation manifest themselves in children's play pretty reasonable. She also talks insightfully about how these dynamics are connected to the child's phantasy world, so that, for example, when a child conjures up images of monsters, these images can be viewed as representations of certain bad or scary aspects of parental figures (such as the devouring mother or the terrifying phallic father). All of this seems less wildly implausible than the way she continually insists on reading the primal scene into every instance of children playing with trains going through tunnels.

I realize that this isn't an argument: it's just me confessing that when it comes to certain aspects of Klein's work, I think, "I'm not going there."

MR: That's how I feel about Lacan's graph of sexuation, which Badiou, among others, has taken such an interest in.[44] I experience a visceral recoil from—a hugely negative affective response to—this aspect of Lacanian theory. Some critics would argue that sexuality is the only thing that truly matters in psychoanalysis. But for me, it's the most dated, least engaging part. This may have to do with the fact that, in our era, sexuality is no longer repressed but so endemic that it has become boring: it's impossible to avoid in our public culture, in the omnipresence of internet porn, and so on. On this issue I find myself in agreement with Žižek's analysis of the "injunction to enjoy" that governs our society: we're no longer told to curtail our enjoyment but instead urged to pursue it with the kind of voracity and indiscrimination that's ultimately tyrannical.[45] Constant enjoyment isn't necessarily that enjoyable.

I'm more interested in how people live than in how they have sex. Sex is certainly an important part of life, but its significance has been exaggerated in our culture to the point that it can overshadow other equally meaningful experiences. Incidentally, the centrality of a certain kind of story about sexuality in psychoanalysis may be one of the main reasons that affect theory has distanced itself from it. You just mentioned Klein's heteronormativity. There's less of this in Lacan—at least if you read him the way that I do—but it's woven into the fabric of psychoanalysis so deeply that it's hard to sidestep. One can see why affect theory, with its close ties to queer theory, finds this exasperating. I can't but agree with this assessment. This is why my strategy regarding psychoanalysis has been the same as yours: take what's valuable—the account of subject formation, the repetition compulsion, the death drive, the unconscious, and so on—and leave behind what no longer seems useful.

AA: I couldn't agree more. On this point, I'm inclined to follow Foucault. Although many Foucauldians believe that he rejects psychoanalysis completely, he actually makes a distinction between the theory of psychosexual development, which he does indeed refute as normalizing, and the theory of the unconscious, which he thinks is profoundly important, and on which he explicitly—at least in his early work—models his methodological approach to rethinking history archaeologically and genealogically.[46]

With respect to normalization, I can see how Klein's view that psychoanalysis aims at the integration of the personality could be read as a belief in the possibility of seamless adaptation. But as I've emphasized all along, I don't think that this is what she has in mind, nor do I think that this is implied by her views on subjectivity or object relations. To be sure, Klein talks a fair amount about the reality principle and about the importance of getting one's internal representations to align more closely with external reality. In that sense, there's an important strand of Klein's work that takes up Freud's idea of adapting to the reality principle. If you were worried about the possibility of normalization in Kleinian psychoanalysis, it would make sense to focus on this idea, particularly if you thought that the last thing we want is to adapt to reality, that we should instead want to resist it, and that this is where the radical potential of psychoanalysis resides. I take it that this attitude is what's behind the Lacanian idea of tapping into the drive energies of the real as a way of avoiding complete inscription into the normative demands of the symbolic order.

But when Klein talks about adaptation to reality, I don't think that she means adaptation to *social* reality, which is why her model doesn't necessarily imply social normalization. As I read her, adaptation to reality is simply a matter of resignation to the inevitability of loss; it's fundamentally about the acceptance of the loss of the idealized version of the good object, a loss that's in part the result of the expression of one's own destructive impulses but also in part a function of the fact that the idealized good object never really existed as such because it was always a part-object constructed through the persecutory defenses of splitting and idealization. Adaptation to—coming to terms with—this reality is, for Klein, the key not only to the reparative work of mourning but also central to psychic growth and intellectual and artistic creativity.

It's true that Klein emphasizes the importance of aligning one's internal phantasmatic representations of one's primary objects more closely with the actual people on whom these representations are based. But I don't think that she believes that this gap can ever be fully closed, that we can ever relate to our parents—or anyone, for that matter—in a way that isn't filtered through psychic reality. To suggest that the gap could be completely closed would be to deny the important role of phantasy and of our internal objects in how we experience the world—and these ideas form the crux of her theory.

Moreover, the idea that we should strive to bring our internal and external objects into closer alignment is, for Klein, bound up with the attempt to loosen the severity of the superego. We touched on this briefly the other day: although Klein agrees with Freud that the superego results from the internalization of parental authority, she famously argues that the cruelty of the superego isn't based on an accurate representation of parental discipline or strictness. Rather, it's based on the child's own aggression and sadism, which the child first projects onto the primary object and then subsequently introjects as an internalized object that forms the basis of the superego. As Klein puts it:

> The child himself desires to destroy the libidinal object by biting, devouring and cutting it, which leads to anxiety, since awakening the Oedipus tendencies is followed by introjection of the object, which then becomes one from which punishment is to be expected. The child then dreads a punishment corresponding to the offence: the super-ego becomes something which bites, devours and cuts.[47]

The issue of the superego caused one of Klein's major disagreements with Anna Freud, who thought that analysis should aim to strengthen not only the ego but also the superego as a means of holding the impulses of id in check. Based on Klein's ideas regarding the harshness of the child's superego, she went in the opposite direction, arguing that the goal of analysis isn't to reinforce the superego but rather to "tone it down."[48] On her view, making the strengthening of the superego the goal of analysis would be to turn the analyst into an agent of repression, whereas the analyst's job should be precisely the opposite.[49] Given that the superego, in the classical Freudian conception, is the bearer of social norms, which are inscribed into the subject through the mediation of parental authority, Klein's insistence that the goal of psychoanalysis is to lessen the severity of the superego has clear antinormalizing implications.

MR: It seems to me that this disagreement that Klein had with Anna Freud is central to rescuing her from accusations of normalization. I'm also fascinated by the idea that, for Klein, adaptation to reality is a matter of resignation to the inevitability of loss, the loss of the idealized version of the good object. This sounds more or less akin to the Lacanian idea that there's no cure for your lack, so that the best you can do is to learn to accept it. The idealized version of the good object, in Lacan, would be the Thing.

Maybe what's confusing—what's making it difficult for critics to discern the similarities between Lacan and Klein—is that while Lacan tends to talk about lack, Klein tends to talk about loss. But I don't think that the Lacanian lack is something that you only experience once and then you're done with losing. It's an experience of lack, of being rendered lacking, that's repeated indefinitely (until death—the ultimate loss). In other words, what the subject repeats—through the repetition compulsion, through the death drive—is its failure to reach completion. It keeps returning to the task of trying to make itself whole, cruelly optimistic that *this time* it might be able to accomplish this. But it can't, which is why adaptation is ultimately unattainable.

5

Love

MR: The topic of this conversation is love. I'll admit right away that talking about love in the Lacanian context is challenging because he doesn't use any of the tropes that are usually associated with the theme, such as harmony, generosity, or complementarity. If anything, love in the Lacanian paradigm is about derailment and even traumatization. My understanding from what you have said is that love is also complicated for Klein: filled with ambivalence, ambiguity, conflict, and tension and intertwined with aggression, anxiety, and hatred. In that sense, there might be some intersections.

Nevertheless, you have suggested that, for Klein, there's the possibility that love—or at least reparation, which I've come to see as affiliated with love in the Kleinian context—might function as an antidote to aggression, anxiety, and hatred. It would be great to hear more about this idea because I've never found it in Lacan. For Lacan, there's no possibility of harmony between people for the simple reason that there's no possibility of harmony *within* the self: the subject's self-alienation—what I've been describing as its deformation and maladaptation—presents a fundamental obstacle to any notion of love as a remedy for aggression, anxiety, hatred, or any manifestation of intersubjective or collective strife.

It's hard to overstate how seriously Lacan takes the notion that with the intervention of the signifier, the subject loses the capacity for balance, stability, and equilibrium. Thus: forget about harmony, even in the context of love. This is why throughout his work—and especially in his seminar on transference, *Seminar VIII*—one of the main points Lacan makes about love is that it's an illusion because the beloved can't provide the wholeness and healing that the subject covets. On this view, love is an imaginary fantasy linked to the mirror stage.

The Kleinian picture doesn't sound much rosier. Yet if Freud came to the conclusion that there's something beyond the pleasure principle—the death drive—you seem to have suggested that Klein came to the conclusion that there's something beyond the death drive: reparation. I don't mean to say that Klein believes that it's possible to get rid of the death drive: you have made it clear that she doesn't. Yet you seem to believe that love might be able to mitigate it. Also, am I right in thinking that reparation in Klein is directly linked to love? Or would you draw a distinction between them?

AA: I think that what—always incompletely—lies beyond the death drive for Klein is the working through of the depressive position in the sense that in this position, love or the erotic drive, understood as a drive for binding things into greater unities—as a drive for the kind of integration that doesn't eliminate but rather tolerates difference and ambivalence—is ascendant. Here is one of the few passages where Klein describes working through or overcoming the depressive position:

> The strengthened ego, with its greater trust in people, can then make still further steps towards unification of its imagos—external, internal, loved and hated—and towards further mitigation of hatred by means of love, and thus to a general process of integration. When the child's belief and trust in his capacity to love, in his reparative powers and in the integration and security of his good inner world increase as a result of the constant and manifold proofs and counter-proofs gained by the testing of external reality, manic omnipotence decreases ... which means in general that the infantile neurosis has passed.[1]

Reparation, as you know by now, is the impulse to mend things that have been destroyed, fragmented, or torn to bits by the operation of the death drive: it allows the subject to work through the depressive position, thereby alleviating primary aggression and the hatred to which this aggression gives rise.[2]

Regarding the relationship between reparation and love, I don't think that they are exactly the same, though they are closely connected. Love in its most general sense is one of the two basic drives: if the death drive is the drive to destroy oneself, the other, and/or the connection between the two, love is the drive to preserve life and to bind people together. The urge for reparation, in turn, emerges as a consequence of the "anxiety, guilt, and depressive feelings" that signpost the remorse that the child feels for the harm done by the aggression that it has directed toward its primary object.[3] In Klein's words, "The urge to undo or repair this harm results from the feeling that the subject has caused it, i.e., from guilt."[4] In this sense, reparation is the corollary of guilt and depressive anxiety: it's the "urge to preserve, repair or revive the loved objects."[5]

The relationship between reparation and love is therefore complex. The urge for reparation serves to protect the loved object by compelling the subject to undo the effects of its aggressive phantasies and actions. But the reparative impulse also reinforces and is reinforced by love. As Klein explains:

> It seems probable that depressive anxiety, guilt, and the reparative tendency are only experienced when feelings of love for the object predominate over destructive impulses. In other words, we may assume that recurrent experiences of love surmounting hatred—ultimately the life instinct surmounting the death instinct—are an essential condition for the ego's tendency to integrate itself and to synthesize the contrasting aspects of the object.[6]

With respect to your point about harmony, it's fair to say that Kleinian psychoanalysis aims at a certain kind of harmony, a harmony that's achieved through the overcoming of splitting and other manic defenses in the depressive position. But this is an ambivalent harmony of disparate, disharmonious parts. Because the integration of personality doesn't mean fully transcending the death drive, Klein doesn't entertain even the *ideal* of eliminating ambivalence, of attaining perfect harmony. Instead, the goal for her is the ability to tolerate the continued existence of aggression without having it destroy the self and its relations with others. For this reason, I think that Klein would agree with Lacan that complete harmony is impossible and perhaps even a dangerous illusion.

MR: The Kleinian account of love sounds fairly guarded and distrustful. The idea that love is a matter of mitigating one's aggressiveness—and of learning to tolerate the continued existence of destructiveness in the relational space—makes it sound like love is a *defensive* stance at best. I understand what you mean when you say that love, for Klein, is a fragile achievement: a volatile edifice that can collapse at any moment. It's far from the image of undying passion that our society associates with "true" love. Do you think that a dose of Kleinianism might be a corrective to our culture's overvalorization of love as the ultimate solution to our problems, as the most meaningful part of human life? Or do you think that, for Klein, love still deserves the adulation that our culture bestows upon it?

AA: It's true that Klein believes that love is a delicate achievement that can fall apart at any moment and that must hence be continually established and re-established. But as is so frequently the case with Klein—who, in my view, is one of the preeminent theorists of ambivalence—I think that the best answer to your question is: a bit of both. The ambivalence of Klein's account of love can be traced back to the idea that the child's relationship with its primary caretaker is both the first love relationship—in the sense that it satisfies the infant's basic needs for care, support, and nourishment—and the first hate relationship, partly because it necessarily frustrates some of the infant's desires, and partly because the goodness of the caregiver, which is evidenced by the very fact that they satisfy the infant's basic needs, generates the envy that we spoke about at the end of yesterday's session. As a result, as Klein sees it, "The first love is already disturbed at its roots by destructive impulses. Love and hate are struggling together in the baby's mind; and this struggle to a certain extent persists throughout life and is liable to become a source of danger in human relationships."[7]

This dynamic sets up a challenge for the subject, who must "find the way to bear inevitable and necessary frustrations and the conflicts of love and hate which are in part caused by them: that is, to find his way between his hate which is increased by frustrations, and his love and wish for reparation which bring in their train sufferings of remorse."[8] In other words, even though Klein regards love as a powerful force that can help the subject to break up the vicious circle of aggression, anxiety, and hatred,[9] she nevertheless has a clear-eyed, realistic view of it, so that her perspective could function as a corrective to an overly idealized picture of love. At the same time, inasmuch as love is the only thing that can help the subject to work through and—to the limited extent that this is possible—mitigate its aggressiveness, it could be said to deserve the adulation that our culture bestows upon it. However, love for Klein isn't so much about undying passion as it is about gratitude, generosity, tolerance of difference and ambivalence, and the drive for affirming bonds with others.

MR: That's all extremely helpful and unquestionably quite different from Lacan, for whom things always seem to come back to the fact that there's no cure for our lack, that the repetition of loss is the human condition. This doesn't mean that we can't work toward finding better ways to repeat our losses, but—and this is the gist of Lacan's realism regarding love—it does, as I've stressed repeatedly, mean that we have to give up the fantasy of an object that can redeem our suffering. At the same time, and perhaps somewhat surprisingly, Lacan does allow for the possibility of "truly" loving someone: in *Seminar VIII*, he explicitly refers to scenarios where "we truly love."[10] Such scenarios bypass the illusions of the mirror stage by tapping directly into the jouissance of the real, though—for reasons that I'll explain later—a certain version of fantasy may still play an important role in them. For now, I'll risk proposing that there's something "real" about "truly" loving. But this of course also means—to return to the first point I made today—that this type of love is derailing and traumatizing.

I'm here talking about the kind of love that touches the real rather than about romance as a concrete manifestation of the imaginary structure of the mirror stage and the subject's illusory quest for wholeness. This distinction between love and romance has recently been a strong preoccupation for Badiou, Žižek, and McGowan.[11] All three maintain that romance is a capitalist plot that's meant not only to make money—through expensive dates, dinners, flowers, chocolates, rings, wedding dresses, and so on—but also to make the subject believe that love is safe, that the other will in fact mend its lack.

Even independently of romance, McGowan illustrates how easy it is for capitalism to manipulate our desire for wholeness by promising healing through the objects that the market economy makes available to us at the same time as it banks on the fact that these objects will never definitively satisfy us. This is why we keep going back to the stores. Through this understanding of capitalism's power to trap us in repetitive circuits of hope and disappointment, McGowan approaches Berlant's notion of cruel optimism: it's almost like we're constitutionally "designed" to chase objects, scenes of desire, and relationships that can ultimately only disappoint us.[12]

McGowan speculates that romance functions exactly in this manner, which is why it usually doesn't last long: the realization that the other won't redeem my lack leads to the failure of romance by introducing what Roland Barthes astutely describes as a crack, or a "speck of corruption," in the perfect image of the other (the other as mirror).[13] All of a sudden, the (imaginary) other is fractured, stained, smudged, tarnished, or revealed to be banal and commonplace. This is to say that the other is shown to be just as lacking as I am, which is a reality that romance can't tolerate.

In contrast, in the kind of love that relates to the real—in the self, the other, and/or the relational space between self and other—rather than to the fantasy of the other as redeeming, it's exactly the other's lack that's cherished. One of the maxims that Lacan repeats throughout *Seminar VIII* is that when we truly love, what we love is the lack in the other. In this scenario, what captivates the lover are the other's inadequacies, weaknesses, and failures; its inability to understand itself; its incompatibility with the symbolic order; its deformation and maladaptation. This is one reason that love, from a Lacanian perspective, is derailing and traumatizing: the other in its deformation and maladaptation isn't a reassuring entity but rather one whose jouissance to some extent overrides the stabilizing influence of the symbolic and the imaginary.

AA: It sounds like in this scenario what you love about the other person is what you have in your work called the singularity of its being.[14] Is that right?

MR: Yes, I think so, because the singularity of the other's being has a lot to do with its inner unruliness: its jouissance and its consequent inability to fully adjust to the dictates of the symbolic order.

AA: My question is this: Do you know that this unruliness is what you're loving when you love the other? Suppose you love someone because they are incredibly passionate and intense, but then it turns out that the flipside of these qualities is a certain kind of self-absorption and single-mindedness, and perhaps even volatility, that absolutely drives you crazy.

MR: This is a tricky question because it implies that "truly" loving someone might come uncomfortably close to a masochistic surrender to a person who possesses undesirable, and perhaps even dangerous, qualities. But for me, unruliness is more strongly associated with the other's disorientation in the world (which is comparable to the subject's own disorientation). It's clearly easy to end up in the scenario that you describe, but it's not what I have in mind when I talk about singularity as an effect of the real. The Lacanian notion of love as derailing and traumatizing has more to do with ontological disorder than with the kind of potentially abusive situation you allude to. I would never want to suggest that you should stay in a damaging relationship: if the other's unruliness takes forms that are hurtful to you, you should probably get the hell out of there.

At the same time, for me, unpredictability—and the lack of guarantees that comes with this unpredictability—resides at the core of love, as it also does for Badiou, Žižek, and McGowan. I think that this is because the real is such an important concept for all of us. With the real—with the kind of love that touches the real—comes volatility. But we tend to view this volatility in a positive light, not as a seed of abusive relationships, but as what energizes the relational space, what animates the amorous event. However, I can see why it would be equally possible to view it in a negative light and point out that it's a recipe for disaster, an impediment to "healthy" relating.

AA: I suppose I wasn't thinking so much about how volatility might tip over into abusiveness—though of course that's definitely something to worry about!—but rather about how the kind of blazing love that you describe can easily transform into frustration, anger, and even hatred. It seems to me that frequently what most draws us to someone we love—that feature of them that most represents the singularity of their being—is also the thing that we later can't stand about them. So, for example, you love someone for their passion and intensity and later hate them for their single-mindedness and self-absorption, or you love them for being even-keeled and easy-going and later hate their passivity—that kind of thing. For me, this is where Klein's conception of the fundamentally ambivalent nature of love is insightful with respect to adult romantic relationships.

MR: That's astute. Klein gives us a lot to think about regarding how the ambivalence of early object relations might impact adult relationships. Lacan of course agrees with this in the sense that, for him, every amorous relationship in some ways replicates the fantasy of the Thing. This is why he characterizes every new love object as a "refound" object,[15] meaning that love is always a matter of finding a trace of the Thing in the beloved. The *objet a* is this trace. But Klein takes us in a more concrete direction of thinking about the implications of early object relations with real-life (even if phantasy-infused) caretakers.

AA: It's probably fair to say that Klein's conception of love takes parental love rather than passionate, romantic love as its paradigm. Of course, psychoanalysis tells us that we can never fully separate the two: all love is transference love, as Freud already recognized. Still, I think that there's a difference between Lacan's emphasis on the passionate relationship between lovers—and the destabilizing, derailing, and even traumatizing force of such passion—and Klein's emphasis on the relationship between a child and its primary caregiver. Klein's account is perhaps more relevant for thinking about the relationship between lovers after the first rush of derailing passion has subsided and the lovers are trying to figure out how to sustain their attachment through the loss, pain, aggression, and destructiveness that are—it seems to me—part of all long-term love relationships. Indeed, although I appreciate the critique of romance that Badiou, Žižek, and McGowan have staged, which implies that romance is about safety whereas love is about derailment, I wonder whether any adult love relationship could in reality sustain an experience of derailment over a long period of time. If I'm right to suspect that it couldn't, Klein's conception of love could perhaps be understood as what takes hold once the passionate experience of love—Badiou's amorous event—fades.

MR: Badiou's ideal of staying faithful to the amorous event regardless of the obstacles that it might face as the relationship matures may be an attempt to grapple with the dilemma you describe. But it's true that his expectation is that even in the aftermath of the event proper, love is going to remain volatile. It doesn't sound like Klein would disagree with this: it's just that for her working toward harmony might be a goal in a way that it isn't for Badiou, for whom preserving the twoness of the Two—the unbridgeable gap between the lovers—is essential for love. In general, the Lacanians I have named appear to assume that taming love's ability to disorient the lovers amounts to killing it.

Bruce Fink's account of love in *Lacan on Love*, which is largely based on *Seminar VIII*, might have some bearing on what you say because he's the most level-headed—though also unnecessarily heteronormative—of the Lacanians who have recently written on love.[16] Essentially, Fink breaks Lacan's analysis down to three components that he then aligns with the symbolic, the imaginary, and the real. The convenience of this trinity is a little dubious, but I think that something useful still comes out of the exercise.

Fink argues that when you love within the symbolic register, you—and this is a catchphrase that runs through Lacan's seminar—give the other what you don't have. The idea is that insofar as lack is the foundation of desire, you can only desire—and here there seems to be a conflation of desire with love—the other because you lack. So when you say, "I love you," you automatically declare, "I lack." This implies that the act of loving is on some level an acknowledgment that you have nothing to give, that you are a being-of-lack.

The imaginary register of love is the one that critics are most familiar with and also, rightly, most suspicious of. It implies the kind of blissful fusion that you have criticized in the context of Honneth. It takes place within the space of the mirror stage, narcissism, and the attempt to complete the self through the other. This is what Badiou, Žižek, and McGowan all align with romance. Fink also views imaginary love negatively, as a questionable search for redemption through the other.

Finally, on the level of the real, we're dealing with the drive, with jouissance, with what Fink calls the "thunderbolt" of love and describes in terms that are similar to how Badiou describes the amorous event.[17] Like you, Fink is more wary of this thunderbolt of love than the other Lacanians I've mentioned, but the relevant point for our purposes is that Fink regards Lacanian love as a combination of all three of these registers. Even though he's critical of both the imaginary and "thunderbolt" (real) aspects of love—leaning surprisingly strongly toward valorizing the ability of the symbolic order to institutionalize love—he nevertheless maintains that in *Seminar VIII* Lacan activates all three registers to analyze love.

AA: That's fascinating. And even if Fink's account is relatively level-headed, it still confirms my sense that Lacan's vision of love is modeled on romantic love between adults, whereas Klein's vision centers on parental (for her, maternal) love. The choice of starting points is interestingly different.

MR: This might have something to do with the fact that, for Lacan, it's the *objet a* rather than the object relation, as Klein theorizes it, that truly matters in love: simply put, "love" is never just—or even primarily—about the person you adore; it's about the *objet a*. This may sound incredibly callous, but I believe that there's a lot that this perspective can teach us.

Lacan's *Seminar VIII* is interesting not the least because of the way in which his reading of the *objet a* vacillates between the imaginary and the real valences of this concept. In his early work—and the 1960–1961 *Seminar VIII* is still relatively early—Lacan *usually* associates the *objet a* with the imaginary, reading it as a fantasmatic substitute for the lost Thing that the subject pursues because it promises narcissistic completion: the *a* promises to return to the subject a sliver of the lost Thing. This reading is evident in *Seminar VII*, the seminar Lacan delivered right before the one on transference. And in *Seminar XI*—delivered three years after *Seminar VIII*—Lacan describes the *a* as what's "in you more than you."[18]

In this manner, Lacan calls attention to the idea that the *a* is a partial object that I, the lover, install in you in order to render you desirable. We're not here talking about an object relation, but rather about the *a* as the cause, the trigger, of desire. Let me put it this way: it's not the shoe—let's imagine a Louboutin—that you want to fuck; instead, the shoe can become the *a* that causes you to want to fuck. So it's not *you* as a whole person I desire; rather, I desire what's "in you more than you" (the *a* that I have placed in you). This is a suspicious operation at best.

It's undeniable that parts of *Seminar VIII*, which is a close reading of Plato's *Symposium*, follow this reasoning. Lacan keeps cycling back to Alcibiades's obsession with Socrates, demonstrating how Alcibiades deposits the *objet a*—actually a whole bunch of them—in Socrates, how he sees within Socrates a treasure trove of jewels. Lacan uses the Greek word *ágalma* (or *agálmata* in the plural) to represent what he usually calls the *objet a*. He explains that, for Alcibiades, Socrates is full of *agálmata*: gleaming gems of unfathomable worth. But Socrates has no patience with this dynamic: he's wise enough to recognize that he doesn't possess the gems that Alcibiades sees in him. In other words, he understands the imaginary nature of desire, which is why he refuses to enter the game of love by bluntly rejecting Alcibiades's advances.

However, Alcibiades is convinced that Socrates contains a treasure. Lacan proposes that, for Alcibiades, Socrates is like a jewelry box that conceals a gift. Lacan basically likens Socrates to Ancient Greek wrapping paper: "What is important is what is inside. *Ágalma* may well mean ornamentation or ornament, but here it means above all gem or precious object—something that is inside."[19] Lacan then steps into Alcibiades's voice to express the utter wonder of what's inside Socrates: "No one has ever seen what is in question as I managed to. ... I saw them, the *agálmata* that are already divine ... they're wonderful, they're golden—totally beautiful, so utterly amazing that there was only one thing to do ... which was to do everything that Socrates ordered."[20]

On some level, Lacan is obviously talking about the imaginary nature of desire. As he specifies, "What the one is missing is not what is hidden in the other."[21] That is, what the lover is missing can't be found in the beloved. This is why Socrates says to Alcibiades, "Pay attention—where you see something, I am nothing."[22] At the same time, it's difficult to deny that there's something engaging about Alcibiades's description of Socrates as a jewelry box that contains golden, "totally beautiful" gems. Even though it's obvious that the gems originate from Alcibiades, there's also something very "real" about their impact on Alcibiades. The text doesn't give you the impression that Alcibiades's desire for Socrates is purely fantasmatic.

This is why I think that Lacan is doing something interesting with the *objet a* in this text in the sense that even if, on one level, the *a* is imaginary, on another, there are times when it functions as a remainder or residue of the real that persists after the cut of the signifier has brought the subject into existence. In other words, the *a* is a part of the self that the subject has been forced to give up as the price of its subjectivity, which is why it's so valuable, why the subject wants it so badly. This could obviously be read as a matter of seeking narcissistic self-completion. But I'm more inclined to read it as an encounter with something compellingly "real." Moreover, Lacan's analysis implies—and this is what I had in mind when I said that even "truly" loving may contain an aspect of fantasy—that fantasy, the *a*, may be the only way to access the real.

This isn't the first time during my ruminations about Lacan that I've proposed that the *objet a* isn't all bad.[23] But the reason I think that *Seminar VIII* lends special support to the idea that there may be something "real" about the *objet a* is that Lacan explains that when you chance upon—or yourself place—the *objet a* in another person, the *a* stops the sliding of the signifier. In the usual current of life, you're always gliding from one signifier to the next, and to be human is to do exactly that. But when you're enticed by the singularity of the other, by the *a* as a manifestation of jouissance, the sliding of the signifier comes to a halt. I read this as Lacan arguing that, through the *a*, you manage to access a bit of the real so that you're no longer purely a servant of the signifier. From this perspective, it's almost like Lacan is asserting, "This *is* an event in your life; it *is* a thunderbolt; it stops you in your tracks; these gorgeous gems in the other yank you out of the realm of the signifier; of course you'll eventually return to this realm but only as an altered being; your life will never be the same."

This is why I believe that although Lacan acknowledges that Socrates doesn't enter the game of love because he's aware of its illusory character, he's also on some level saying that Socrates makes a mistake in being so mistrustful of Alcibiades's desire. Lacan specifies that "Socrates is just as caught up in the deception … as Alcibiades is."[24] He admits that Alcibiades is the more deceived of the two but he also appears to suggest that Socrates makes the grave mistake of not understanding that "real" love—the act of "truly" loving—can only be attained by entering the illusion. In other words, if Socrates in fact had the desire for Alcibiades that Alcibiades claims he did— and Lacan notes that Alcibiades was Socrates's first love[25]—perhaps he should have had more respect for this desire. Socrates should have grasped that the fact that he knew himself to be hollow—

devoid of the gems that Alcibiades saw in him—didn't in any way diminish the "truthfulness" of Alcibiades's desire.

At one point in the seminar, Lacan says—again pretending that he's speaking in Alcibiades's voice—"I want it because I want it."[26] Alcibiades's desire is non-negotiable. I guess you could read this in two ways. If you wanted proof for the imaginary nature of love, you would propose that Alcibiades can't live without Socrates because he expects Socrates to complete his being. But if you wanted proof for the idea that there's something "real" about Alcibiades's love, you would say that Socrates's singularity is so gripping that Alcibiades can't resist it no matter how hard he tries.

AA: That was amazing. I'm trying to think about how to connect your explanation to Klein's account of love. As I said earlier, I think that Klein would agree that all love relationships are modeled on the primary object relation, which would perhaps be her version of the idea that when we love someone, it's because we invest that person with some aspect of *das Ding*. But as I've noted repeatedly, Klein views this primary object relation as fundamentally ambivalent. This is partly because of the ambivalence of the drives that operate within the infant, which means that the primary attachment has both libidinal and aggressive/destructive features. This is why the breast is split into good and bad part-objects.

For Klein, the goal of both psychological development and psychoanalysis is to foster gratitude, which is another way of telling the story about how love can mitigate the forces of envy, hatred, aggression, and destructiveness. But this suggests that Klein distinguishes between two kinds of love. First, there's love in the form of the attachment to the good breast, which corresponds with the paranoid-schizoid position. This type of love idealizes the object and experiences it as a source of all that's good, nourishing, and life-sustaining. But precisely for this reason, it also experiences the object as all powerful and itself as radically dependent on that object. Perhaps there's a connection to be made here to your description of romantic love, in which we idealize the other and experience ourselves as utterly dependent on it, to the extent that we might even feel and say that we would die without it. Yet, for Klein, the tendency to idealize is intrinsically connected to the tendency to demonize: the good breast easily turns into the bad—persecuting—breast.[27] This brings us back to how romantic love can and often does flip into extreme hatred, aggression, and demonization when the relationship comes to an end.

Second, there's what we might call mature love, which corresponds with the depressive position. This kind of love recognizes and tolerates ambivalence; it accepts that the relationship to the object is characterized by both love and hate, and that the other itself has both good—loving, gratifying, supportive—and bad—hateful, destructive, and undermining—features. In this sense, mature love is grounded in the acceptance of the fact that the other is just as internally split and fragmented as I am, just as riven by conflicting drives as I am, rather than in the infantile wish to overcome ambivalence. This is why mature love necessarily has elements of aggression in it. In addition, because it's depressive, mature love requires coming to terms with the loss of the phantasy of the wholly good, ideal, or pure breast. Judith Butler has a lovely (and funny) description of this in her 2016 Tanner Lectures:

> I love you, but you are already me, carrying the burden of my unrepaired past, my deprivation and my destructiveness. And I am doubtless that for you, taking the brunt of punishment for what you never received; we are for one another already faulty substitutions for irreversible pasts, neither one of us ever really getting past the desire for repairing what cannot be repaired. And yet here we are, hopefully sharing a decent glass of wine.[28]

These different types of ambivalence—the unreconciled dualities of love and hate, idealization and demonization, and so on—seem central to Klein's account of mature, authentic love, the type of love that characterizes the depressive position. My question is: how does ambivalence feature in Lacan's account of love?

MR: That's well articulated. And honestly, it sounds pretty Lacanian. You said that, for Klein, "mature love is grounded in the acceptance of the fact that the other is just as internally split and fragmented as I am, just as riven by conflicting drives as I am, rather than in the infantile wish to overcome ambivalence." This is the gist of what I was getting at earlier when I talked about the subject loving the other's lack as well as its deformation and maladaptation.

I also think that ambivalence is part of Lacan's account of love even on the level of the Thing. The Thing is a lot like the Kantian sublime: both appealing and terrifying. As I've explained, coming too close to the Thing would destroy the subject, which is why the task of the *objet a* is to maintain some distance between the two. This already seems like a deeply ambivalent endeavor because the danger of falling into the Thing's orbit is ever present. Indeed, everything I've stressed about love's capacity to derail the subject touches on the subject's ambivalent relationship to the Thing as what's (unconsciously) both most desired and most dreaded.

Moreover, the way in which Alcibiades is completely dependent on Socrates—subjugated by his desire for Socrates, ready to do Socrates's bidding—obviously drives him bonkers even if he also can't break the spell. The power of the *objet a* to render the subject vulnerable by definition implies ambivalence. Along related lines, the scenario where "love"—or more precisely, romance—entails an imaginary attempt to redeem the self is a cradle of ambiguity because, in this scenario, when the other rejects me, I not only lose the other but I'm also deprived of the (fantasized) possibility of wholeness.

On the level of Badiou's amorous event—which is supposed to be the "real" antidote to the romantic quest for wholeness—there must also be ambivalence. Otherwise Badiou wouldn't place so much weight on how important it is to stay faithful to the event regardless of the kinds of impediments you encounter. This emphasis on faithfulness applies to all of his events—the political, scientific, artistic, and amorous—but let's stick to the amorous event. Badiou admits that it's easy to start doubting your commitment to this event, particularly if the outside world is telling you that you have made a mistake or if the person you're with starts to drive you crazy. So it's almost like Badiou is protesting too much—is attempting to conjure away the ambivalence of the amorous event—when he maintains that once this event happens, you *must* stay loyal to it, that the worst thing you could do would be to betray it.

AA: That brings up the difficult question of what you're supposed to do if you're in the midst of living out your commitment to one love event when another love event happens. What happens then?

MR: That's an excellent question. Badiou admits that something like this could happen because he acknowledges that a person could have multiple love events in their life. But he attempts to get around the obvious problem that this raises by insisting that the new love event doesn't cancel out the "truthfulness" of the previous one.

This argument is easier to grasp on the level of the other kinds of events that Badiou references: the fact that the Russian revolution failed doesn't mean that it has lost its status as a political event; we can never return to a world that has no awareness of communism. And the fact that Einstein overcame some of the limitations of Galileo's scientific paradigm doesn't mean that Galileo wasn't a genuine scientific event. Finally, jazz doesn't diminish the importance of classical music. Supposedly the same holds for the amorous event: your new love doesn't neutralize the "eventness" of your previous love. However, I admit that I've never been entirely convinced by Badiou's argument regarding multiple love events: it seems to me that your new love is bound to diminish the significance of your previous love.

But I have a question about Klein. Do you think that Klein is the thinker whom we should most accredit for developing the notion of the partial object? Obviously the concept wasn't alien to Freud. And Winnicott talks about the transitional object. Moreover, the *objet a* is central to Lacan's thinking. But isn't it really Klein who takes this concept the furthest?

AA: Absolutely! The paradigmatic partial object for Klein is the breast, which obviously plays a central role in her theory. In addition, her distinction between the two positions—the paranoid-schizoid and the depressive—could productively be understood as turning on the shift from relating to partial objects, or part-objects, to an ability to relate to a whole object. As Klein states, "The step from the introjection of part-objects to whole loved objects with all its implications is of the most crucial importance in development."[29]

As I've explained, this transition is facilitated by the introjection of the good breast, which forms the core of the developing ego. "This internal good breast," Klein writes, "strengthens the infant's capacity to love and trust his objects, heightens the stimulus for introjection of good objects and situations, and is therefore an essential source of reassurance against anxiety; it becomes the representative of the life instinct within."[30] In other words, the good breast is a part-object that, somewhat paradoxically, enables us to make the transition to relating to whole objects and therefore to tolerating ambivalence by combining love and hatred, the good and the bad breast, in ourselves and in our primary object. In that sense, you could say that it's all about the part-object for Klein.

MR: Interestingly, as apprehensive as Lacan often is regarding the *objet a* as a partial object, he nevertheless berates other psychoanalysts—and in light of what you just said, this would presumably include Klein—for wanting to turn the partial object into a whole one. Lacan postulates, "The function of the partial object is one of the great discoveries of psychoanalysis": "We had a real find there, that of the fundamentally partial nature of the object insofar as it is the pivotal point, crux, or key of human desire."[31] After this insight about how the *objet a* explains the workings of desire, Lacan asserts that it was a giant mistake for psychoanalysis to enter into "a dialectic of totalization" that attempts to turn this partial object into a whole person.[32] Lacan believes that the impulse to totalize the other arises from the fact that we—even psychoanalysts—find it too disturbing to think that it's the *objet a*—the partial object—that we want rather than the whole person. So we do everything in our power to convince ourselves that we love the other as a whole person.

You said that it's crucial for Klein that the subject—the child—learns to turn its part-objects into a whole object. I understand that this is a matter of transcending a false conception of people as either all good or all bad, which is obviously important. But I'm wondering if you would be willing to say more about this translation of partial objects into a whole object in light of Lacan's criticism. You have talked so much about the ambivalence of love that it sounds like it might be impossible to actually ever create a genuinely "whole" object. But is this still a goal for Klein, something that the subject should seek to approximate?

AA: My sense is that Lacan and Klein might mean something different by the term *whole object*. I take it that for Lacan a whole object would be one that isn't split by the signifier, contains no lack, and therefore also feels no desire. For reasons that I've talked about extensively, the whole object for Klein is still internally split in the sense that it contains unresolved ambivalence.

MR: In this particular context, I conjecture that by the whole object Lacan simply means—in the colloquial sense—the whole person rather than the *objet a*. I don't think that he's talking about an undivided subject without lack or desire: there's no possibility of such a subject in his theory. He's merely saying that because psychoanalysts other than himself are uncomfortable with the idea that the cause of desire isn't the beloved's entire personality but rather the *objet a*, they overlook Freud's insights about desire's link to partial objects and instead focus on how the lover desires the beloved as a whole person. He's referring to a sentimentalization of desire in psychoanalytic theory that bothers him.

AA: I see. Yet the fact that Lacan refers to the "dialectic of totalization" as what transforms the part-object into a whole object suggests to me that he's also worried about the creation of a fantasy of an undivided subject. Indeed, he proceeds to explain that what psychoanalysts who are committed to the whole object fail to see is that "this other, as an object of desire, is perhaps the summation of a pile of partial objects, which is not at all the same as a total object."[33] I think that this way of understanding the other as an object of desire—as the summation of a pile of partial objects—is consistent with the way that I've been interpreting Klein's understanding of integration as the enrichment, expansion, and enhancement of personality.

These intersections between the Kleinian and Lacanian models regarding partial objects bring me back to my earlier question about whether Badiou's love event can be repeated: it seems to me that if you take seriously the idea that all love is transference love, it doesn't matter if you stick with your first love event or pick a different one. For both Klein and Lacan, when you're in love, what you experience as exerting such a compelling pull on you is something that you have placed in the other person in the first place. And the placing of this entity—*objet a* or whatever you want to call it—into the other is a way of trying to work through the lack or loss that you have experienced in relation to your primary object.

This implies that whether or not someone embodies *das Ding* for you is to some degree almost arbitrary. Is this right?

MR: I agree that depositing the *a* in the other is a matter of working through the lack or loss that you have experienced in relation to the primary object, which for Lacan is more fantasmatic than for

Klein but nevertheless powerful. Moreover, what you just said about the arbitrariness of subsequent objects is pretty much exactly what Lacan says at the end of his seminar on transference, namely that what both Socrates and the analyst understand is that there's a degree of randomness to object choice. Regarding the subject's desire for love, Lacan states:

> The analyst cannot help but think that *any object whatsoever can fill it*. This is where we analysts are led to vacillate, regarding the limit where—with any object whatsoever, once it has entered into the field of desire—the following question arises: 'What are you?' *There is no object that is of any greater value than another*—this is the mourning around which desire for the analyst ... is centered.[34]

So, yes, on some level, any object will do. That the analysand can desire the analyst is one manifestation of this insight. In addition, the sadness of being an analyst—or perhaps just analytically informed—is that you're cognizant that this is how desire functions. In this sense, Socrates was a better analyst than lover: he grasped that it was a fantasmatic cluster of gems rather than himself that Alcibiades was after and that these gems could in principle be found in a number of objects, that objects of desire are on some level interchangeable.

Yet Lacan's analysis of the *objet a* also reveals that desire is extremely specific, that it's not usually the case that just anyone will do. The extent to which a particular person approximates *das Ding* makes a difference, for some people emit a stronger aura of the missing Thing than others. Certainly more than one person can fulfill the role of being a substitute for the Thing. However, I don't think that every person can. In my experience, it's quite difficult to find people who elicit the type of desire that we see in Lacan's account of Alcibiades and that Badiou is getting at with his notion of the love event. Barthes describes marvelously the enigmatic, indefinable nature of the tiny detail that draws us to some people in ways that we ourselves don't necessarily comprehend. In addition, as I suggested earlier—and this has been an intellectual point of fixation for me for a long time—I believe that there's something "real" about the kind of desire that the *objet a*, when it's fully operational, can elicit.

Of course we can fleetingly or casually desire all kinds of people. But it seems to me that there are different frequencies of desire and that when the *a* really gets under our skin—even if it, paradoxically, originates from us—something genuine is going on. I mean "genuine" in the sense that the encounter with a particular person jolts us awake, making us feel fully alive. Unquestionably, the whole thing could be a ruse, a form of cruel optimism, but I try to hold onto moments that feel meaningful. And there simply aren't that many of those in life. Or maybe that's just my life.

This may also be related to what I said earlier about loving the lack in the other: desire that touches the real isn't looking for a perfect object; instead, frequently the person who attracts us on this fundamental level is a flawed one. This doesn't sound compatible with the idea that our desire is so superficial that *anyone* could become its object. In addition, if anyone could become its object, our desire wouldn't make us as vulnerable as it routinely does. We could be much more rational about it: we would pick the gentle, reliable, reasonable, and high-earning person. But do we do this? Sometimes, yes. But often, no.

Another indication that our desire is quite picky—and tremendously irrational—is that we sometimes fixate on people who don't want us: we can be in love with someone for *years* even if that person couldn't care less (and in some instances even if that person treats us badly). In addition, for many people—not everyone, but many—the nature of desire seems to be such that once they get attached to a specific object, it's impossible for them to shift their desire to an other object even if this other object is amazing in every possible way. Even if the person they are attached to abandons them or otherwise hurts them, they may find it hard to get excited about a new object. It's almost like mourning and desiring are incompatible: we can't desire when we're still mourning a loved one we have lost.

There's therefore a stubborn irrationality to our attachment to specific—unique—others, which can lead to a great deal of pathology, desperation, and traumatization. This may be related to the fact that it takes so long for the child to become an independently viable creature. You have described astutely the vulnerability that results from the child's dependence on its caretakers. Butler likewise analyzes this dependency compellingly, spelling out how precarious it makes us in the sense that we're sometimes forced to attach ourselves to people who treat us badly because doing so is our only way of surviving.³⁵ Berlant in turn develops this idea by positing that sometimes a bad attachment is the only thing that's holding us together—the only thing that's lending coherence to our identity—so that giving up the attachment would be even worse than staying attached.³⁶

Because of the lengthy period that it takes for us to become semi-independent, by the time we get to the point where we could in principle make decisions about whether or not we want a certain relationship, it's almost like it's too late: our patterns of relating have solidified, with the consequence that we don't always know how to break them even when we want to. One reason that the psychoanalytic account of desire is so convincing is that it explains why this happens, why we keep repeating the same aggravating or damaging relational scenarios throughout our lives. From this perspective, what Klein has to say about early object relations seems right on target.

AA: Perhaps I was conflating two different senses in which the decision to commit to a love event could be arbitrary. It's true that it isn't arbitrary in the sense that just anyone could be the object of desire. It seems right to me to say that only some objects can serve as compelling approximations of the Thing, and people definitely get stubbornly attached to such objects. But given that for each person there can be multiple objects who embody the Thing, the choice of which of *these* objects to declare fidelity to is arbitrary, at least from the viewpoint of psychoanalysis. This isn't to suggest that there might not be other reasons for remaining faithful to one rather than the others.

Your response also reminds me of our earlier discussion of the relationship between the intrapsychic and the intersubjective. If it's true that, for Lacan, it's not only that you place the *a* in the object of your desire but also that there has to be something real (in the non-technical sense) or genuine about the other person, such that you want to place the *a* in them, this appears to come close to Klein's understanding of the interplay between the intrapsychic (or phantasized) and intersubjective aspects of our ways of relating to others. This interplay seems important for thinking about how relationships, perhaps especially love relationships, work because when you fall in love with someone new, it can be difficult to sort out how much of your attraction arises from your (usually idealized) phantasized projections and how much of it arises from what the other person really is like.

    This is where Klein's idea of trying to bring the intrapsychic and the intersubjective into better alignment is useful. I think that she is right that—as difficult, painful, and time consuming as this can be—the more you can bring the phantasmatic aspects of your relationship to your love object in line with some semblance of who that person actually is, the better the relationship will be. This requires realizing that the other isn't the idealized phantasy that you were projecting onto it without this realization flipping over into demonization—into a situation where you're screaming at the other person that if they aren't the perfect object you have put on a pedestal, they must be a horrible bitch. Bringing psychic reality and external reality together means realizing that the other you love is both good and bad and that you both love and hate them—and loving them all the same.

MR: I may have less patience than you do with putting up with the hated parts of the other: in some cases, solitude seems preferable. But more to the point, although I agree with you that multiple people can function as objects of our desire, I'm wondering if it might be accurate to say that, from a psychoanalytic perspective, far from being arbitrary, our object choices are determined. I don't mean "meant to be" in the pop cultural sense of needing to find our soulmate, but rather in the sense that psychoanalysis suggests that there's something about our early object relations that determines the shape of our love lives, which is another way of saying that the repetition compulsion has something to do with it.

AA: That depiction fits well with the Kleinian perspective. Our early object relations establish our internal object world, which in turn sets down certain patterns of relating. For instance, being parented by a caregiver who is emotionally distant or unavailable—perhaps because she's depressed and unable to cope—might well lead an individual to seek out lovers who are emotionally withdrawn or have a tendency to become self-absorbed, because that's what love feels like to them. This is an example of what you said earlier about getting stuck in a pattern of relating that becomes difficult to even recognize as a pattern, let alone to change. That's how I would think about the repetition compulsion in Kleinian terms.

But can we talk more about love, ambivalence, and the death drive in Lacan? I'm thinking about the part toward the end of *Seminar VII*, where he's talking about Freud's critique of the idea of loving one's neighbor as oneself.

MR: *Nebenmensch?*

AA: Yes. The passage I want to look at is in a chapter entitled "Love of One's Neighbor." Lacan argues that, in *Civilization and Its Discontents*, Freud reveals that "we cannot avoid the formula that *jouissance* is evil."[37] Moreover, this evil jouissance—this beyond the pleasure principle—has something to do with the neighbor, which is why loving one's neighbor is an impossible command. As Lacan puts it, "Those who like fairy stories turn a deaf ear to talk of man's innate tendencies to 'evil, aggression, destruction, and thus also to cruelty.'"[38] Lacan then quotes the following passage from Freud: "Man tries to satisfy his need for aggression at the expense of his neighbor, to exploit his work without compensation, to use him sexually without his consent, to appropriate his goods, to humiliate him, to inflict suffering on him, to torture and kill him."[39] Lacan concludes—now speaking as himself—that "Freud was literally horrified by the idea of love for one's neighbor [because] the neighbor ... is bad."[40]

MR: I see where you're going with this. Here is the fundamental—even constitutive—aggressivity that you find in Klein. It sounds a lot like the passage about the individual's ineradicable aggressiveness that you quoted from Klein the other day. Precisely because jouissance, in Lacan, is linked to destruction—aggression toward the self or toward the other—aggression is central for him. It's in fact so central that the reparative love of the child for the mother, or the love of the mother for the child, that's at least a part of the Kleinian story is hard to find in Lacan. This may be among the reasons that Lacanian theory has been so off-putting to some other analytic schools, such as the relational school, for which love is essential.

And then we get to the point about the neighbor being intrinsically evil. If love between mother and child is already difficult, you can well imagine what happens in relation to the neighbor who wants to exploit the subject, to use it sexually, to steal its goods, to humiliate it, to inflict suffering on it, and to torture and kill it. Loving such a neighbor is, as Lacan suggests, impossible.

AA: That makes sense. But Lacan goes on to say:

> Every time that Freud stops short in horror at the consequences of the commandment to love one's neighbor, we see evoked the presence of that fundamental evil which dwells within this neighbor. But if that is the case, then it also dwells within me. And what is more of a neighbor to me than this heart within which is that of my *jouissance* and which I don't dare go near? For as soon as I go near it … there rises up the unfathomable aggressivity from which I flee, that I turn against me, and which in the very place of the vanished Law adds its weight to that which prevents me from crossing a certain frontier at the limit of the Thing.[41]

Earlier I asked whether love for Lacan is ambivalent in the sense that it's ambivalent for Klein, and it seems to me that he's quite close to Klein here. But it also seems like he's actually saying something stronger, harsher, and darker than anything Klein would say, for all her relentless negativity. It sounds like he's saying that love isn't possible because the neighbor is evil and so am I.

MR: That's right. On the one hand, I think that Lacan is close to Klein in suggesting that aggression (or "evil") is primary. On the other, I think that his position is more extreme than Klein's in the sense that, as I just suggested, he doesn't posit reparation (or love) as a possible palliative to aggressivity—the evil in the other and in yourself—that you find in Klein. The closest you might come to this idea in Lacan is the admission that when you love the lack in the other, you must also tolerate its jouissance, the very "evil" that Lacan is referring to. That is, love can't just be about appreciating the symbolic and imaginary facets of the other—that's too easy. Love has to account for the other's jouissance as well.

However, loving the derailing jouissance of one person is hard enough. Trying to love this jouissance (or "evil") in everyone is daunting, to say the least. One reason Lacan emphasizes Freud's horror at the idea of loving the neighbor as yourself is that doing so would mean loving the jouissance of everyone, inasmuch as everyone is ultimately your neighbor. This seems impossible. This is why Žižek has argued that the ultimate ethical challenge in relation to the other arises whenever we have to face this other as a "real" creature, as a creature of jouissance, of chaos, suffering, overagitation, overanimation, and, yes, evilness.[42]

As I've mentioned, under normal circumstances, we operate under the protection of symbolic and imaginary support systems—systems that allow us to communicate with others (the symbolic) and empathize with others (the imaginary, where the other can be judged to be "like" me because in some ways it's my mirror). That is, in our everyday lives, we don't usually have to confront the depth of the other's death drive. To be sure, there are deprivileged people in our society for whom the other's aggression is a palpable quotidian reality. But in principle our society is premised upon the notion that the death drive can be disciplined by symbolic and imaginary structures of meaning. However, this social edifice is a sham in the sense that underneath these structures bubbles an evil that—as Lacan highlights—is in me as much as it's in my neighbor. This is why the real—"real" also in the technical Lacanian sense—ethical dilemma arises when we're forced to confront the other's jouissance, the other's monstrosity. In that situation, what do we do? What is the ethical thing to do? This is an incredibly difficult question.

In the ethical act, what's central is your *own* death drive. But then there's the dicey question of how you relate to the other on the level of its death drive. It seems to me that this is a genuine ethical dilemma in the contemporary political context. It probably always has been, but right now it feels acutely pronounced, with the school shootings, acts of police brutality, suicide bombings, and other scenes of violence—all the way to ethnic cleansings, mass rape as a weapon of war, and deadly drone strikes—that are taking place with staggering regularity. When we're dealing with the "real" of the other's death drive, we're up against the kind of situation that language (the symbolic) or fantasy (the imaginary) can't mediate. Lacanian ethics—inasmuch as it has focused on the terror of having to face the jouissance of the other—has been able to diagnose the problem. But it hasn't been able to provide a solution. I'm not sure there's a solution, actually.

AA: I'm not sure there's a solution either, at least not any easy solution. But perhaps this is a predicament where Klein could help us to think beyond—not against, but beyond—Lacan. Klein's notion of reparation dovetails with theories and practices of reparative or restorative justice that focus more on the healing of relationships and communities that have been fractured by crime or political violence than on retribution or punishment. Such models of justice have been implemented—with mixed success, to be sure—in post-conflict situations including, for example, the wake of the Rwandan genocide. Similarly, Angela Davis, in her work on prison abolitionism, suggests reparative or restorative justice as an abolitionist alternative that, when combined with broader decarceration efforts, could replace our current retributive model.[43] Although Klein's work isn't directly invoked in these discussions, her model of integration as a toleration of internal ambivalence, differentiation, and negativity that emerges in response to an experience of loss seems apt here, and could be extended to think about how communities might heal in the aftermath of loss, trauma, and violence.

The connection between Klein's notion of reparation and theories of reparative or restorative justice has been developed extensively by David McIvor in his terrific book, *Mourning in America*.[44] McIvor draws on Klein to discuss truth and reconciliation commissions (TRCs) as potential spaces for a democratic politics of mourning. Although such commissions are far from perfect, he reads them as entities that have the capacity to help communities to work through traumatic events and violent pasts without appealing to impossible and exclusionary ideals of social unity, harmony, or integration. While McIvor cautions us against turning the "reconciliation" pursued in TRCs into a manic attempt to overcome all social conflict—in which case such commissions could easily become instances of a problematic "sentimental humanitarianism"[45]—Klein's account enables him to envision them as contributions to an open-ended process of integration. As McIvor understands them, TRCs are "less a collective form of healing or forgiveness than the possibility of ongoing interactions across social divides through which democratic norms and practices might extend and deepen their reach."[46] Reconciliation is therefore an ongoing democratic practice by means of which communities can form and reform a fractured, fractious, and internally contested—and thus necessarily incomplete and open-ended—whole.

MR: I appreciate these points about reparative or restorative justice. Finding ways to heal from collective traumas is incredibly demanding, and I can see how Klein would be more helpful than Lacan in thinking about how we might approach these types of challenges: there's something about her account of reparation—a reparation, moreover, that arises from a place of *depression*—that feels intuitively compelling even if it's hard to envision how to put it into practice because dealing with collective situations demands not only communication but also the willingness to tolerate prolonged ambiguity, to curtail one's aggression, and to risk the possibility of retraumatization. The urge to just walk away might be difficult to contain.

Badiou and Žižek have analyzed the ethical dilemmas of facing the other's traumatization from a perspective that might be related to this problematic of reparative or restorative justice. They have asked the following question: What do we do when the other no longer appears human to us, not because it displays a monstrous aggressivity, but because it has been the target of such extreme aggression that it has been stripped of its social intelligibility and now appears to us in the pure "realness" of its being? The "real" here isn't the destructive force that we have been discussing this far. Rather, it's the real of the body deprived of its symbolic and imaginary wrappings.

As an example of this predicament, Badiou and Žižek use Agamben's notion of bare life, particularly the figure of the *Muselmann*: the emaciated, catatonic, and almost-dead concentration camp survivor who is a mere "shell of a man" because of the terrible suffering they have undergone. This situation is yet another illustration of why love—or reparation and restoration— is such a difficult endeavor in relation to the neighbor. On the one hand, my assumption is that the *Muselmann* would elicit the impulse to help, to be loving, supportive, and compassionate—to "hold" the damaged other in the sense that psychoanalysts use this term in the clinical context. On the other, there might be a strong impulse to turn away because the other's suffering is too unbearable to witness, let alone to engage with. We see this latter impulse in relation to beggars on the streets, in relation to refugees in camps. Their deprivation is so immense that we don't always know how to respond. Sometimes we give the beggar money. But other times we avert our eyes.

Finally, love, reparation, and restoration are such difficult concepts to reconcile with Lacanian theory because, as the passage you read reveals, Lacan believes that the evil that dwells within the neighbor also dwells within me. This implies that the very jouissance that I recoil from in the neighbor I equally recoil from in myself: as soon as I go anywhere near it, as soon as I get too close to the Thing, I experience an aggression that feels unbearable. In addition, when I love a person on the level of their jouissance—meaning, when I "truly" love—I can't avoid the "evil" in them. I may want to flee from it, but it always hovers in the background. So ultimately the answer to your question regarding whether love in Lacan, like love in Klein, is ambivalent is a resounding *yes*. It's totally ambivalent. The moment I touch the real in the other, the thing that draws me …

AA: … is also aggressive and evil.

MR: Yes, I'm automatically exposing myself to the possibility of tremendous aggression, to the "evil" jouissance of the other—and of myself.

AA: Okay, good. [laughter]

6

Creativity

MR: As we continue our Klein-Lacan dialogue, our topic is creativity—or sublimation—as it relates to lack, loss, and mourning. We have already noted that, for both Klein and Lacan, at the root of creativity resides lack or loss. Lacan's theorization of lack takes the concept in various directions, but he appears to agree with Klein that creativity can't be dissociated from the loss of the first object of psychic, affective, and bodily cathexis. For Lacan, this object is more fantasized than actual. Nevertheless, as is the case with Klein, he sees a connection between mourning the lost object and creativity.

One could say that, for Lacan, the flipside of accepting that there's no cure for one's lack is the potential for creativity (or sublimation). I mean creativity in the broadest possible sense rather than merely in the sense of creating works of art. For instance, self-fashioning—as theorized, among others, by Nietzsche and the late Foucault[1]—could be thought of as a creative undertaking, as could much of what we do in the course of everyday life. Indeed, although Lacan regards the big Other mostly as a hegemonic entity to be resisted, he also—and I've already mentioned this because I feel that it's a point that many critics miss—has an appreciation for the rewards that the Other grants us by giving us access to the signifier as a tool for navigating daily life as creatures of communicative ability.

I'll return to some of these themes later in today's conversation. But the most logical place to start might be Lacan's scathing critique of Klein on the topic of sublimation because by now, having learned so much about the nuances of Kleinian theory from you, Amy, I suspect that this critique may be excessively harsh. It can be found in *Seminar VII*, where—as we already know—Lacan accuses Klein of equating *das Ding* with the mother's body. In this context, he states: "In that register which currently interests us, namely, the notion of sublimation in the Freudian economy, the Kleinian school is full of interesting ideas."[2] Lacan therefore recognizes that, like he himself, the Kleinians—and in this instance he's referring more to the Kleinian school than to Klein herself—are drawing a connection between *das Ding* and sublimation. However, it quickly becomes clear that his motivation for bringing up the Kleinians in this context is to prove them wrong.

Lacan begins his critique by referring to an American author, M. Lee, who isn't a Kleinian but who apparently has written "on sublimation as the principle of creation in the fine arts" along Kleinian lines because she attributes to sublimation "a restitutive function": "She finds there more or less of an attempt at symbolic repair of the imaginary lesions that have occurred to the fundamental image of the maternal body."[3] This is how Lacan arrives at the Kleinian reparative impulse: the mother's body has been lacerated, and sublimation is a means of repairing the damage.

This idea genuinely irritates Lacan, causing him to exclaim: "I can tell you right away that the reduction of the notion of sublimation to a restitutive effort of the subject relative to the injured body of the mother is certainly not the best solution to the problem of sublimation."[4] Lacan thus believes that it's a colossal blunder to reduce sublimation to the attempt to repair the mother's injured body. Although he admits that there's a link between *das Ding* and sublimation, he complains that the Kleinians are turning this link into a narrow, overly literal preoccupation with the mother's body, thereby perpetuating what he mockingly calls "the Kleinian myth."[5]

Because of these disagreements, Lacan accuses Kleinian clinicians of exercising "a rather limited and puerile notion of what might be called an atherapy."[6] That is, according to Lacan, Kleinian clinicians are no longer doing psychoanalysis proper but rather undertaking a nonanalytic form of therapy, which means that they seek solutions to the analysand's problems in the fine arts, dance, and other exercises that are supposed to give the subject satisfaction or a measure of equilibrium.[7] Reading the Kleinians, Lacan concludes, leads one "to realize how such an orientation reduces the problem of sublimation ... The approach involves valorizing activities that seem to be located in the register of a more or less transitory explosion of supposedly artistic gifts, gifts which appear in the cases described to be highly doubtful."[8]

What are your thoughts on this?

AA: It sounds like the Kleinian analysts that Lacan is referring to are taking Kleinian theory in the direction of art or play therapy. As far as I know, Klein herself didn't do this. It's true that she pioneered the use of the play technique in analyzing children, but the idea behind this technique wasn't to use play as a form of therapy. Rather, it was Klein's attempt to adapt psychoanalytic technique to analysands who weren't yet linguistically developed, and so weren't capable of the kinds of free associations that are so central to analytic work with adults. Play, for Klein, became the analogue to linguistic associations—and in this sense, play might have a very interesting relationship to the Lacanian symbolic order. This way of thinking about play strikes me as different from using the arts to give analysands satisfaction and provide solutions to their emotional problems.

Although sublimation isn't extensively thematized in Klein's work, she acknowledges not only that aggression can be sublimated but also that the sublimation of aggression is key to anything productive. I'll come back to the details of this point in a moment. For now, I want to note that in making it, Klein goes beyond the caricature that Lacan offers, where sublimation is understood as the restitutive effort to repair the mother's injured body. When Klein and her disciples talk about the sublimation of aggression, their position actually seems fairly close to some of the things that Lacan says in *Seminar VII* about the relationship between the death drive and the will to create *ex nihilo*. I assume that you'll come back to this part of *Seminar VII* because it seems central to Lacan's understanding of creativity.

MR: Yes, definitely.

AA: I would say in response to Lacan's critique that he flattens out what, for me, seems like the most important aspect of Klein's work, namely the relationship between the intrapsychic and the intersubjective that we have already discussed extensively—and I think that we keep returning to this topic for a good reason. In the present context, it's noteworthy that Lacan makes it sound as if Klein's understanding of the subject's relationship to the primary object is completely intersubjective, with no intrapsychic element, no phantasy, at all. Although this is certainly a possible reading of Klein—one that takes her talk about the good and bad breast, milk, and so forth, literally—for reasons that we have discussed I don't think that this is the best interpretation of her approach because it completely ignores the phantasmatic aspects of the primary object relation.

MR: It's interesting that the mediating role that phantasy plays in Kleinian theory—the intrapsychic aspects of her theory—has been overlooked by so many critics, including Lacan, and certainly most contemporary critical theorists. As I've suggested, this may be the main reason that Klein hasn't, until recently, been taken seriously by my version of critical theory, which, for valid reasons, is averse to any hint of essentialism. Because of this, the fact that you're bringing out this side of Kleinian theory—and emphasizing the centrality of aggression to this theory—is a terrific contribution to my field. Furthermore, I can't but concede that even if Lacan's critique is valid in relation to some analysts who saw themselves as adopting the mantle of Klein, when it comes to Klein herself, he may once again be overcompensating for the fact that some of his ideas may not necessarily be that different from those of Klein.

I'm wondering if mourning, which both Klein and Lacan connect to creativity, might provide a productive entry point for us. How does Klein conceptualize mourning?

AA: Klein's key texts on mourning are "Love, Guilt and Reparation" and "Mourning and Its Relation to Manic-Depressive States."[9] I'll state up front that my interpretation of Klein's account of the productivity of mourning is influenced by Whitebook's reading of Freud, which contains a fascinating examination of the relationship between mourning and creativity. At the core of Whitebook's depiction of this relationship is resignation, by which he means the acceptance of the reality principle. However, it's important to keep in mind that—as I noted when we discussed affect—this needn't imply an acceptance of the existing social reality (the Lacanian symbolic). Rather, in this context, the acceptance of the reality principle refers to the acknowledgment of human finitude and, thus, to the ubiquity and inevitability of loss.

Whitebook regards resignation to a painful reality—the realization that I and everyone I care for will die—as the opposite of the desire for transcendence or immortality, both of which he deems to be infantile, omnipotent wishes. Although Freud is Whitebook's point of reference for this argument, which he develops into a thought-provoking critique of philosophical projects that incite a desire for transcendence, it can also be connected to Klein's critique of all forms of idealization.

As I read her, Klein is working in the same vein as Whitebook's Freud: she connects mourning to the acceptance of painful reality and to the working through of the loss of ideality that this acceptance necessarily entails. Moreover, she views this process as central to the formation of the subject, which means that the subject has a melancholic structure. In addition, Klein characteristically believes that mourning—exemplified by the depressive position—is connected to the drive for love, reparation, and integration. More specifically, she develops the link between the melancholic incorporation of lost objects and the creation of psychic structure that emerges in Freud's late work.

Recall that in "Mourning and Melancholia," Freud contrasts melancholia with mourning: although both of these psychic states are responses to the loss of a loved object that are characterized by painful sadness, lack of interest in the world, and difficulty of moving on, Freud depicts mourning as a normal reaction to an experience of loss that's overcome in due course while portraying melancholia as a pathological state in which the subject gets stuck. The melancholic internalizes the lost object, forging an identification with it. This means that the melancholic subject never truly gives up the lost object but instead sets it up inside its ego, thereby replacing object love with an identification. The result is that the subject is never able to move on. Its object loss is translated into ego loss, which explains why melancholia—unlike mourning—is accompanied by feelings of extreme worthlessness and self-beratement.[10]

Later, Freud rethought this pathologization of melancholia. In an important passage at the beginning of Chapter 2 of *The Ego and the Id*, he acknowledges that in his earlier essay he "did not appreciate the full significance of this process and how typical it is," adding that he has come to realize that "this kind of substitution has a great share in determining the form taken by the ego."[11] He now admits that the process of melancholic identification may be the "sole condition under which the id can give up its objects."[12] As a consequence, for the later Freud—and this idea has an important resonance with Klein's work—the character of the ego might best be understood as "a precipitate of abandoned object-cathexes" that "contains the history of those object-choices."[13] In other words, the ego (and also the superego) has a melancholic structure: it's forged through the response to an experience of loss.

In "Mourning and Its Relation to Manic-Depressive States," Klein explicitly links the depressive position to mourning and melancholia (without distinguishing between the two). But given that the depressive position emerges so early in life, when the baby is between four and six months old, you might wonder what the baby could be mourning? The answer, as we already know, is that it's mourning the loss of the good breast, which it feels it has destroyed through its aggressive phantasies. As Klein puts the point: "The object which is being mourned is the mother's breast and all that the breast and the milk have come to stand for in the infant's mind: namely, love, goodness and security. All these are felt by the baby to be lost, and lost as a result of his own uncontrollable greedy and destructive phantasies."[14] This feeling is probably connected to an omnipotence of thoughts or magical thinking on the baby's part, inasmuch as it can't distinguish between destroying the good breast in phantasy and destroying it in reality. But in any case, it's the baby's realization of the implications of its destructiveness that gives rise to depressive anxiety.

Once the depressive position is achieved, the baby experiences the loss of the good breast. This breast obviously never existed, but what matters is the perception that it's lost. At the same time, pieces of it survive and become part of the whole object together with the bad breast that the baby earlier perceived as its persecutor. The baby thus mourns the loss of the wholly good breast that it never had. Yet in another sense it doesn't lose this breast after all; rather, it internalizes it and this internalization enables the creation of psychic structure, and therefore of symbolization, language, and creativity. But in order to gain access to these things, the baby has to give up its idealized phantasy of the purity of the good breast. This loss is required by the depressive position.

MR: I've always loved the late Freud's idea that the melancholic incorporation of lost objects can lead to the enrichment of the psyche. I have—rightly or wrongly—expanded upon this concept by analyzing the gradual construction of "character" through repeated experiences of loss.[15] That is, I've linked melancholia to self-fashioning. But in the present context, I'm struck by your description of how the baby mourns the loss of something that it never had: the phantasy of the purity of the good breast. This sounds more or less identical to the Lacanian claim that the subject never possessed the Thing that it imagines having lost. Furthermore, the notion of having to relinquish the phantasy of the good breast aligns nicely with the Lacanian notion that the subject needs to give up the pursuit of a cure. Ditto for Whitebook's argument about the need to relinquish the fantasy of transcendence, which you link to Klein's rejection of idealizations. These prominent connections reinforce my sense that Klein and Lacan share much more than psychoanalytic scholars and critical theorists have recognized.

AA: I couldn't agree more. I've also tried to emphasize the melancholic structure of the subject for Klein, which is a theme that you have raised repeatedly in relation to Lacan's understanding of the subject as a creature of lack.

Earlier you wondered about the link between mourning and creativity that Klein and Lacan also seem to share. For Klein, mourning a loss is undoubtedly a precondition of creativity: it's only by entering the depressive position that the child becomes capable of reparation, which is one form of creativity. But Klein also connects the internalization of the good breast to creativity because the good breast is the representative of the life instinct, and hence a source of creativity. However, internalization alone isn't enough: the child must also come to relate to its object as a whole object because the enrichment of its personality—including the integration of its ego—depends on its ability to undertake this process of synthesizing the good with the bad.

In "On the Development of Mental Functioning," Klein explains the matter as follows:

> The more the ego can integrate its destructive impulses and synthesize the different aspects of its objects, the richer it becomes; for the split-off parts of the self and of impulses which are rejected because they arouse anxiety and give pain also contain valuable aspects of the personality and of the phantasy life which is impoverished by splitting them off. Though the rejected aspects of the self and of internalized objects contribute to instability, they are also at the source of inspiration in artistic productions and in various intellectual activities.[16]

Here Klein asserts that the split-off parts of the self and the impulses that are rejected because they arouse anxiety and give pain are nevertheless valuable parts of the psyche. While they add to the subject's instability, they are also "the source of inspiration in artistic productions and in various intellectual activities." In other words, even if there are times when creativity for Klein is about engaging in the reconstructive work of repair, it's also about harnessing the instability of split-off parts of the self—that is, about harnessing the energy of the death drive.

This is a much more complicated picture of sublimation than Lacan's depiction of the urge to repair the maternal body. It's not so much that Klein wanted to use the creative arts to facilitate the work of analysis, as Lacan suggests in his critique of the Kleinians that you outlined a moment ago, but rather that the work of analysis aims to enhance the creativity of the analysand by allowing for the kind of integration and augmentation of personality that involves accepting parts of the self and of one's internal objects that were previously split off.

MR: Interesting. In an earlier conversation, you mentioned that Klein views the death drive mostly diagnostically, that she doesn't celebrate it in the way that some Lacanians do. But here you seem to suggest that the death drive—or aggressivity—is fundamental to Klein's notion of creativity. Does this mean that the paranoid-schizoid position is intrinsically linked to creativity? Does one have to destroy things, tear them to bits, in order to create something new?

AA: You're right that Klein doesn't celebrate the death drive. However, some later thinkers who draw inspiration from Klein take a different view. Thomas Ogden, for instance, argues that Klein and her followers were too quick to "valorize the depressive mode and villainize the paranoid-schizoid mode."[17] Ogden claims that these two modes are dialectically related in the sense that each serves to redress the dangers inherent in the other. Regarding the depressive position, he proposes that although it enables reparation and integration, thereby mitigating the dangers posed by the paranoid-schizoid position, it can also lead to "certainty, stagnation, closure, arrogance, and deadness."[18] The paranoid-schizoid position, then, "provides the necessary splitting of linkages and opening up of the closures of the depressive position, thus reestablishing the possibility of fresh linkages and fresh thoughts."[19] On this view, the aggressiveness that holds sway in the paranoid-schizoid position has its distinctive value: it plays a crucial role in clearing space for something new by breaking up hegemonic patterns. This is fundamental to creativity.

There's *some* suggestion of this view of aggression in Klein's work, but it's very brief. In a footnote to "Love, Guilt and Reparation," Klein asserts that even in individuals who have a highly developed capacity for love, aggression and hatred remain active. "In such people," she writes, "both aggression and hatred ... is used very greatly in constructive ways ('sublimated,' as it has been termed). There is actually no productive activity into which some aggression does not enter in one way or another."[20] In other words, not only does Klein believe—contra Freud—that aggression can be sublimated, but she also suggests that all productive activity involves some sublimation of aggression.

The examples she offers involve things like politicians, lawyers, and critics who combat each other for a living; games and sports in which one attacks one's opponent; and, interestingly, the housewife who cleans in order to make life pleasant for her family but in so doing also wages an ongoing war against dirt and disorder. In this manner, Klein points toward the productive potential of aggression, and the intrinsic link between destruction and creation.

MR: This makes sense. Julia Kristeva said something related during one of her lectures that I've never forgotten because it helped me to break my writing block. She claimed that the most difficult thing about writing is the violence that you have to inflict in order to carve a path through your knowledge: you have more material in your mind than you can possibly put on the written page, so that you need to make *the cut*—this has obvious Lacanian resonances—that gives you the path you need; being able to sever the necessary bits of material from all the material that you have is essential for creativity. Many people find this task difficult because it's uncomfortably violent. The implication is that your inability to be aggressive—your fear of your own aggression—can paralyze you. From this perspective, perfectionism, thinking that you need to fit *everything* you know into your book, is the Achilles' heel of writers.

AA: This perspective is compatible with Klein's view. You're paralyzed because you're afraid of the destructive force of your aggression, the possibility that it might destroy all the intellectual material you have gathered, break it up into fragmentary, unusable bits. Extending Klein's model a bit, perhaps one could also say that there's an anxiety here about whether your reparative powers will be up to the job: once you have broken your knowledge into bits, will you be able to reassemble them in a way that's compelling?

MR: I'm also wondering whether, in the Kleinian paradigm, creativity could be thought of as not just a matter of fashioning external objects but also of self-fashioning. You have talked about integration as a process of accepting previously split-off parts of the self and of one's internal objects. And you have drawn a connection between this process and the enrichment of the subject's personality. Does this mean that working through the depressive position—which entails integration—is intrinsically a creative act?

AA: That's right. For Klein, as I mentioned a moment ago, creativity is ultimately connected with the good breast, which, she claims, is "the representative of the life instinct and is also felt as the first manifestation of creativeness."[21] Recall that for Klein the internalization of the good breast forms the core of the developing ego. Given the connection between the good breast and creativity, this suggests that, as you just said, the project of enriching the ego by working through the depressive position is a creative act—perhaps the original creative act.

MR: I suppose that if self-fashioning is a form of creativity, within the clinical practice of psychoanalysis transference is the tool of this self-fashioning. For Lacan, this might mean gaining a greater degree of detachment from the demands of the big Other as well as from the demands of others, such as various authority figures. I'm inferring that for Klein it would mean a greater integration of the ego in the sense that you have defined the process. Do you agree with this?

AA: Yes. Klein links the analysis of transference to the "general enrichment of the personality."[22] For example, she describes the goal of analyzing transference as the diminishment of anxiety and guilt, the overcoming of splitting through the synthesis of love and hate, and the greater incorporation of unconscious content. This implies the integration of the ego (in her sense of that process). She moreover views the task of transference to be the more secure establishment of the internal good object, which in turn helps to facilitate integration. She proposes that in comparison to Oedipal jealousy and hostility, the envy and hatred directed at the breast are much more intense, with the result that helping "a patient to go through these deep conflicts and sufferings is the most effective means of furthering his stability and integration, because it enables him, by means of the transference, to establish more securely his good object and his love for it and to gain some confidence in himself."[23] In this way, given the connection between the good object and creativity, we could say that transference is designed to foster the analysand's creativity—first and foremost in their own creative process of self-fashioning, but perhaps in creative or intellectual work as well.

MR: In the context of transference, Hanna Segal's essay on creativity is useful because she gives four examples of her adult patients.[24] These are analysands who are blocked in their creativity, and she's trying to get them to a point where they can begin to create. She claims that the capacity to mourn is essential for creativity, the implication being that if her patients are unable to create, it's because they are unable to mourn. Kristeva argues along related lines when she hypothesizes that as long as you're stuck in melancholia, there might be seeds of creativity sprouting within you, but you remain incapable of symbolization; it's only when you're able to enter the process of mourning that you're able to create.

Segal makes this point concrete by describing Proust as a quintessentially successful mourner. According to Segal—and I think she's right—*À la recherche du temps perdu* is about recovering (almost repairing) the past by bringing together all the people that Proust has lost. Proust's multi-volume treatise is largely autobiographical, so he's talking about the loss of his mother, grandmother, Albertine, and a whole host of other people. Moreover, he explicitly reflects on what it means to resurrect these people in his writing when in reality he has lost them or when his connection to them has been destroyed. In this sense, Proust's process of writing is an attempt to repair the damage, obviously not literally—not in the sense of being able to revive the dead or mend his broken relationships—but in a substitutive sense. Segal relates this to the depressive position's reparative impulse.

Segal also proposes that in order to create, "the artist must acknowledge the death instinct, both in its aggressive and self-destructive aspects."[25] This is pretty much what you said a moment ago. So Segal is talking about patients who are either ensnared in melancholia or avoiding the death drive by putting up the kinds of manic defenses that you have referred to, thereby pretending that things are just fine. Either way, they aren't able to enter the process of mourning, with the consequence that nothing comes out of their attempts to create.

AA: That's interesting. Whitebook also describes Freud as an excellent mourner insofar as he was able to turn all the major losses in his life—his damaged relationship with Josef Fliess, his break with Carl Jung, and the death of his daughter Sophie—into occasions for intellectual growth and creativity that were transformative for his thinking. For example, Whitebook reads Freud's famous discussion of the fort-da game in *Beyond the Pleasure Principle*—which Whitebook presents as a meditation on how human beings tolerate loss, given that the child creates the fort-da game as a means of mastering its mother's absence—as Freud's attempt to "come to grips with [Sophie's] loss through the creation of meaning."[26] I confess that I worry a bit about this way of talking because it might seem to pathologize or judge people who get stuck in mourning or who are unable to respond to a tragic loss by engaging in forms of sublimation that result in creative acts such as writing a great novel or producing significant intellectual work. Still, there's something quite persuasive about this picture.

I don't know if you remember this moment at the workshop on psychoanalysis and critical theory that we did at The New School a few years ago, where Robyn Marasco gave an interesting paper on Klein, and during the discussion she made this throwaway comment about how strange it is that Klein calls the position that we should all strive to achieve the depressive position, that she seems to posit depression as an achievement, as a hallmark of maturity. Whitebook was in the audience and said something along the following lines: "Well, when you think about it, life is all about loss, so what else could psychological maturity be, other than being able to manage loss without letting it derail you but instead turning it into something productive?" It was a simple moment, but I found it both profound and utterly compelling.

MR: I remember that moment vividly because I also thought that Whitebook's comment was incredibly insightful. And I don't think that you could get more Lacanian than this: accepting your lack—and coming to terms with the inevitable string of losses that follow the constitutive loss that brings you into being as a subject of lack—is the only way to live a meaningful life. You're right that this perspective potentially pathologizes those who can't perform the transformation of loss into creativity. But perhaps just being able to live with loss—to sit with it while you mourn—and then eventually being able to move on can be thought of as a creative act because it's an act of self-renewal and therefore of self-fashioning.

The Lacanian rhetoric of accepting your lack, castration, deformation, and maladaptation sounds so harsh that other psychoanalytic schools tend to recoil from it. But he's saying exactly what Whitebook said: life is about loss and your task is to manage this reality so that it doesn't derail you but instead functions as a catalyst for something generative. I know that I'm here putting my distinctive gloss on Lacanian theory. But this is how I've always read him, why I find him comforting. This is why it's difficult for me to understand why so many analysts and academics hate him so much, why his name elicits such aggression. There's a deeply compassionate—both tragic and comic, tragically comic and comically tragic—understanding of human life at the core of his teachings.

For me, there are two ways of thinking about creativity (or sublimation) in the context of Lacanian theory, and one of these pertains precisely to this relationship between lack and creativity. Simply put, it's only because you're a being of lack—because the signifier has cut you irrevocably—that you have any interest in the outside world to begin with; if you didn't have this lack, you would be self-contained and you wouldn't care about anything beyond yourself. I've emphasized that the idea of having lost your wholeness is a retroactive fantasy, but this doesn't change the *effect* that the sense of having lost something irreplaceable has: your feeling of lack gives rise to the desire to connect to the outside world, to pursue the *objets a* I've talked about so much. However, this pursuit isn't necessarily the most reliable means of dealing with your lack, particularly as it can so easily veer into commodity fetishism. A more productive route might be to fill your void with creative activity, with sublimation. This activity can never definitively heal you, which is why it needs to be continually renewed—which is why I usually start to write a new book the day after I finalize the previous one—but the fleetingness of the solution doesn't diminish its value.

AA: Right—that reminds me of Lacan's discussion of the vase in *Seminar VII*.

MR: Yes, that's the passage where Lacan refers to creation *ex nihilo*. Before I get to the vase, let me make a more general point, namely that, broadly speaking, Lacan is talking about how it's the subject's capacity to manipulate the signifier—not just mindlessly to glide from one signifier to the next but to work with them innovatively—that allows it to make its life manageable, avoid complete derailment, and keep itself from crossing the line to the death drive. Another way to state the matter is to say that the fashioning of signifiers allows the subject to represent something about the Thing rather than to either completely collapse into it or avoid it. And importantly, this isn't a matter of pursuing substitutes (*objets a*) for the Thing but rather of *making* them.

When Lacan talks about a potter molding a vase out of emptiness, he's also on some level depicting the fashioning of a signifier. I'll quote the passage that has for me always been most central:

> Now if you consider the vase from the point of view I first proposed, as an object made to represent the existence of the emptiness at the center of the real that is called the Thing, this emptiness as represented in the representation presents itself as a *nihil*, as nothing. And that is why the potter, just like you to whom I am speaking, creates the vase with his hand around this emptiness, creates it, just like the mythical creator, *ex nihilo*, starting with a hole. ... the fashioning of the signifier and the introduction of a gap or a hole in the real is identical.[27]

This passage clarifies why the Thing, for Lacan, is a nonobject: it's the emptiness at the center of the real. Yet the potter is able to create a vase around this emptiness, starting with a hole. But because the vase also contains the emptiness, the signifier (the vase) and the hole (emptiness) emerge at the same time; the hole is just as much a part of the vase as the rest of it. Likewise, gaps between signifiers—which could be described as dwelling places of the real—are just as important for signification as signifiers themselves because without these gaps, signifiers would run into each other in a manner that would impede the creation of meaning. However, the less technical point I want to extract from this section of *Seminar VII* is that the subject's capacity to deploy signifiers is an antidote to existential despair—a way of dealing with the nothingness within its being.

There's another moment in the text regarding this dynamic that I want to flag: it's the story of a woman called Ruth Kjar, the details of which Lacan, interestingly, gleans from an article by Klein. Kjar's brother-in-law is a painter. She has many of his paintings on her walls, but one day he decides to sell one of them, with the result that suddenly there's an empty spot on the wall. Kjar isn't a painter, but she begins to paint in order to fill the blank space, to get rid of the disturbing emptiness, and it turns out that she's a phenomenal painter. Her brother-in-law gets furious and doesn't believe that she has painted something that, in his assessment, only a mature painter could ever have created. Lacan himself has reservations about Kjar's expertise. But that's beside the point. What's important is that he's presenting an example of how emptiness (lack) can be generative, can cause the subject to want to create something to compensate for it.

For Lacan, the Thing is the primary site of lack: the psychic equivalent of the empty spot on the wall. It's a nothingness around which our desire hovers because it remains veiled and therefore shrouded in mystery; without the veil we would see that there's nothing to covet. As Lacan explains: "If the Thing were not fundamentally veiled, we wouldn't be in the kind of relationship to it that obliges us, as the whole of psychic life is obliged, to encircle it or bypass it in order to conceive it."[28] In other words, it's only because the Thing is veiled that we're forced to approach it obliquely—circle around it or bypass it—by manufacturing substitutes for it; it's only because we lack the Thing that we're induced to create anything.

Lacan also describes sublimation as a matter of elevating a mundane object "to the dignity of the Thing."[29] This isn't about creating something entirely new but rather about stumbling upon an object that entices us so strongly that we bestow upon it the preciousness of the Thing, thereby, in a sense, recreating it: sublimation as recreation rather than creation. This is related to my commentary on the treasure that Alcibiades discovers in Socrates: Alcibiades obviously raises Socrates to the dignity of the Thing. He takes a mundane person—someone who exists in the real world—and elevates him to the level of the revered Thing. Admittedly, Socrates should probably not be characterized as a "mundane" person. But my point is more general, namely that when we fall in love, we raise the beloved—the mundane object—to the dignity of the Thing.

I've already mentioned that, like the Kantian sublime, the Thing has two faces: the monstrous and the astounding, the deadly and the enticing. This means that even though the Thing is clearly connected to the death drive, the sublime also enters the picture. Without the sublime aspect of the Thing, why would we want anything to do with it, unless we're all total masochists? The sublime aspect—the aspect that seems so full of gleaming gems that it feels irresistible—is what draws us in the amorous event. Sublimation in Lacan can thus be understood in two ways: either we take an already existing "object" (Socrates) and elevate it to the dignity of the Thing or we fashion objects, ideals, or concepts (paintings, books, and intellectual aspirations, among other things) that can convey something about that dignity.

AA: Does the Thing represent transcendence?

MR: I can see why it might be easy to assume so because Lacan talks about *raising* a mundane object to "the dignity of the Thing." But I don't think that sublimation in the two ways that I've described it is a matter of transcendence in the usual sense of the term. It might be better characterized as immanent transcendence: a matter of finding the sublime within the folds of the world, in your beloved object, or in the object you create.

An evocative example of this type of immanent transcendence is Lacan's story about his friend's collection of match boxes: his friend has fashioned a string of match boxes that he has hung over his fireplace. When Lacan looks at this string, he finds the sublime kernel of *das Ding* shimmering in this completely mundane object.

He claims that the collection of match boxes reveals that "a box of matches is not simply an object, but that, in the form of an *Erscheinung*, as it appeared in its truly imposing multiplicity, it may be a Thing," adding that his friend's motivation for his creation "concerns less the match box than the Thing that subsists in a match box."[30] I've always loved this image because it's a way of talking about sublimation that isn't about escaping the world but rather about finding the sublime within the world.

AA: For Klein, sublimation isn't about escaping the world either but about relating to it differently, through the reparative urge to establish connections, unities, and bonds rather than through the aggressive urge to destroy.

MR: Both Klein and Lacan thus sidestep metaphysical models of transcendence by situating sublimation on the level of worldly experience. This is one of the many ways in which psychoanalysis offers an alternative to earlier philosophical models of human life, including the so-called "good life." This is one reason that it has been so productive for both your and my versions of critical theory insofar as this theory is by definition looking for alternatives to how life has historically been, and currently is, configured. Inasmuch as the "now" isn't satisfactory, psychoanalysis provides some powerful tools for envisioning new possibilities.

But let me round up the theme of creativity in Lacan by outlining the second model of creativity that I've extracted from him in my previous work.[31] Not surprisingly, this model has to do with the death drive. I'm tempted to connect this model—which has to do with the sometimes tumultuous commingling of the signifier and the real—to the paranoid-schizoid position because it conjures up the very fine line between creativity and psychosis that we have already identified as a theme that interests both Klein and Lacan. Rudiments of this model are probably already present in Lacan's early seminar on psychoses, *Seminar III*, which is a close reading of the Schreber case. But it's Lacan's late seminar on James Joyce, *Seminar XXIII*, that fully develops it.

I've alluded a few times to the fact that in his later work, Lacan focuses strongly on the jouissance of the real, and this is the case in the seminar on Joyce. This seminar, which was delivered in 1974–1975, is the linchpin of Lacanian theory for me, which is probably the reason that I read Lacan in ways that are alien to those who are mostly only familiar with the early structuralist Lacan.

One of Lacan's aims in this seminar is to illustrate how close creativity really can come to psychosis: for instance, he notes Joyce's uncontrollable laughter while writing. In addition, we both know that Joyce's writing is formally unique. Simply put—and this is why I asked that question about the creative potential of the paranoid-schizoid position and the death drive—Lacan proposes that in order to invent his singular manner of writing, Joyce has to obliterate language, to demolish conventional ways of using language. And the way Joyce does this is by allowing the jouissance of the real to overtake the signifier.

If in the earlier seminars, there's frequently a juxtapositioning of the signifier and the jouissance of the real, in the context of Joyce Lacan describes how the signifier and jouissance can merge in productive ways. If earlier the idea was that the signifier takes over the real, murdering the Thing—in *Seminar VII* Lacan's wording is that the Thing "suffers from the signifier"[32]—in *Seminar XXIII* Lacan postulates that Joyce's creative activity takes on the intensity that it does because Joyce is able to bring the signifier and the real together in such a way that he nudges the signifier into a new place.[33] The energy of the real reanimates Joyce's signifiers, with the consequence that they are able to operate differently from how signifiers usually operate. From this reanimation of the signifier arises something genuinely innovative. But this process presupposes the willingness—or the capacity—to destroy previous forms of signification.

Lacan implies that the line between creativity and psychosis is so precarious because when you allow the jouissance of the real to infiltrate your signifiers, you're automatically allowing your social (symbolic and imaginary) being to be overwhelmed by this jouissance; you're allowing yourself to brush the limit of the death drive that the *objets a* are trying to prevent you from crossing. At the same time, it's almost like Lacan is saying that you can't create anything genuinely new unless you're willing to risk this encounter with the death drive. And this encounter entails a degree of aggression against preexisting signifiers. So on the one hand, there's the shredding into bits of established forms of signification, which reminds me of the paranoid-schizoid position; on the other, there's the fashioning of new signifiers, which reminds me of the reparative impulse of the depressive position.

Against these tentative conceptual connections, I want to return to the link that Segal makes between the death drive and creativity. She writes:

> Thus far my contention has been that a satisfactory work of art is achieved by a realization and sublimation of the depressive position. ... But to realize and symbolically express depression the artist must acknowledge the death instinct, both in its aggressive and self-destructive aspects, and accept the reality of death for the object and the self. One of the patients I described could not use symbols because of her failure to work through the depressive position; her failure clearly lay in her inability to accept and use her death instinct and acknowledge death. Restated in terms of instincts, ugliness—destruction—is the expression of the death instinct; beauty—the desire to unite into rhythms and wholes—is that of the life instinct. The achievement of the artist is in giving the fullest expression to the conflict and the union between the two.[34]

What Segal conveys here about the acknowledgment of the death instinct, both in its aggressive and self-destructive aspects, as being necessary for creativity, as well as about how the artist's achievement lies in their ability to express the conflict between the life and death instincts, sounds similar to what Lacan argues regarding the commingling of the signifier and jouissance. It's like you have to be willing to dive into jouissance (death) before you can resurface on the level of new signifiers (life).

Note also that Segal posits that her patient's inability to create was due to her failure to work through the depressive position. This failure, in turn, resulted from her inability "to accept and use her death instinct." During our first session on subjectivity, I said that my intuition was that if there's something "beyond" the depressive position in Klein, it might be creativity. It feels like Segal is here lending some support to this intuition.

AA: I agree, absolutely. Moreover, her claim that the artist's achievement lies in the ability to express the conflict and the union between the life and death instincts—which she associates with beauty and ugliness, respectively—is quintessentially Kleinian. As I have emphasized repeatedly, the depressive position is marked by the ability to tolerate ambivalence without resorting to splitting. So it makes sense for Segal to argue that the type of creative sublimation that becomes possible beyond the depressive position (via its working through) has ambivalence—the conflict of the life and death drives, beauty and ugliness, harmony and disharmony—at its core.

In this essay, I was also struck by Segal's description of an unconscious awareness that she believes that all artists share. She depicts this awareness as follows:

> all creation is really a re-creation of a once loved and once whole, but now lost and ruined object, a ruined internal world and self. It is when the world within us is destroyed, when it is dead and loveless, when our loved ones are in fragments, and we ourselves in helpless despair—it is then that we must re-create our world anew, reassemble the pieces, infuse life into dead fragments, re-create life.[35]

This is the lesson that she draws from her reading of Proust. I'm fascinated by this passage because it's not only an incredibly moving depiction of the link between loss, mourning, and creativity but also because it resonates in interesting ways with Adorno's understanding of the project of critique.

In the opening to *Minima Moralia*, Adorno describes critique as a "melancholy science."[36] Readers typically see this reference as a play on Nietzsche's gay science, which makes sense because *Minima Moralia* is obviously inspired by Nietzsche and is even written in the same aphoristic style as *The Gay Science*. But I think that there's also a psychoanalytic valence to Adorno's understanding of melancholy, and even though (as far as I know) he never read Klein, it can be read in Kleinian terms. This is because, for Adorno, critique emerges in response to an experience of loss and fragmentation: it can be understood as an attempt to make meaning in the wake of, and even out of, that experience. As he states, "The light that is kindled in the phenomena as they fragment, disintegrate and fly apart is the only source of hope that can set philosophy alight."[37]

In his early, programmatic essay, "The Actuality of Philosophy," Adorno argues that the task of philosophy is interpretation, but, importantly, this doesn't mean that its goal is to discern the hidden meaning underlying perceptible reality. For Adorno, there's no hidden meaning: reality is intrinsically meaningless. Therefore, the task of philosophy, he maintains, is "to interpret unintentional reality"—in other words, to create meaning where there is none.[38] This is done through the construction of what Adorno, following Walter Benjamin, describes as constellations that function as "keys, before which reality springs open" or that serve to illuminate social reality in a new, conclusively striking way.[39]

Connecting Adorno to Klein—via Segal—we could hence understand critique as a creative response to experiences of loss, dislocation, and fragmentation, as an attempt to metabolize these experiences by turning them into critical-philosophical insight. Resigned to the inevitability of loss and the dead, loveless, and inherently meaningless nature of reality, critique nonetheless generates meaning by gathering the remaining fragments into constellations that can light up social reality. Critique is a melancholy science not because it's pessimistic or sad but because it has a melancholic structure: not a structure that "remains stuck fast in an unhappy consciousness," but rather one that "exteriorizes itself as a critique of existing phenomena."[40] In other words, the critical stance requires a mature resignation to the painfulness of reality without giving in to the temptation to wallow in conservative despair. To say that critique is a melancholy science is to say that it resigns itself to the ubiquity of loss while resolving to construct meaning out of the decaying fragments left in its wake.

MR: That's beautiful. These images of sorting through the rubble in search of usable bits—of breathing life into dead fragments, of finding the kernel of renewal in decay, of gathering sparkling constellations to light up something that's worth seeing—speak to me both theoretically and personally. They are a poetic way of expressing what I take to be the crux of what Lacan has taught me with all of his talk about lack, loss, deformation, maladaptation, and the rest of the melancholy tropes that I have resorted to during our conversations. I'm not sure why I've always taken these tropes toward creativity. I don't think that I've done so from a place of sugarcoated optimism; rather, I've tried to turn suffering into something that isn't just a pure loss. And perhaps I've attempted to place some distance between myself and a now dead psychotic who was once a genuine role model because he was both brilliant and humane. I don't think that I've ever gotten over witnessing the gleam of his eyes fade as the illness—or perhaps the lithium—gradually extinguished his immense creativity. This may be why the friable line between psychosis and creativity intrigues me.

The psychotic dwells close to the real, devoid of the necessary signifiers—what Lacan calls "quilting points"—to anchor him in the world. The artist, in contrast, is able to periodically and temporarily risk the encounter with the real, the death drive, without losing the ability to hold onto enough signifiers to yank herself out of this fragmenting and disorienting space when she needs to. A hugely simplified—perhaps too simplified yet still potentially useful—way to describe the matter is to say that creativity arises from the ability to dip into the real without drowning in it.

Roberto Harari, when discussing Lacan's seminar on Joyce, talks about Joyce's ability to "bite into bits of the real" so as to reignite the signifier.[41] This suggests that creativity can entail a fall into a state of near-psychosis. This can obviously generate a great deal of anxiety insofar as it's about—even if just fleetingly—surrendering your symbolic and imaginary supports, your socially intelligible being, so it's understandable that most people don't want to go anywhere near this experience. But the price of their caution can be the inability to create, which is why both Segal and Lacan, in their own ways, are working to undo the various defenses that their patients construct against the death drive. I guess in the Kleinian model, among the most powerful of these defenses is the manic defense.

AA: That makes a lot of sense. If one has to tap into the death drive in order to create, in Kleinian terms—as you suggested earlier—this would mean risking falling back into the paranoid-schizoid position, which is more or less equivalent to psychosis for Klein. The challenge is precisely to do this without becoming completely disintegrated. However, this is the very tightrope that the subject in the depressive position has to walk all the time because this position represents not the elimination of the death drive but the toleration of the ambivalence that this drive necessarily generates.

MR: I assume that this is a challenge that many creators—artists and other creative individuals—face: how to risk the encounter with psychosis, and to do so *repeatedly*, without falling into it irrevocably?

AA: This reminds me of the early Foucault's argument in the *History of Madness*, where he repeatedly links madness and creative genius.[42] Many of his examples—Nietzsche, van Gogh, Artaud—didn't successfully maintain the line between creativity and psychosis that you have described, or at any rate, they had a difficult time tapping into psychosis without disintegrating. They exemplify what Foucault describes as a tragic experience of madness that has been covered over by our society's critical consciousness regarding madness, a consciousness that presents madness in scientific, medical, and moral terms—that essentially transforms it into mental illness. Foucault refrains from discussing this phenomenon in psychoanalytic terms because the *History of Madness* is, among other things, a complex—though, in my view, not entirely negative—critique of psychoanalysis. However, there's one sentence in the text where Foucault connects the insights of the mad geniuses whom he repeatedly invokes to Freud's discovery of the death drive. Foucault claims that the tragic experience of madness that "is visible in the last words of Nietzsche and the last visions of van Gogh" is also "that same element that Freud began to perceive at the furthest point of his journey, the great wound that he tried to symbolise in the mythological struggle between the libido and the death instinct."[43]

In this manner, Foucault links the death drive to unreason, and therefore to figures of genius who refused to be wholly subjected to the discourse of modern reason. For Foucault, this stance evokes a kind of beauty and transgressive freedom. I don't mean to suggest that freedom for the early Foucault consists in taking up the position of unreason or embracing the descent into madness. Although this is a fairly common reading of the *History of Madness*,[44] it's not my reading. Rather, as I see it, Foucault connects the figure of unreason to freedom because this figure serves to illuminate lines of fragility and fracture in our historical a priori in ways that open up spaces of freedom within this historical a priori. It's only as a result of the illumination provided by the lightning flashes of unreason that we witness in the figures of Nietzsche, van Gogh, and Artaud—as well as in Freud's notion of the death drive—that we can start to glimpse the outlines of our system of thought. Doing so, in turn, is necessary for freeing ourselves from this system, so that we might think beyond it.

MR: I love your reading of the early Foucault. And I see the connection between your account of Foucault's analysis of the lightning flashes of unreason and what you said a moment ago about Adorno's analysis of the constellations of critical insight that light up social reality. Both analyses seem compatible with what I've said about dipping into the real without being engulfed by it, though, as you noted, Nietzsche, van Gogh, and Artaud in the end found it impossible to maintain this line. In contrast, I've never been convinced by Deleuze and Guattari's valorization of schizophrenia as a transgressive (and creative) mode of being because it seems completely unlivable; it feels that, for them, permanent psychosis is the valorized state of being.[45]

AA: I agree, and for reasons I just explained, I would distinguish Foucault's account from Deleuze and Guattari's. Far from glorifying the descent into schizophrenia, Foucault proposes that the mad, creative geniuses he analyzes offer a vantage point from which it's possible to challenge the social order and the conception of reason that defines the geniuses in question as mad in the first place. This isn't exactly the same as how you have portrayed Lacan's attempt to think about the fine line between creativity and psychosis. But I agree that it's not incompatible with this attempt either.

MR: One of the many things that I appreciate about your work is your attempt to rescue a certain version of rationality—a less arrogant version of rationality than the one that we have inherited from the Enlightenment—from a generation of critics who appear to just want to destroy reason and present unreason (madness, schizophrenia, or related notions of self-disintegration) as the only possible antidote to our society's ills. This antidote has never seemed feasible to me. And frankly, it has seemed somewhat preposterous coming from academics who are constantly trying to outreason each other, for whom reason is among the main tools of their craft. I mean, is it possible to do "critique"—which critical theorists presumably don't want to give up—without the input of reason? I don't think so, which is why I value the ways in which you have endeavored to resurrect reason in a less oppressive, more humble register.

For instance, in one of your essays, you propose—and here I'm simply elaborating on what you just said—that the aim of the *History of Madness* is "not a rejection of reason in favor of a romantic embrace of madness or unreason, but rather a *critique* of reason that foregrounds the ongoing spiral of rationality and power."[46] In other words, you demonstrate that Foucault's relationship to reason is ambivalent—there's that word again!—in the sense that it leaves the door open for the possibility of a different conceptualization of reason from the one that has been fueling power (or biopolitics and necropolitics) as an instrument of oppression.

You also touch on the fine line between madness and creativity that we have been discussing by positing that if one completely crosses this line to madness, creativity becomes impossible. Referring to Foucault's argument about unreason, you state:

> The gesture toward Nietzsche, Nerval, Artaud and others isn't a lyrical glorification of their *madness*, for it is precisely their descent into madness that ruptures their philosophical and artistic oeuvres. "*Where there is an oeuvre,*" Foucault insists, "*there is no madness*"; madness is the absence of an oeuvre, and these men are geniuses precisely because they were able to create an oeuvre.[47]

That is, where there is creativity, there's no madness: creativity holds madness at bay.

I guess that this is in part what I was getting at when I, in the context of our discussion of anxiety, mentioned that creativity could be understood as an antidote to anxiety. If anxiety, as I've hypothesized, is related to a too-muchness of energy, to an overagitation of the psyche and the body, creativity might be a means of burning off some of this excess. That is, if creativity entails attaching some of the energy of the real to the signifier (or to an image on a canvas, a rhythm of a song, etc.), my assumption is that creativity might decrease the overanimation that's part of anxiety. And if creativity can (sometimes) rescue us from anxiety, perhaps it can also (sometimes) rescue us from madness.

In any case, I think that your interpretation of Foucault is one that contemporary theory—meaning, my field, critical theory broadly understood—would do well to take seriously. I've used your insights in two of my recent books in an attempt to counter the default demonization of reason that's rampant in my field. This demonization is by now so automatic that it's no longer genuinely critical. This is why it's important that there are thinkers like you who resist this position without thereby lapsing back into a celebration of Enlightenment reason. My challenge to Deleuze and Guattari, and also to critics such as Edelman is: "Okay, show me how you're going to live in the aftermath of the complete destruction of reason." Your work, Amy, offers livable alternatives, which are sorely needed in my version of critical theory.

AA: Thank you for that—I appreciate it. It's funny, though, how much context matters. Within the world of contemporary Frankfurt School critical theory there are those who regard me as a dangerous irrationalist!

MR: [Laughter] And in my world of critical theory, there are those who see me as a traitor to progressive causes—even as an upholder of neoliberal values—because I'm not fully on board with the complete demolition of reason, agency, and normative limits. I guess a part of being a scholar is that you can't please everyone. Indeed, doing so would be the end of critique. At the same time, it's true that both of us have the tendency to go against the grain of our respective fields. This is probably why we end up agreeing on so many issues: the attempt to flee the extreme positions of our fields brings us to a place where we can meet intellectually in ways that make sense to both of us.

Amy Allen: a dangerous irrationalist—seriously? I would like to remind those who judge you in this way that you have argued convincingly that feminists have profited from the use of reason, that feminist theory has used reason to …

AA: Combat gender-based subordination?

MR: Exactly! So reason can't *always*, in every situation, be an entirely bad thing.

I'm also thinking that one way to productively analyze the role of the death drive in creativity might be through a version of the Lacanian ethical act that allows for the possibility of rebuilding after destruction. Badiou's notion of the event in some ways leans toward this vision, in which you plunge into the jouissance of the real—you plunge into a place of self-destructive (or destructive) asociality—yet eventually you're able to resurface and refashion yourself as a different kind of social being.

I also want to add that, despite my reservations about the fetishization of destructiveness in contemporary theory, what I like about the Lacanian ethical act is that, on the individual level, it allows the subject to stop caring about what others think of it. In other words, the Lacanian subject of the act—and perhaps even just the well-analyzed Lacanian subject—isn't looking for recognition from the Other/other. Indeed, one of the objectives of Lacanian analysis is to get the analysand to the point where they don't give a damn about whether or not the other recognizes them. I guess this is yet another way of giving up the fantasy of a cure. And it may be the only way to survive as a critical theorist. [Laughter]

This means that Honneth's emphasis on the need for recognition is absent in Lacanian theory. This is one reason that hard-core Lacanians don't appreciate Judith Butler's valorization of relationality: in her Levinasian work on ethics, revering the humanity of the other is essential, which suggests that, in ethical relationships, there's always a play of mutual recognition at stake.[48] For Butler, the ethical impulse is to retain a connection to the other at almost any cost, to the point that she at times implies that the other is inviolable regardless of what it has done, that breaking ties with the other is an instant ethical failure.

For Lacan, things are more or less the reverse: the ethical act is about being able to sever a social or intersubjective connection when you need to. For instance, if you're associated with someone who is demanding the kind of recognition that's oppressive to you, the ethical thing to do is to break this association. This is why so many Lacanians are (theoretically) antisocial or antirelational. I myself don't go this far. I don't want to neglect relationality as an important component of human life. Still, I don't have nearly the same degree of respect for it as Butler does, in part because Lacan has taught me to discern the toxic and pathological components of relationality. This is part of the coldness of Lacanian theory.

Not caring about what the Other/other wants can be incredibly liberating, and not necessarily in a selfish sense. We both know how oppressive the big Other—and some others—can be, so that being able to renounce your dependence on it/them isn't automatically individualistic or self-centered; it can be a matter of survival. While it may be impossible to dwell in the world without ever caring about what other people think of you, loosening your reliance on the opinions of others is a portal to a certain kind of freedom.

Furthermore, it's easy to leap from this insight to collective ethical and political matters by calling attention to the ways in which ceasing to seek the recognition of the big Other—of dominant ideology— is essential for social movements searching for better modes of organizing human life than our current neoliberal capitalist system, which brutally purchases some people's well-being at the expense of the suffering of others.

All of this is to say that the goal of analysis, for Lacan, is to allow the analysand to break its dependence on the Other/others. I suspect that this is entirely different from the Kleinian perspective on what analysis is supposed to accomplish.

AA: For Klein, the goal of analysis is for the analyst to *be* the good object for the analysand so that the analysand can internalize this object more securely and therefore have a more stable internal world than they were able to develop as a child. This provides the basis for the analysand's ability to develop a more integrated ego. In a sense, then, the analyst, for Klein, is like the good breast. The analyst's job is to supply love, support, and nourishment so that the analysand can more securely internalize the good object and draw on it for the integration, expansion, and enrichment of the ego.

But we have to be careful here because to say that the analyst's job is to be the good breast might make it seem as if analysis for Klein is about the analyst offering unconditional affirmation to the analysand. In fact, nothing could be further from the truth. If the analyst occupies the role of the good breast, the analogue for the milk that the analyst/good breast provides isn't affirmation but rather interpretations. As Klein states: "As in infancy, repeated happy experiences of being fed and loved are instrumental in establishing securely the good object, so during an analysis repeated experiences of the effectiveness and truth of interpretations given lead to the analyst—and retrospectively the primal object—being built up as good figures."[49] In other words, Klein doesn't believe that the analyst should tell the analysand how wonderful they are. Rather, the analyst's task is to give the analysand good, nourishing interpretations. This might well mean that the analyst has to withhold praise or tell the analysand things that they don't want to hear.

Moreover, the love, support, and nourishment provided by the analyst aren't necessarily received positively by the analysand. As

I've mentioned before, Klein speaks of envy as it manifests itself in the clinical setting, for example when the analysand not only rejects a good interpretation, but then goes further and expresses hostility toward the analyst. Klein understands this as an instance of wanting to spoil the milk from the good breast, and by extension, of wanting to spoil the analyst as a good object. As is the case with her understanding of love more generally, analytic transference is a highly ambivalent experience.

MR: That's definitely different from Lacan, for whom being the good object isn't a goal at all. Instead, the role of the analyst is to be an enigmatic, unreadable object, so that the analysand is left in a constant state of questioning. The analyst serves as the big Other, or—and this amounts to more or less the same thing—the *sujet supposé à savoir*: a subject that the analysand expects to hold some special knowledge about their suffering. However, the aim of analysis is to get the analysand to recognize that the analyst doesn't in fact have any privileged insight into their suffering, so that it's up to them to figure things out, and more profoundly—as I've said many times—to learn to accept that there's no ultimate cure, no Sovereign Good that will heal them.

This is related to the idea that, for Lacan, the big Other is hollow, doesn't possess any epistemological support for its claims. As he puts it, there's no Other of the Other: no guarantee of the Other's consistency or veracity. This is one reason that the subject needs to learn to distrust the Other's injunctions. This insight about the unreliability of the Other's discourse brings me back to what you said about Klein and good interpretations because the way you phrased it—good, nourishing interpretations—implies that Klein is also operating on the level of language. You have said that Klein doesn't have a good model for the symbolic, but as soon as you're dealing with language, you're on the level of …

AA: The symbolic.

MR: Yes. It's also interesting that Klein believes that the analysand who rejects a good interpretation envies the analyst. I think that Lacan's response would be more along the lines of—and I already suggested this a moment ago when I said that the well-analyzed Lacanian subject isn't looking for recognition—"You're rejecting my interpretation? Good for you! You need to learn that I don't have the answers; you need to learn to detach yourself from the interpretations of the big Other."

If rejecting a good interpretation means that you envy—or even hate—your analyst, you don't have much room for disagreement, do you? How do you know that what the analyst deems as a good interpretation in reality is good? Maybe it's dismal, so that you *should* reject it. But if you do, your disagreement can be used to accuse you of resisting the analysis, which was already a problem in Freud. In reading Klein—as well as Segal—I was struck by the fact that in most of the case studies they presented, the analyst became an object of hostility. I was wondering whether this hostility was in fact coming from the patient or whether the analyst assumed it, or maybe even projected it onto the patient.

AA: That's a valid concern. Klein's interest in aggression and anxiety stems in part from wanting to understand the negative therapeutic reaction, but she does seem to have a very particular explanation for this reaction: it's in them, it's not in me.

MR: Does she not have a notion of countertransference?

AA: Klein says very little about countertransference in her published writings, and the standard story about her is that she viewed countertransference mostly negatively, as something that interferes with analytic work rather than as something that should itself be analyzed. However, later Kleinians and post-Kleinians have made countertransference central to their understanding of analytic technique.[50] And I don't think that Klein is any worse than Freud on this issue. Any time you talk about psychoanalytic resistance, there's this worry: is the analysand rejecting the analyst's interpretation because of resistance or because what the analyst says is completely crazy?

7

Politics

MR: This is our final session, and our topic is the political potential of psychoanalysis, particularly the relationship of Kleinian and Lacanian theory to critical theory. In this context, it's helpful to keep in mind that, as we explained in the preface, Amy and I work with different conceptions of critical theory. We understand each other's conceptions fairly well—and as our conversations have revealed, we agree on many issues—but our intellectual milieus are nevertheless quite different. For instance, where Amy's version of Frankfurt School critical theory regards normativity—not the kind of idealist normativity that transcends its historical context that the Western philosophical tradition, including the Enlightenment and its liberal inheritors, has promoted, but nevertheless normativity that contains ethical ideals—as an important component of social theory, my version of progressive critical theory has mostly rejected models of normativity in favor of models of antinormative rebellion.

As should be clear by now, on this issue I'm closer to Amy than I am to many of the leading scholars of my field, which hasn't always made things easy for me. As I mentioned yesterday, in my version of critical theory the assumption appears to be that any endorsement of normativity, however cautiously defined, immediately renders one complicit with neoliberal, imperialist capitalism. I hope that one of the things that gets clarified during today's conversation is that this isn't necessarily the case. Amy, you have taught me valuable new ways of thinking about normativity, so I hope that you can guide us to our topic.

AA: For me, what's most important and interesting about the Frankfurt School of critical theory isn't a particular position or series of beliefs, but rather its methodological approach, which is grounded in a diagnosis of existing social, cultural, historical, and political conditions at the same time as it seeks to develop a critical perspective on these conditions. This critical perspective means that critical theory always has a normative edge, that it strives toward a set of ethical standards. But whatever normative project it articulates has to be based on a *diagnosis* that takes seriously the contingent historical conditions, ongoing power relations, and forces of irrationality that form our present. Foregrounding this diagnostic dimension of critical theory, in turn, puts constraints on how one can conceptualize normativity.

Once you say that critical theory's normative analysis has to be based on a diagnosis of existing historically contingent power relations, it becomes impossible to endorse a strongly idealist conception of normativity that would be grounded in standards that are presumed to transcend their historical context. Instead, Frankfurt School critical theory conceptualizes normativity as a matter of transcendence from *within* a historical context: the kind of immanent transcendence—a transcendence that doesn't leave behind the specific sociohistorical situation that we find ourselves in—that's conceptually related to your understanding of Lacan's notion of raising a mundane object to the dignity of the Thing.

There are stronger and weaker ways of understanding this notion of immanent transcendence. For example, Habermas has developed a theory of transcendence from within a sociohistorical context in a relatively strong sense. His model of communicative action relies on language as a medium of the kind of communication that's supposed to give rise to norms that everyone can agree on. Moreover, he posits that once these norms have emerged, they become capable of transcending their original context, become "context-transcendent."[1] This is what makes his version of immanent transcendence strong, and as I've argued elsewhere, it's bound up with problematically teleological and even informally imperialist conceptions of social evolution, progress, and modernity. Partly for this reason, I favor a weaker version of immanent transcendence: one that situates ethical and political norms within an analysis of power relations in their social, cultural, and historical specificity and contingency. That is, I don't aim for context-transcendent normative models.

The need to avoid overly strong conceptions of normative transcendence is also related to critical theory's engagement with psychoanalysis. There's a complicated history here because, as we have noted, the first generation of Frankfurt School thinkers—Adorno, Horkheimer, and Marcuse—considered psychoanalysis to be central to the project of critical theory. Among other things, this had to do with their assessment that Marxism alone was an insufficient critical framework because it was unable to explain, for example, why the German workers not only failed to fulfill their world historical mission of engaging in a communist revolution but also why they embraced fascism. In other words, the early Frankfurt School critics thought that Marxism on its own was incapable of explaining some of the most important historical developments of their time, and that what was needed was a social psychology that could illuminate why and how individuals could be brought to embrace and uphold their own oppression and exploitation. Psychoanalysis gave them the necessary tools for such a social psychology.

In this sense, there's an important historical relationship between critical social theory and psychoanalysis. But this relationship has to a large extent broken down in the second, third, and now we might even say fourth generations of the Frankfurt School. Many of the thinkers who currently write in the mainstream of this tradition—I'm thinking of people like Nancy Fraser, Seyla Benhabib, and Rainer Forst—work in a broadly Habermasian vein, and although Habermas engaged extensively and seriously with psychoanalysis early in his career, even using it as a model for his understanding of critique,[2] he later broke with psychoanalysis and turned instead to the developmental psychological work of Jean Piaget and Lawrence Kohlberg. The models of Piaget and Kohlberg fit much better than psychoanalysis does with the progressivist, developmentalist understanding of the individual and society that forms the core of Habermas's theory of communicative action.

However, Honneth has recently argued compellingly for a return to psychoanalysis within Frankfurt School critical theory.[3] He proposes that critical theory needs to begin with a realistic conception of the person, which—as you know—I agree with. It's just that I'm dissatisfied with the version of psychoanalysis that he develops. Honneth works mainly with Winnicott and relational psychoanalysis, with the consequence that his vision of psychoanalysis doesn't include the drives or primary aggression. In contrast, I agree with the early Frankfurt School thinkers, who regarded the death drive as perhaps *the* crucial psychoanalytic concept for critical theory.

One reason I've turned to Klein is that she offers a theory of the drives and primary aggression at the same time as she—as we have seen—also provides a realistic conception of what people are like. This conception takes seriously the fragmented, decentered, and deeply ambivalent nature of the psyche without thereby glorifying rupture or psychotic incoherence. I believe that without such a complicated conception of the subject and its tendencies toward irrationality, critical theory risks assuming too high a degree of rationality and autonomy in its addressees. Klein has also helped me consider how the theory of the death drive might be formulated in a way that's compatible with the basic methodological assumptions of critical social theory, one of which is the idea that the self is socially constituted.

This background might help to explain why, throughout our conversations, I've brought up the relationship between the intrapsychic and the intersubjective. I find Klein incredibly productive for critical theory because even though she has a complex account of intrapsychic dynamics and phantasies, she also has a thoroughly intersubjective and social view of the self. In other words, she's an intersubjectivist who also believes in the drives and primary aggression. From my point of view, this makes her an ideal psychoanalytic interlocutor for critical theory.

In some of his recent work, Honneth suggests, rightly I think, that the historical relationship between the Frankfurt School and psychoanalysis doesn't by itself establish the current importance of psychoanalysis for critical theory. Given the historically situated nature of critical theory, this relationship stands in need of ongoing re-evaluation.[4] Following Honneth's lead, we might ask whether critical social theory today still needs psychoanalysis, and if so, why?

My view is that critical theory needs psychoanalysis now more than ever. This is for a number of reasons. The first is that the realistic conception of the person that I've just outlined—an understanding of the subject as fragmented, decentered, ambivalent, and irrational—allows us to avoid problematic forms of normative (or moral) idealism. Equally importantly, psychoanalysis can help us to think about normativity in alternative, and in my opinion, more productive ways. For example, one of Klein's strengths is that her realistic conception of the person disallows normative idealism without thereby giving up on the possibility of the development of moral capacities—the feeling of guilt for the damage done by one's destructiveness which gives rise to the impulse to engage in acts of reparation—which for her are consolidated in the move to the depressive position.

Yet it's also the case that—and here I'm summarizing some of the main points I've made about Klein during our dialogue—even though Klein's subject has these moral capacities, it remains a fundamentally split subject. For Klein, the loss that's foundational to the subject can never be fully healed; the subject can never be made whole. On this point Klein and Lacan clearly agree. To be sure, the depressive position involves a kind of holding together or containing of the various split, fragmented aspects of the self, but I don't see this as a simple reconciliation, where all the splits are eliminated and the fragments are fully integrated. For Klein, this sort of false reconciliation would involve a manic form of (spurious) reparation that would deny the reality and severity of loss. In contrast, the key to the depressive position is ambivalence, which means that there's no elimination of conflict and disharmony; rather, there's simply the ability to tolerate one's internal fragmentation without falling into incoherence and breaking up into bits. This, as we have seen, is a fragile achievement—one that can and often does break down.

In short, then, Klein provides a realistic understanding of the subject that nonetheless—because of her account of the depressive position and the reparative impulse that this position entails—preserves and even explains the emergence of moral capacities. Starting from her account of subjectivity has important ramifications for a host of important concepts in Frankfurt School critical theory, including normativity, progress, and emancipation. I'll come back to some of these ramifications later.

The second reason that critical theory needs psychoanalysis—and here I'm still following Honneth—has to do with our ability to diagnose contemporary social and political events. On this issue, we have to be careful because extending psychoanalytic categories to thinking about social and political situations is tricky and can't be done hastily. At the same time, it seems to me that some basic Kleinian categories—such as splitting, idealization, projection, and the inability to tolerate ambivalence—are at the very least powerful metaphors for thinking about certain aspects of our contemporary political situation: for instance, one might think in Kleinian terms about the dynamics of splitting and demonization at work in defining groups of immigrants or refugees as outside the existing social and political order, as well as about the related inability to tolerate internal ambivalence, ambiguity, and difference.

These are arguably persistent features of political life that have recently returned with a vengeance, perhaps in part as a consequence of the stress that the aftermath of the 2008 financial crisis has placed on polities. I suspect that Klein would go further and propose that these are ineliminable dangers stemming from the kinds of creatures we are. However, as I've explained, I believe that if statements about human nature are to be serviceable for critical theory, they need to be recast in a more historicist vein as claims about certain features of the human condition that can take very different forms in different times and places.

At the same time, Klein's account of love and reparation offers possibilities for rethinking justice in the context of the violent tendencies of contemporary social and political life. We have discussed the influence of Klein's notion of reparation on affect theory, and I've mentioned the connections between her work and theories of reparative or restorative justice. In addition, in her Tanner Lectures Butler draws on Klein to develop an ethics of non-violence whose motivation is the preservation of the life of the other. This is an interesting move to make because, as Butler acknowledges, Klein's starting point is in a way quite violent: as I've stressed, Klein believes that aggression and destructiveness come first in the development of the subject, and she conceives of love and reparation as achievements that are motivated by depressive anxiety and guilt. All of this leads to an ambivalent, complicated, and chastened conception of non-violent ethics. Yet it's an ethics that nonetheless prioritizes preserving the life of the other.

The third reason that critical theory needs psychoanalysis has to do with conceptualizing resistance to existing social reality. For this task, Lacan may admittedly be a better resource than Klein. Nevertheless—and I'm once again summarizing some of the main Kleinian themes that have emerged during our exchange—I don't think that it would be fair to accuse Klein of advocating adaptation to existing social reality: I don't think that her conception of the integration of the ego or personality has this implication, and she's quite clear, in contrast to Anna Freud, on the idea that an important objective of psychoanalysis is to weaken the superego, to mitigate its cruelty. That is, although Klein does advocate a kind of adaptation to reality, this merely means the acceptance of the ubiquity and inevitability of finitude and loss and of one's own (and the other's) ineliminable destructiveness. As far as I can see, this is entirely different from the problematic kind of adaptation that involves the attempt to fit into existing social norms and expectations.

That said, I don't necessarily see in Klein a well-developed account of how psychoanalytic resources could be deployed for thinking about resistance to the social order, whereas this is clearly an important theme in Lacan. Since this is something that you have developed at great length and convincingly in your work, I'll let you speak about it. But before you do, I'll add that the Lacanian idea of tapping into the chaotic drive energies of the real as a way of refusing the demands of the big Other could be connected to the early Frankfurt School, and to Marcuse in particular, because he was interested in the unconscious as a possible resource for resistance to the existing social order.

MR: Thank you so much for your amazing explanation! I can see why you regard Klein as a fantastic resource for thinking about ethics and politics, especially in today's charged situation where everything seems so drastically split, where there's so much aggression toward and demonization of "the other," and where people don't seem at all capable of handling ambivalence and ambiguity. It's like the paranoid-schizoid position has become the norm for our political landscape.

The death drive dominates. If the death drive is constitutive of the subject, and reparation is an always tenuous attempt to counter its destructiveness, at the moment we're spectacularly failing at this attempt. Against this backdrop, I want to ask you a question. You have suggested that Klein's account of reparation might give us ways to reconsider questions of justice. But if we start from the realistic view of subjectivity that we have determined that Klein and Lacan share, namely that aggression (or the death drive) is foundational to human subjectivity, how can reparation ever have a real chance? How do we begin to activate the ethical potential that the Kleinian depressive position and reparation might hold?

AA: Here's where I think that Butler's engagement with Klein is interesting, because through this engagement she moves beyond or at least significantly expands her Levinasian conception of ethics. The very starting point of her attempt to develop an ethics of nonviolence is the recognition of and reckoning with the death drive. As she states: "Any position against violence cannot afford to be naïve: it has to take seriously the destructive potential that is a constitutive part of the social bond."[5] Then the question becomes: How do we go about alleviating violence without setting for ourselves the impossible task of eliminating a constitutive part of the psyche? Does the recognition of the ineradicability of aggressiveness leave us in the conservative and ultimately paradoxical position of siding with the cruelty and severity of the superego—a position that's paradoxical because the superego enlists the forces of aggression in its attempt to contain aggression?

It's in the context of Butler's attempt to think through this impasse that she turns to Klein, for Klein provides a story about how an ethical orientation—an orientation toward love and reparation—is compatible with and indeed emerges out of primary aggression. For Klein, the ability to identify with or put yourself in the place of the other—an ability that's fundamental to ethics—emerges out of the dynamics of dependency, frustration, aggression, loss, and guilt that characterize early childhood. As Butler puts it, "We cannot understand the reparative trajectory of identification without first understanding the way that sympathetic identification, according to Klein, is wrought from efforts to replay and reverse scenes of loss, deprivation, and the kind of hatred that follows from nonnegotiable dependency."[6]

Because our primary object relation, for Klein, is characterized by ambivalence—by a complicated mixture of dependence, love, and hate—destructiveness gives rise to guilt and reparation. As I've explained, when the child moves to the depressive position and experiences its primary caregiver as a whole object, it realizes that the object it hates and has attempted to destroy whether in reality or in phantasy is also the object that it loves and on whom it depends. This means that guilt and the drive for reparation don't need to be imposed from without in the form of strict moral rules and laws that then get anchored in the superego; they emerge from within, as a consequence of the move to the depressive position. Furthermore, when I engage in reparative acts, as Butler postulates, "I do not disavow my destructiveness, but I seek to reverse its damaging effects. It is not that destructiveness converts into repair, but that I repair even as I am driven with destructiveness, or precisely because I am so driven."[7] As far as I can see, this is far from the claim that human beings are fundamentally good, but it does make a compelling case for how ethics is nonetheless possible.

MR: This is very helpful because it counters the sense that I've gotten from Butler's Levinasian work on ethics that her ethical paradigm can only work if we assume that people are fundamentally good. In this context, I also want to note that Noëlle McAfee, in *Fear of Breakdown: Politics and Psychoanalysis*, combines psychoanalysis and critical theory—mostly the Frankfurt School genre of critical theory—to analyze mourning in ways that seem relevant, not the least because she explicitly draws on Klein.[8] McAfee also draws on Winnicott, from whom she borrows the idea of the fear of the kind of breakdown that—like the Lacanian lack-in-being—has always already taken place. According to McAfee, this fear of breakdown can be used to explain political defensiveness, fundamentalism, and all manner of violent and misguided self-protectiveness. But perhaps most usefully for our purposes, McAfee describes the kind of everyday mourning that takes place when we, in the course of quotidian life, are forced to choose between two tasks, such as working on our book or taking our child to an appointment. Neither task may be intrinsically unsatisfying, but there can be a sense of loss—and therefore the necessity to mourn what we have to give up—when we're asked to drop one task for another. From such quotidian concerns, McAfee fans out to larger sociopolitical dilemmas and the mourning that's a necessary (but often disavowed) result of the fact that these dilemmas cannot be easily resolved.

At the core of McAfee's argument resides a question that I think that we're also implicitly dealing with: a question regarding what psychoanalysis can contribute to deliberative politics. Working with the legacies of Freud, Winnicott, and Klein, and with Habermasian and post-Habermasian versions of Frankfurt School critical theory, McAfee maintains that deliberative politics cannot be merely a matter of rational consensus building—where the unforced force of the better argument wins—but additionally demands an affective process that allows participants to collectively mourn the loss of ideal arrangements and definitive resolutions. That is, deliberative politics must recognize that because we can't have it all, we need to make difficult political choices without the security of knowing how things will turn out, and that every choice we make entails the discarding of other possibilities, of other possible paths. This in turn means that we must—both individually and collectively—learn to mourn the loss of these possibilities and paths; as you have argued all along in the context of Klein, we have to learn to come to terms with ambivalence, uncertainty, the lack of flawless solutions, and the fact that every choice implies a loss, sometimes even an excruciating one.

McAfee argues persuasively that without this capacity to mourn losses and to tolerate ambiguity, politics too easily degenerates into what she, following Kristeva, describes as an adolescent fundamentalist faith in ideality that can only lead to an inability to compromise, to see other people's points of view, and to accept less than perfect solutions. Another way to state the matter is to say that the inability to mourn our losses and to tolerate ambiguity can lead to a reversion (or regression) to the Kleinian paranoid-schizoid position, so that one categorically splits the world into good and bad components, projects all the badness to the (threatening) other, and idealizes one's own position. This is a politics of defensiveness, the type of politics that we see happening globally today, from the fundamentalism of ISIS to Donald Trump's ability to rally people around the notion of returning America to "real" Americans by keeping out all intruders (Muslims, Mexicans, etc.).

As an analysis of our contemporary political dilemmas—the mess we find ourselves in—McAfee's treatise managed to change my views on some important issues, including, most centrally, the place of mourning in politics. In some of my recent work, I've been critical of Butler's ethics of precarity and her related account of mourning because this account has made me feel that there's too short a step from arguing for the importance of mourning to the idea that mourning *in itself* is a political act that absolves us from having to do anything more concrete.[9] I've worried that it can too easily lead to the notion that as long as "we"—relatively privileged Western critics—mourn the pitiful lot of the victimized "other," we have done our ethical or political duty. But McAfee's analysis of mourning convinces me because it illustrates that without the capacity to mourn the loss of ideality, we'll inevitably demonize the other as the enemy of the ideality that we fantasize about, would like to see come about, or fear that we're in the process of losing.

McAfee makes a tremendous contribution to theories of deliberative politics, discourse ethics, and radical democracy by emphasizing the importance of affect—as opposed to just reason—for these theories, like you have also always done, Amy. In addition, although she doesn't use affect theory explicitly, many of her insights are related to recent work in the field, which demonstrates that without attention to the affective valences of human life, we can't understand much about ethics, politics, or the general human condition. Finally, McAfee's clear-sighted pragmatism about the fact that every choice we make, every direction we take, comes at a cost—forecloses other choices, directions, and options—is refreshing.

Sometimes I think that one of the biggest problems with contemporary progressive theory—with my version of critical theory—is that it's conceptually greedy: it wants to have its cake and eat it too. For instance, it routinely denounces normative ethics in favor of unmitigated antinormativity, yet when a given critic's back truly is against an (ethical or political) wall, they often fall back on quasi-Kantian ways of deciding what the right course of action should be. It feels to me that we can't have it both ways: we can't ridicule all norms but then resort to them whenever our argument happens to demand them. This is why I appreciate the fact that although McAfee isn't a proponent of liberal normative ethics—ethics based on a priori metaphysical principles or other "objective" factors—she recognizes that we routinely need to make some extremely difficult ethical choices, that some of these choices hurt, and that this is why mourning is so important for political deliberation.

McAfee doesn't promote normative ethics in either the Kantian or Rawlsian sense, or even in a strictly Habermasian sense, yet she's looking for a theoretical edifice for understanding how we can nevertheless come to open-ended agreements about how to proceed in complicated situations that require an ethical choice of some kind. Like you have done in your work, she emphasizes that all norms are human creations—and therefore historically specific and without any ultimate metaphysical, divine, or other external grounding—without thereby minimizing the fact that we nevertheless need to be able to make judgments about how to proceed.

It's also pertinent to our dialogue that McAfee believes that an appreciation for a "dark" form of psychoanalysis—a form that follows Freud's relatively pessimistic vision rather than the more sanguine one advanced by the early Habermas, and more recently, Honneth—is necessary for deliberative ethics. Without the death drive, and the related understanding of loss, psychoanalysis loses its critical edge. McAfee's argument in fact makes me realize that one of the main points I've been striving to convey throughout our conversations is that Lacan adopted the mantle of Freud's pessimistic vision: Lacan truly understood the need to mourn the losses that are intrinsic to human life, that subjectivity is essentially a process of mourning the collapse of ideality. This is why his theory is at odds with so many other psychoanalytic schools, which took the opposite route of downplaying the death drive, destructiveness, aggression, and the constitutive role of loss in human life.

AA: I agree, absolutely. And I think that McAfee's book is extremely relevant for our discussion. All three of us clearly agree about the importance of recovering the "dark" side of psychoanalysis—specifically the death drive, but also the focus on negativity, loss, and mourning more generally—for Frankfurt School critical social theory. And I think that the two of us are both on board with McAfee's criticisms of Habermas and Honneth on the grounds that they domesticate psychoanalytic concepts. Moreover, like you, I find her use of psychoanalysis for diagnosing contemporary political realities to be exemplary: her work demonstrates how psychoanalysis can be useful for critical theory at our current historical moment. It beautifully analyzes the destructiveness of phantasies of idealization and demonization in political life; the limits of reason in overcoming such phantasies; and the important role that a tolerance for ambivalence, complexity, and loss plays in the functioning of democratic politics. Her conception of deliberation as not simply cognitive and rational but also affective and particularistic is helpful, as is her account of the importance of working through loss and mourning. Her vision of democratic politics mobilizes Kleinian insights in an utterly compelling way.

However, it may be worth pointing out that McAfee seems (at least to me) more committed to the notion of primary fusion—or what she calls plenum—than either of us. In fact, for McAfee the plenum is crucial since it—or, more precisely, the terror that accompanies its loss—is what gives rise to the fear of breakdown. For reasons that we have analyzed at length, both of us are more skeptical of this notion of primary fusion than she is. As I've argued throughout this book, I believe that Klein sidesteps a falsely reassuring picture of infantile experience by avoiding dubious claims about an originary plenum. Klein would agree with McAfee that "the passage to reflexive sociality is contingent, fraught, and easily derailed."[10] But for Klein this is because of the centrality of aggression in early object relationships rather than because of a primordial experience of plenum.

This technical metapsychological disagreement notwithstanding, I think that McAfee makes a fascinating psychoanalytic intervention into democratic theory. However, as is probably clear by now, my interest in bringing Klein into conversation with critical theory has less to do with deliberative politics—not, to be sure, because I don't believe in the significance of this topic, but just because it isn't where my primary interest lies—than with the conceptual ramifications that psychoanalysis has for critical theory. For example, if we accept the psychoanalytic theory of the subject, what implications does this have for our understanding of critique, progress, and emancipation?

Along these lines, I'm interested in thinking about how we might connect what you have said about the Lacanian idea that there's no cure—that the only "cure" is to accept that there's no cure—with my recent work on progress and emancipation. As you know, I've criticized appeals to the concept of progress in contemporary Frankfurt School critical theory, but I've tried to do so in a way that allows me to recuperate a certain understanding of progress that I believe that you probably share, because it's implied in the very idea of "progressive critical theory"—which is how you describe your field. In other words, the little bit of the idea of progress that I want to retain is the one that allows us to think about our theory or politics as progressive.

In order to do this, I distinguish between what I call backward-looking claims about history read as a story of progress and forward-looking claims about progress as a moral or political aspiration. The former have the tendency to be both self-congratulatory and potentially ideological. Self-congratulation seems to me to be endemic to reading history as a story of progress. This approach seems particularly problematic for *critical* theorists inasmuch as the task of the critical theorist is to try to uncover our investments in or entanglements within relations of power and domination that we don't yet quite see. Telling history as a story of progress runs counter to this task: it leans toward the vindication rather than the problematization of the present. As a result, it's not the best way to interpret history if our goal is to interrogate our situatedness within ongoing but possibly obscure or as-yet-not-widely acknowledged relations of power and domination.

This self-congratulatory streak takes a particularly pernicious form when Europeans and Euro-Americans read the history of European modernity as a story of progress because doing so requires explicitly or implicitly positioning themselves as superior to those—premodern, traditional, racialized, or subaltern others— who have yet to learn what "we" already know. For this reason, there's a deep danger of an imperialist sensibility creeping into this particular Eurocentric narrative of historical progress.

Nevertheless, in order for our politics to be progressive (as opposed to reactionary or conservative), we seem to need some sort of—perhaps very minimal—conception of what we're striving to achieve. I would even say that such a conception is implied by the very critique of the backward-looking notion of progress that I just sketched: to criticize the notion of historical progress for being Eurocentric and ideological is to claim, implicitly at least, that it would be better to rid ourselves of this way of thinking about history and that doing so would count as a kind of progress. It's only in this very minimal forward-looking sense that I want to hold onto the notion of progress.

Here's where the death drive and the impossibility of a cure come in because critics have frequently thought that the death drive undermines any and all possibilities of progress, that it destroys all possibility of hope. And forward-looking conceptions of progress are often thought to be closely connected to utopian visions, in that a utopian vision gives us an ideal toward which we strive and then progress is just a measure of whether we're moving closer to that ideal. But if we accept the idea that there's no cure—which means that there's no possibility of wholeness or utopia whether on the individual or social level—and if we place the death drive at the center of our theory of subjectivity, what sense can we possibly make of the idea of progress in this forward-looking sense?

I've attempted to address this question in my recent work partly by developing a thoroughly negativistic understanding of emancipation, where emancipation is understood as the minimization or transformation of relations of domination rather than as breaking free from power relations altogether.[11] I develop this idea through a reading of Foucault, picking up on his somewhat under-appreciated distinction between power and domination. I realize that when we talked about affect theory, I mentioned that the early Foucault allows for the possibility of breaking with one's social context so that a new *episteme*, a new historical a priori, can emerge. Here I'm working with a different component of his theory, which posits that while power relations are always fluid, mobile, and reversible, states of domination are situations where power relations have become so congealed that reversibility is impossible. Developing this idea, I propose that we can think about emancipation—or progress in a forward-looking sense—not as a utopian ideal of getting outside of or beyond power altogether but rather simply as a matter of transforming existing states of domination into more fluid, mobile, and reversible relations of power.

This is a way of understanding progress in a forward-looking sense that doesn't rely on the possibility of a cure. It also strikes me as quite congenial to how Bruce Fink describes the goal of Lacanian analysis to be to transform "stopping points or dead ends ... into through streets,"[12] though of course transcribed to the social level. The common thread is the idea that in the same way as analysis aims to open up blockages, to enable the analysand to engage with new possibilities—and in that sense to transform dead ends into through streets—emancipation could be understood as a process of opening up states of domination by transforming them into open-ended and reversible relations of power.

I think that there's something like this minimalistic and negativistic view of progress implicit in Klein as well. We have discussed several times the passage where she points out that people have been naïve about the possibilities for progress because they have underestimated the depth and vigor of the aggressive drive, and that this is why their efforts to improve society have been doomed from the start. Yet although psychoanalysis, according to this vision, cannot eliminate aggression, Klein suggests that it can help us to figure out ways to break up the cycle of mutual reinforcement between our fear and our hatred. In other words, there's no cure, no overcoming of the death drive, of the repetition compulsion, but there are better and worse ways to manage this lack of a cure, both individually and collectively.

Something like this idea is also a theme in Lacan's *Seminar VII*, where he insists that Freud "was a humanitarian [but] he was no progressive."[13] I'm inclined to read this claim as positing that Freud was interested in ameliorating suffering, and that in that sense he was a humanitarian, but that he wasn't a utopian idealist, which is what Lacan means by a progressive. This reminds me of the famous line from the end of the *Studies on Hysteria* where Freud claims that the goal of analysis is to transform hysterical misery into ordinary unhappiness.[14] Again, there's a kind of minimalist and negativistic understanding of progress implied here—progress as an amelioration of hysterical misery—that doesn't at all rely on any notion of a cure, the Sovereign Good, or utopia.

MR: That was amazing. Let me start with Lacan's statement about how Freud was a humanitarian but not a progressive. My reading of this statement is the same as yours, namely that although Freud wanted to alleviate suffering, he—like Klein and Lacan—had a realistic vision of subjectivity: he didn't have any utopian hopes about an ultimate cure or resolution either on the individual or collective level. In *Seminar II*, Lacan in fact claims that Freud—and Lacan is referring to *Beyond the Pleasure Principle* specifically— "cannot find the slightest tendency towards progress in any of the concrete and historical manifestations of human functions, and this really has a value for the person who invented our method. All forms of life are as surprising, as miraculous, there is no tendency towards superior forms."[15] I take this to mean that Lacan believes that the realization that there's no tendency toward progress was a paradigm-shifting discovery for Freud. Yet even though there's no tendency toward superior forms of life, all forms of life are "as surprising, as miraculous." For me, this suggests that, according to Lacan, the lack of progress doesn't render life worthless.

Obviously, Lacan's lack of faith in progress is related to his conviction that there's no cure. However, as I've tried to get across, this doesn't mean that there's no possibility of things changing, sometimes even for the better. This is where Lacan's account of the repetition compulsion—and I think that one could make the argument that he's mostly following Freud's lead on this—becomes important because he isn't merely saying that we keep repeating our failures. He's saying that even though it's our fate to keep repeating—and that the manner in which we repeat conditions our fate—we can nevertheless learn to repeat differently. Indeed, if there was no possibility of intervening in the repetition compulsion, there would be no point to psychoanalysis as a clinical practice. This may be one way of thinking about your minimalist and negativist conception of progress.

In addition, as I've suggested throughout our dialogue, for Lacan, accepting lack, deformation, maladaptation, alienation, and castration—and I guess the Kleinian analogy would be accepting one's aggression—isn't a defeatist notion; rather, the idea, on my reading at least, is that it's only through this acceptance that a degree of creative living becomes possible. As long as we're hoping for a cure, we remain caught up in the meshes of cruel optimism in ways that—as Berlant so brilliantly conveys—undermine our ability to move through the world with any degree of fluidity. There are of course countless structural obstacles to our ability to break out of this predicament. But if we stay on the existential level, the idea is that the quest for a cure can only keep us from stepping into what Eric Santner calls "the midst of life."[16] From a Lacanian point of view, the quest for a cure—for wholeness, perfection, or complete happiness—is more or less the antithesis of life.

If we shift to the collective level, it's possible to argue that the Lacanian point about the lack of a cure is somewhat compatible with Butler's ethics of precarity in the sense that it implies that if I truly understand—and accept—that there's no cure for my lack, deformation, maladaptation, alienation, and castration, maybe I might grasp that this is true of everyone. In Butler, correctly, there's a greater emphasis on different degrees of precariousness and vulnerability because she's thinking about these states in connection to social power. Lacan doesn't do the work of considering power differentials explicitly, in part because this wasn't part of the French way of thinking back then (in fact it still doesn't seem to be). But there's nothing to prevent us, post-Lacan, from acknowledging that signifiers—whether linguistic or affective—impact different subjects differently, so that power differentials are always part of the equation. For instance, racist, sexist, or homophobic language has vastly different effects on people depending on their subject positions. Lacan doesn't deliberate on this, but we can use his theory of the hegemonic symbolic order to make this argument. In addition, we can use his insight about the lack of a cure as a starting point for attempting to figure out how we might get to a place where we understand that all of us—however differently—are precarious and vulnerable.

Some people are obviously much better off than others, and structural inequalities can't be fixed by asserting that there's no ultimate cure for our precariousness and vulnerability. And there are people who go to great lengths to deny their woundability, frequently by lashing out against others. But there's nonetheless something powerful about the recognition of our shared woundability, not the least because it can reveal forms of traumatization that might otherwise remain invisible. I saw the value of this revelation last semester in my graduate seminar on bad feelings. As soon as my students—many of whom came from backgrounds of damaging social inequalities—grasped that we can't always tell by looking at someone what kinds of challenges they may have had to face, something marvelous happened: the kinds of students who might under normal circumstances have resented each other—say, because of assumptions of privilege—began talking to each other with genuine generosity. For me, the ethical and political potential of the idea that there's no cure for my lack arises from the realization that there's a direct line from accepting this fact about myself to acting more charitably toward others.

Both Klein and Lacan make it hard to think about progress. But this doesn't mean that we should sink into despair. This is why your notion of "a negativistic understanding of emancipation"— premised on minimizing relations of domination, on transforming states of domination into reversible relations of power—is indispensable. If we give up this notion, I don't think that we can talk about progressive critical theory. And as I've mentioned, I hugely appreciate the manner in which you strive to recuperate a version of progressive theory that retains a degree of normative purchase.

In this context, you ask what happens when we place the death drive at the center of our theory of subjectivity; you wonder whether doing so makes it impossible to think about progress in the forward-looking sense that you're still hoping to preserve. This is where Lacanian political theory might be useful because it places the death drive at the center not only of subjectivity but also of politics without thereby abandoning the possibility of social change. I'm referring to the ways in which critics such as Žižek, Badiou, Eisenstein, and McGowan have conceptualized the act, event, or rupture that I've already discussed extensively. As I've explained, what's central for these thinkers is the idea that the death drive, the jouissance of the real, erupts within the symbolic order in destructive yet world-altering ways. This eruption of the real within the symbolic marks moments when the system shifts in a seismic way that brings something genuinely new onto the collective stage; at such moments, the social fabric rips so that an opening is created for possibilities that previously appeared impossible. Undoubtedly this vision may be impossible to reconcile with your more minimalist approach, which is precisely why the later Foucault sometimes seems incompatible with Lacanian theory. At the same time, if there's a notion of progress in the Lacanian perspective, I would argue that it's the forward-looking version of progress that you also want to preserve. Indeed, given the Marxist inclinations of the Lacanians I'm referring to, it would be impossible for them to valorize the backward-looking version of progress that you find problematic because they can't possibly posit that our neoliberal capitalist society represents historical progress.

That said, there's a component of Lacanian political theory that at first glance at least goes against the grain of your approach, namely its defense of a universalist ethics of freedom and equality that transcends the specificity of culture, custom, and tradition. Although the Lacanians I've named shun Habermas, they present a strongly context-transcendent notion of ethics. I hope that in a moment it will become clear that their vision isn't necessarily entirely antithetical to yours, but I might as well say right away that they have no qualms about promoting context-transcendent ethical norms (even if they go about this task in a completely non-Habermasian and anti-liberal manner).

Eisenstein and McGowan's definition of rupture gives you a good sense of what I mean: "The rupture is always a traumatic cut. Though the rupture gives birth to political values like freedom and equality, it does so through disconnecting individuals from the bonds of tradition through which they receive a sense of identity and belonging. To remain within the rupture is to exist without the security of a place in the world."[17] On the one hand, Eisenstein and McGowan encourage giving up the quest for a secure place in the world in a manner that can be linked both to the Lacanian notion of there not being a cure and to the Kleinian notion of tolerating ambivalence. On the other, their endorsement of freedom and equality over "the bonds of tradition"—over cultural belonging—can sound problematically universalist, context-transcendent, and even Eurocentric.

I've stressed that progressive critical theory has largely discarded normative ethics. Lacanians are the exception, along with Marxists such as Michael Hardt and Antonio Negri, in the sense that they unapologetically defend a universalist understanding of freedom and equality. Furthermore, they believe that genuine equality can only be purchased at the expense of the particularity of culture, custom, and tradition. This is a hard pill to swallow for critics trained in cultural studies, ethnic studies, feminist theory, queer theory, certain versions of postcolonial theory, and related fields, who have spent decades deconstructing universalism for its Western, white masculinist bias. As a result, when Lacanians propose, say, that the universality of equality can only be achieved by breaking the bonds of culture, custom, and tradition, many non-Lacanian critics—and both Sara Ahmed and Maggie Nelson have noted this explicitly[18]—hear white male identity politics in disguise.

I've mixed feelings about this issue because I appreciate the logic and validity of both perspectives: on the one hand, I hate the idea of coercively imposing universal ideals on those who don't want them; on the other, it's hard for me to accept the notion that equality should *not* be a universal ideal for progressive critics. I know that a great deal depends on how we define this ideal, but if we assume that at issue is a genuine version of equality rather than, for instance, a watered-down neoliberal, rights-based version, how can we possibly oppose it? *How can progressive critics claim that the equality of all people isn't an ideal worth upholding? Should we be voting for inequality just to avoid the charge of universalism?*

It seems to me that this is a situation where there's no way around universalism, that the ideal equality can't be theorized or practiced from a place of relativism: either it applies to everyone or it has no meaning. In addition, there are times when I literally feel bullied into silence about this issue by my field, which is one reason that I have respect for Lacanians who don't yield to it. But perhaps more pertinently for our purposes, I've come to realize that the divide between Lacanian theory and the rest of progressive theory on this topic arises from the fact that these theoretical orientations are working with antithetical understandings of universalism. When progressive critics outside of Lacanian circles hear the term *universalism*, they immediately think of the Enlightenment, of the "parochialism" of white male universalism, and of the related atrocities of Western imperialism, slavery, and sexism. In contrast, Lacanians don't associate universalism with the Enlightenment or its liberal inheritors, whom they regard as the enemies of true universalism. Rather, their universalism is supposed to be built from the bottom up, from the position of the disenfranchised, the dispossessed; it's related to the argument that Hardt and Negri make about "the common."[19] Furthermore, it's always a historically specific, continuously renegotiated universalism. And it can't be rationally constituted, which is why the (irrational, unpremeditated) act, event, or rupture is so central to Lacanian ethics.

Lacanian universalism is essentially Hegelian: it has to do with the singular universal. The Lacanians I've named explicitly or implicitly conceptualize three levels of "being." First, there's the irreducible singularity of the subject, which has to do with the real, the drives, and the unconscious—in a way, with what is most "inhuman" about the human. That is, your singularity is related to your fundamental fantasy and the unique ways in which you have been derailed by a process of subject formation that has fashioned you into a person who can't be exchanged for another—that, in short, has made you irreplaceable. Second, there's the level of particularity: the culture, customs, and traditions that you have been raised in, the bonds of belonging that suture you to your specific situation. This type of particularity coincides loosely with the historically specific symbolic order, which is why Lacanians are so aggravated with it: for them, it's social hegemony, pure and simple. Third, there's the universal, which in this case has to do with Marxist-inspired notions of leveling socioeconomic differences and with a radical notion of emancipation—it's in fact extremely utopian.

The goal, then, is to jump from the singular directly to the universal, bypassing the particular altogether; the goal is to allow every singularity to participate in the universal on an equal footing. We both know how difficult this would be to put into practice. But it's an ethical and political ideal that many Lacanians believe in. If in much of the rest of progressive theory, the particular is considered progressive—as the sheltering antidote to false universalism—and the (false) universal is regarded as oppressive, in the Lacanian vision, the universal is progressive and the particular is oppressive. Interestingly, I believe that the Lacanian perspective is compatible with much of the *early* work in postcolonial theory and diaspora studies that focused on hybridity, nonbelonging, and the impurity (and oppressiveness) of all cultures. I'm thinking of critics such as Edward Said, Homi Bhabha, and Paul Gilroy.[20] In contrast, more recent postcolonial theory sometimes defends cultural specificity and the importance of tradition in ways that I—and this is the Lacanian streak in me—find potentially conservative.

I understand why such defensiveness arises in situations where people feel that Western imperialism is erasing their cultures, customs, and traditions. Nevertheless, I believe that every culture is hegemonic, oppressive, and repressive, and that the kind of immanent critique that you described as the defining feature of the Frankfurt School should be applied to all cultures, albeit with a keen sensitivity to colonial histories and ongoing power differentials. I guess I'm willing to take the risk of admitting that one reason I'm drawn to Lacanian ethics is that I believe that ethical ideals such as freedom and equality are more important than cultural belonging. This may be for idiosyncratic personal reasons, given that I've never felt like I belong anywhere! But my point is that I don't see the defense of cultural specificity and tradition as a feasible political strategy. If anything, what we're witnessing in the world right now is the astounding brutality that this strategy tends to generate.

Consider what's happening in the United States: "outsiders" are being demonized precisely in the name of cultural specificity and tradition ("our way of life"). I comprehend that there's a big difference between the nationalism of a non-Western society under siege by Western imperialism and the nationalism of an imperial power. Nevertheless, even in the former instance, it seems that what's often being defended is the culture, customs, and traditions of the elites (heteropatriarchy, social hierarchies, and financial power). The disenfranchised "masses" might be more interested in the ideals of freedom and equality, and, like me, they might not care that much about where these ideals originated.

To illustrate this point, Eisenstein and McGowan turn to the Haitian revolution. In some ways going all the way back to Hegel, they present the Haitian revolution as the quintessential example of a revolutionary rupture that disrupts the existing social order.

They valorize the Haitian revolution over the French revolution precisely because they aren't convinced by nationalist ideologies of belonging. They reason that whereas a strong sense of national belonging was intrinsic to the French revolution, the Haitian revolution brought the ideals of the French revolution—the ideals of *liberté, égalité,* and *fraternité*—to a different context, thereby universalizing these ideals. By using them for its own purposes, the Haitian revolution proved that they aren't culturally specific (even if they are historically specific, as all ideals are).

I suspect that you might have reservations about this Lacanian celebration of universalist, context-transcendent ethics. However, I see a connection between the Lacanian view and your negativistic understanding of progress in the sense that what functions as the glue for Lacanian universalism isn't the idea that people share positive attributes but rather the idea that all of us are deformed and maladapted beings who don't ever fully feel like we belong in the world. This approach suggests that politics—or any form of collective sociality—can't begin from the assumption that at its root we find "whole," undamaged individuals. In addition, when Lacanians talk about politics, they aren't talking about trying to resolve antagonisms but about accepting that antagonisms are always going to exist. Perhaps inaccurately, I am tempted to align this both with Klein's commentary on the inerasability of aggression and with your negativistic understanding of progress.

AA: The question of universalism is extremely difficult, and you're absolutely right that everything depends on how one defines universality. In my work, I've proposed that accepting that our normative standards are contextual—that, as you noted, they are historically specific and continually renegotiated—isn't incompatible with understanding them as universal in some sense. The opposite of contextualism isn't universalism but rather foundationalism: the assumption that our normative standards can be grounded a priori. Contextualism is a view about how our normative standards are grounded or justified, whereas universalism is a claim about their scope, about how far and in what circumstances they apply. As a result, although I probably place more emphasis than you do on the rootedness of conceptions of freedom, equality, justice, autonomy, and so forth in their social, cultural, and historical context—and in this sense I may be guilty of the kind of particularism that the

Lacanians you just discussed are worried about—I don't think that this rules out the possibility of a bottom-up, historically emergent type of universalism.

I also agree that all cultures can be hegemonic and oppressive and that they should be subject to critique and contestation from within—and also from without, because endorsing contextualism doesn't preclude us from making judgments about whether we think that the institutions, practices, or laws of another culture are wrong, even if it puts some constraints on how these judgments might be grounded or justified. But I would emphasize your point about the importance of keeping power differentials clearly in view. And I would want to understand these power differentials in a complex, multifaceted, and intersectional way. I think that there's a tremendous danger in the attempt to reduce all power relations to one axis and also in the unwillingness or inability to reflect on one's own privileged position in relations of domination. It seems to me that this is where Žižek flounders. This is why even if I might agree with the idea that we should reformulate universalism, I would be cautious about signing onto his critique of particularism since it seems to dovetail with his defense of Eurocentrism.

MR: This is exactly why I find Eisenstein and McGowan more palatable than Žižek: they don't give the same impression of insensitivity to multiple axes of power differentials as Žižek sometimes does. I have in fact staged a critique of precisely this dimension of Žižek's theory even though I respect him as an excellent interpreter of Lacan—and the latter is the case even when my interpretation differs from his, as it often does.[21] What I ultimately find most compelling about Eisenstein and McGowan's argument—and I'm coming back to this because it's important to me—is the idea that if we can truly accept our constitutive derailment, we might gain better ways of relating to others as similarly damaged entities. I suppose that, for me, this is what universalism on the most basic level comes down to.

I'm also the last person to deny that context-specific (circumstantial) forms of suffering are differentially distributed. This is why I have so much esteem for affect theory even though my primary orientation remains psychoanalytic: affect theory has been superbly insightful in bringing to the fore context-specific forms of traumatization. We have noted that for this reason it threatens to drown out any consideration of the death drive, primary aggression, or constitutive lack. But it's hard to fault it for this, given the excess of context-specific derailment that, in the case of many individuals, overshadows constitutive derailment. In other words, it's easy to understand why the affect theoretical focus on context-specific genres of suffering leads to an emphasis on reparation rather than, say, on accepting that there's no cure because *of course* there's a cure for context-specific genres of suffering: a more egalitarian and less performance-oriented social order.

The problem of social inequality persists. On the theoretical level, I can think endlessly—as I've in fact done—about the process of translating loss, lack, and mourning into creativity. Doing this theoretical work has helped me personally not only in relation to existential concerns but also in relation to context-specific forms of affliction. Nonetheless, I'm acutely aware that there are situations where I can't in good conscience tell others to turn their loss, lack, and mourning into creativity. There's just too much violence and discrimination, poverty and abjection, racism and sexism, homophobia and transphobia, among other injustices, in the world.

AA: Perhaps this is one of the places where the psychoanalytic framework ...

MR: Reaches its limit?

AA: Yes, runs up against its limit. When we were talking about your queer theory book in my class this spring,[22] we spent a lot of time discussing this point. We were trying to think about the implications of various psychoanalytic theories for social critique as well as about their limitations. And we kept coming back to your distinction—which I think is compelling—between ontological or constitutive lack on the one hand and more socially or politically specific forms of loss, negation, and wounding on the other. For me, it's easy to see how the Lacanian perspective is helpful for thinking about the former but perhaps less helpful for illuminating the latter. This isn't to say that the Lacanian perspective rules out the possibility of analyzing circumstantial forms of negation that have differential effects; it's just to say that it may not offer us the best way of thinking through such situations. Perhaps we need other tools for that type of work.

It sounds like affect theory is offering some of these alternative tools. That said, listening to how you have described the split between Lacanian theory and affect theory, it seems to me that the two positions might be more compatible than they may at first glance appear. As we have discussed at length, the Kleinian notion of reparation can't mean the elimination of fundamental antagonisms. This means that if affect theorists are drawing on her concept of reparation, this has to—should—entail the preservation of internal ambivalence and primary aggression, and therefore of fundamental antagonisms, which I know Lacan also believes are insurmountable. Only manic reparation—the kind of reparation that refuses to acknowledge the reality of loss, that pretends that no damage has been done, and that consequently attempts to put everything back together without processing the actuality of harm—would enable the denial of fundamental antagonisms. Genuine reparation requires facing the reality of loss and accepting the role that one's destructiveness plays both intrapsychically and intersubjectively, which is far from denying fundamental antagonisms. For this reason, it seems to me that the emphasis on reparation can go together with the claim about the inevitability of fundamental antagonisms.

MR: They definitely go together for me. As we have determined, what Klein and Lacan share—and I wouldn't have known this before our dialogue started, so thank you for this—is a respect for the inerasable nature of antagonisms as well as for the deep psychic ambivalence that ensues from this state of affairs. On this issue, Klein and Lacan are much closer to each other than I expected, and this perhaps separates them from some other psychoanalytic schools.

AA: Let me close by returning to what you said a moment ago about how non-Lacanian progressive critics sometimes accuse Lacanians such as Žižek of advancing a white male identity politics. I have many reasons for turning to Klein in my work, some of which are conceptual. However, one reason I'm interested in her contributions is that, in my view, she's a female thinker who hasn't had nearly the influence that she should have had within academic discussions of psychoanalysis. There's at the moment a resurgence of interest in her work, with Butler, David Eng, and other scholars turning to Klein. And as you have noted, affect theory owes a great deal to

Sedgwick's appropriation of Klein. In addition, Jacqueline Rose has been writing on Klein for quite some time. So it's not that there has been *no* interest in her work. But she certainly hasn't had anything like the kind of massive influence that Lacan has had on critical theory. Even within the somewhat more narrowly demarcated world of Frankfurt School critical theory, there's more written on Lacan than on Klein. I like the idea of helping to recover the work of this brilliant, pioneering, and original woman thinker whose potential contributions to critical theory haven't yet been fully appreciated.

MR: That's an excellent reason. Truly excellent.

Let me merely add that writing this book with you has been a pleasure and a privilege. Your generosity as a collaborator is especially striking given that you're among the most formidable theorists of our generation. I thank my lucky stars that you suggested that we undertake this thrilling project.

AA: Wow. Thank you for saying that. This process has been a pleasure and a privilege for me as well, not least because I have been such a huge admirer of your work since I first encountered it almost a decade ago. I have learned so much from you about Lacan and critical theory and much else besides. I am so grateful that you took my rather offhand suggestion so seriously and made this book a reality.

NOTES

Preface

1. Exceptions to this are Adam Rosen-Carole, *Lacan and Klein, Creation and Discovery: An Essay of Reintroduction* (Lanham, MD: Lexington Books, 2011) and *The New Klein-Lacan Dialogues*, ed. Julia Borossa, Catalina Bronstein, and Claire Pajaczkowska (London: Karnac, 2015).
2. Amy Allen, *The End of Progress: Decolonizing the Normative Foundations of Critical Theory* (New York: Columbia University Press, 2016).
3. Mari Ruti, *The Ethics of Opting Out: Queer Theory's Defiant Subjects* (New York: Columbia University Press, 2017).
4. Mari Ruti, *Between Levinas and Lacan: Self, Other, Ethics* (New York: Bloomsbury Press, 2015).

Chapter 1

1. Hanna Segal, *Introduction to the Work of Melanie Klein* (New York: Routledge, 1988), ix.
2. See, for example, Melanie Klein, "Notes on Some Schizoid Mechanisms," in *Envy and Gratitude and Other Works 1946–1963* (New York: The Free Press, 1975), 1–24.
3. Joel Whitebook, *Freud: An Intellectual Biography* (Cambridge: Cambridge University Press, 2017), 5. Cf. Hans Loewald, "The Waning of the Oedipus Complex," in *Papers on Psychoanalysis* (New Haven, CT: Yale University Press, 1980), 384–404.
4. Melanie Klein, *The Psychoanalysis of Children*, trans. Alix Strachey (New York: The Free Press, 1975), 155.
5. Melanie Klein, "On the Development of Mental Functioning," in *Envy and Gratitude and Other Works 1946–1963* (New York: The Free Press, 1975), 236.

6 Melanie Klein, "On the Theory of Anxiety and Guilt," in *Envy and Gratitude and Other Works 1946–1963* (New York: The Free Press, 1975), 29.
7 Regarding primary narcissism, see, for example, Michael Rustin, "Klein on Human Nature," in *Other Banalities: Melanie Klein Revisited*, ed. Jon Mills (New York: Routledge, 2006), 25–44, 28–30. Rustin believes that Klein accepts the idea of primary fusion whereas I don't, for reasons discussed further in Chapter 2.
8 Melanie Klein, "The Origins of Transference," in *Envy and Gratitude and Other Works 1946–1963* (New York: The Free Press, 1975), 53.
9 See Klein, "Notes on Some Schizoid Mechanisms."
10 Melanie Klein, "Love, Guilt and Reparation," in *Love, Guilt and Reparation and Other Works 1921–1945* (New York: The Free Press, 1975), 311.
11 Klein, "On the Development of Mental Functioning," 239.
12 Klein, "Notes on Some Schizoid Mechanisms," 10.
13 See, for example, the following passage from Klein's "The Emotional Life of the Infant": "The depressive position plays a vital part in the child's early development and, normally, when the infantile neurosis comes to an end at about five years of age, persecutory and depressive anxieties have undergone modification. The fundamental steps in working through the depressive position are, however, made when the infant is establishing the complete object—that is to say, during the second half of the first year—and one might contend that if these processes are successful, one of the preconditions for normal development is fulfilled" (in *Envy and Gratitude and Other Works 1946–1963* [New York: The Free Press, 1975], 80).
14 There's some disagreement among interpreters of Klein on this point. Her student Hanna Segal, for example, contends that the depressive position "is never fully worked through" and that its characteristic anxieties and experiences are always with us (Segal, *Introduction to the Work of Melanie Klein*, 80). Similarly, Eve Sedgwick notes that "it becomes increasingly unclear in Klein's writing after 1940 whether she envisioned a further space beyond the depressive position" (see Sedgwick's "Melanie Klein and the Difference Affect Makes," *South Atlantic Quarterly* 106, no. 3 [2007]: 625–42, 636). However, Meira Likierman maintains that the idea that the depressive position can be overcome is essential to Klein's view and that it distinguishes her view from that of later Kleinians (see Likierman, *Melanie Klein: Her Work in Context* [New York: Continuum, 2001], 112–33).
15 Klein, "The Emotional Life of the Infant," 87.
16 Note that Freud agrees with Klein on this point. See Sigmund Freud, "Civilization and Its Discontents (1930)," in *The Standard Edition of*

the *Complete Psychological Works of Sigmund Freud*, vol. XXI, ed. James Strachey (London: Vintage Press, 2001), 57–146, 130.
17 Melanie Klein, "Envy and Gratitude," in *Envy and Gratitude and Other Works 1946–1963* (New York: The Free Press, 1975), 225.
18 Whitebook, *Freud*, 154–70.
19 Ibid., 154.
20 Ibid., 164.
21 Jacques Lacan, *The Seminar of Jacques Lacan, Book I (1953–1954): Freud's Papers on Technique*, trans. John Forrester (New York: Norton, 1988).
22 Jacques Lacan, *The Seminar of Jacques Lacan, Book X (1962–1963): Anxiety*, trans. A. R. Price (Cambridge: Polity, 2014), 32.
23 Frantz Fanon, *Black Skin, White Masks*, trans. Richard Philcox (New York: Grove Press, 2008).
24 Toni Morrison, *The Bluest Eye* (New York: Vintage, 2007).
25 Slavoj Žižek, *Enjoy Your Symptom! Jacques Lacan in Hollywood and Out* (New York: Routledge, 2008), 59.
26 Sigmund Freud, "New Introductory Lectures on Psycho-Analysis (1933)," in *The Standard Edition of the Complete Psychological Works of Sigmund Freud*, vol. XXII, ed. James Strachey (London: Vintage, 2001), 1–182, 80.
27 Jacques Lacan, *The Seminar of Jacques Lacan, Book II (1954–1955): The Ego in Freud's Theory and in the Technique of Psychoanalysis*, trans. Sylvana Tomaselli (New York: Norton, 1991), 325.
28 Ibid.
29 Ibid., 326.
30 Klein, "Envy and Gratitude," 231.
31 On this point, see Sedgwick, "Melanie Klein and the Difference Affect Makes," 632–3.
32 Melanie Klein, "The Psychoanalytic Play Technique: Its History and Significance," in *Envy and Gratitude and Other Works 1946–1963* (New York: The Free Press, 1975), 123.
33 Amy Allen, *The End of Progress: Decolonizing the Normative Foundations of Critical Theory* (New York: Columbia University Press, 2016).
34 Gilles Deleuze and Félix Guattari, *Anti-Oedipus: Capitalism and Schizophrenia*, trans. Robert Hurley, Mark Seem, and Helen R. Lane (London: Bloomsbury Press, 2013); Lee Edelman, *No Future: Queer Theory and the Death Drive* (Durham, NC: Duke University Press, 2004); Lynne Huffer, *Mad for Foucault: Rethinking the Foundations of Queer Theory* (New York: Columbia University Press, 2010).
35 See, for example, Amy Allen, *The Politics of Our Selves: Power, Autonomy, and Gender in Contemporary Critical Theory* (New York: Columbia University Press, 2008), 22–49.

36 For a discussion of this point, see Rachel Blass, "The Ego According to Klein: Return to Freud and Beyond," in *The New Klein-Lacan Dialogues*, ed. Julia Borossa, Catalina Bronstein, and Claire Pajaczkowska (London: Karnac, 2015), 39–58.
37 The classic discussion of Klein's notion of phantasy can be found in Susan Isaacs, "The Nature and Function of Phantasy," in *The Freud-Klein Controversies: 1941–45*, ed. Pearl King and Riccardo Steiner (London: Routledge, 1991), 199–243.
38 Klein, "Envy and Gratitude," 180.
39 Ibid., 230.
40 See Wilfred Bion, "Container and Contained," in *Attention and Interpretation* (Abingdon: Routledge, 2018), 72–82.
41 Jacques Lacan, *The Seminar of Jacques Lacan, Book VIII (1960–1961): Transference*, trans. Bruce Fink (Cambridge: Polity, 2015), 368.
42 Ibid., 371.
43 Lacan, *Seminar II*, 325–6.
44 See Žižek, *Enjoy Your Symptom!*
45 For a suggestion along similar lines, see Lionel Bailly, "Klein-Lacan: Ego," in *The New Klein-Lacan Dialogues*, ed. Julia Borossa, Catalina Bronstein, and Claire Pajaczkowska (London: Karnac, 2015), 35–8, 35.
46 Julia Kristeva, *Black Sun: Depression and Melancholia*, trans. Leon S. Roudiez (New York: Columbia University Press, 1989), 6.

Chapter 2

1 See Axel Honneth, "Facets of the Presocial Self: Rejoinder to Joel Whitebook," in *The I in We: Studies in the Theory of Recognition*, trans. Joseph Ganahl (Cambridge: Polity, 2012), 217–31, 229.
2 For a compelling critique of Honneth's position along these lines, see Jonathan Lear, "The Slippery Middle," in Axel Honneth, *Reification: A New Look at an Old Idea*, ed. Martin Jay (Oxford: Oxford University Press, 2008), 131–46.
3 See Axel Honneth, *The Struggle for Recognition: The Moral Grammar of Social Conflicts*, trans. Joel Anderson (Cambridge, MA: MIT Press, 1995), 92–130.
4 See, most notably, Daniel Stern, *The Interpersonal World of the Infant: A View from Psychoanalysis and Developmental Psychology* (New York: Basic Books, 1985).
5 Honneth, "Facets of the Presocial Self," 226–8.

6 See Axel Honneth, "The Work of Negativity: A Recognition-Theoretical Revision of Psychoanalysis," in *The I in We: Studies in the Theory of Recognition*, trans. Joseph Ganahl (Cambridge: Polity, 2012), 193–200.
7 See Joel Whitebook, *Freud: An Intellectual Biography* (Cambridge: Cambridge University Press, 2017), 154–70.
8 On the degree of ego organization presupposed by Klein's account of the infant, see Hanna Segal, *Introduction to the Work of Melanie Klein* (New York: Routledge, 1988), 13–14.
9 On this point, see, for example, Melanie Klein, "Love, Guilt and Reparation," in *Love, Guilt and Reparation and Other Works 1921–1945* (New York: The Free Press, 1975), 306–7.
10 Jacques Lacan, *The Seminar of Jacques Lacan, Book I (1953–1954): Freud's Papers on Technique*, trans. John Forrester (New York: Norton, 1988), 210.
11 Ibid., 212.
12 Ibid., 217.
13 Ibid., 213.
14 Ibid., 204.
15 Ibid., 214.
16 Ibid., 218.
17 Paul Eisenstein and Todd McGowan, *Rupture: On the Emergence of the Political* (Evanston, IL: Northwestern University Press, 2012), 193.
18 Ibid.
19 Ibid., 195.
20 Jacques Lacan, *The Seminar of Jacques Lacan, Book X (1962–1963): Anxiety*, trans. A. R. Price (Cambridge: Polity, 2014), 327.
21 Ibid.
22 Jacques Lacan, *The Seminar of Jacques Lacan, Book II (1954–1955): The Ego in Freud's Theory and in the Technique of Psychoanalysis*, trans. Sylvana Tomaselli (New York: Norton, 1991), 257.
23 Ibid.
24 Ibid.
25 Melanie Klein, "Envy and Gratitude," in *Envy and Gratitude and Other Works 1946–1963* (New York: The Free Press, 1975), 179.
26 Jacques Lacan, *The Seminar of Jacques Lacan, Book VII (1959–1960): The Ethics of Psychoanalysis*, trans. Dennis Porter (New York: Norton, 1997), 58.
27 Lacan, *Seminar X*, 313.
28 Ibid., 291, 313.
29 Ibid., 313, 327–8.
30 Ibid., 313.

31 Ibid., 311–16.
32 Ibid., 291.
33 Ibid., 292.
34 See, for instance, Jean Laplanche, *Essays on Otherness*, trans. Luke Thurston et al. (London: Routledge, 1999).
35 Hanna Segal, "Notes on Symbol Formation," *The International Journal of Psycho-Analysis* 38 (1957): 391–7; Wilfred Bion, "A Theory of Thinking," in *Second Thoughts: Selected Papers on Psychoanalysis* (New York: Routledge, 2018), 110–19.
36 See Lauren Berlant, *Cruel Optimism* (Durham, NC: Duke University Press, 2011).
37 Lacan, *Seminar VII*, 106.
38 Ibid., 63.
39 Ibid.
40 Ibid., 67.
41 Klein, "Envy and Gratitude," 178–9; emphasis added.
42 Melanie Klein, *The Psychoanalysis of Children*, trans. Alix Strachey (New York: The Free Press, 1975), 3.
43 Ernest Jones famously suggested that it was precisely because of her shattering of the myth of the paradise of infancy that many people found Klein's work so shocking and difficult to believe. See Ernest Jones, "Introduction," in Melanie Klein, *Contributions to Psychoanalysis, 1921–1945* (London: Hogarth Press, 1948), 9–12.
44 Lacan, *Seminar VII*, 46.
45 Jonathan Lear discusses this notion of too-muchness in many of his books. See, for instance, *Happiness, Death, and the Remainder of Life* (Cambridge, MA: Harvard University Press, 2002).
46 Lacan, *Seminar VII*, 68.
47 Ibid.
48 Ibid., 68, 52.
49 A classic example is Lee Edelman, *No Future: Queer Theory and the Death Drive* (Durham, NC: Duke University Press, 2004).
50 See in particular, Jacques Lacan, *The Seminar of Jacques Lacan, Book III (1955–1956): The Psychoses*, trans. Russell Grigg (New York: Norton, 1993).

Chapter 3

1 Melanie Klein, "Notes on Some Schizoid Mechanisms," in *Envy and Gratitude and Other Works 1946–1963* (New York: The Free Press, 1975), 3. For an interesting discussion of the centrality of anxiety in

Klein's work, also in comparison to Lacan, see Lyndsey Stonebridge, "Anxiety in Klein: The Missing Witch's Letter," in *Reading Melanie Klein*, ed. Lyndsey Stonebridge and John Phillips (New York: Routledge, 1998), 190–202.

2 As Jacqueline Rose argues, this reputation for negativity was a key issue in Klein's early debate with Anna Freud and also a central reason for the rejection of Klein's work by many clinicians in the United States (in stark contrast to her significant influence on clinical work in Britain). See Jacqueline Rose, "Negativity in the Work of Melanie Klein," in *Reading Melanie Klein*, ed. Lyndsey Stonebridge and John Phillips (New York: Routledge, 1998), 126–59.

3 Melanie Klein, "The Origins of Transference," in *Envy and Gratitude and Other Works 1946–1963* (New York: The Free Press, 1975), 56.

4 Ibid.

5 Klein writes: "I recognized, in watching the constant struggle in the young infant's mental processes between an irrepressible urge to destroy as well as to save himself, to attack his objects and to preserve them, that primordial forces struggling with one another were at work" ("On the Development of Mental Functioning," in *Envy and Gratitude and Other Works 1946–1963* [New York: The Free Press, 1975], 236).

6 Ibid., 238–9.

7 Hanna Segal, *Introduction to the Work of Melanie Klein* (New York: Routledge, 1988).

8 See Eric Santner, *On the Psychotheology of Everyday Life: Reflections on Freud and Rosenzweig* (Chicago: University of Chicago Press, 2001). Žižek also uses the concept in several of his books. See, for example, Slavoj Žižek, *The Plague of Fantasies* (London: Verso, 1997), 112–14.

9 Melanie Klein, "The Early Development of Conscience in the Child," in *Love, Guilt and Reparation and Other Works 1921–1945* (New York: The Free Press, 1975), 257.

10 Jacques Lacan, *The Seminar of Jacques Lacan, Book II (1954–1955): The Ego in Freud's Theory and in the Technique of Psychoanalysis*, trans. Sylvana Tomaselli (New York: Norton, 1991), 85–6.

11 Ibid., 90.

12 Amy Allen, "Progress and the Death Drive," in *Transitional Subjects: Critical Theory and Object Relations*, ed. Amy Allen and Brian O'Connor (New York: Columbia University Press, 2019), 109–34, 127.

13 Ibid., 129.

14 Ibid.

15 C. Fred Alford notes a similar connection between Klein and Adorno, though his analysis focuses more on Kleinian aesthetics and also seems to pit Klein's notion of reparation against Adorno's (admittedly

underdeveloped) accounts of mimesis and genuine reconciliation, whereas I see them as more compatible. See Alford, *Melanie Klein and Critical Social Theory* (New Haven, CT: Yale University Press, 1989).
16 Theodor Adorno, *Negative Dialectics*, trans. E. B. Ashton (New York: Continuum, 1973), 362.
17 Theodor Adorno, "Sociology and Psychology (Part 2)," trans. Irving Wohlfarth, *New Left Review* 46 (1968): 79–97, 83.
18 Adorno, *Negative Dialectics*, passim.
19 Ibid., 150.
20 Theodor Adorno, *Minima Moralia: Reflections on a Damaged Life*, trans. E. F. N. Jephcott (London: Verso, 2005), 24.
21 See Theodor Adorno, *History and Freedom: Lectures 1964–1965*, trans. Rodney Livingstone (Cambridge: Polity, 2006).
22 Joel Whitebook, "The Marriage of Marx and Freud: Critical Theory and Psychoanalysis," in *The Cambridge Companion to Critical Theory*, ed. Fred Rush (Cambridge: Cambridge University Press, 2004), 74–102, 88.
23 Ibid., 88–9.
24 See the Introduction and Chapter 1 of Todd McGowan, *Capitalism and Desire: The Psychic Cost of Free Markets* (New York: Columbia University Press, 2016).
25 Jacques Lacan, *The Seminar of Jacques Lacan, Book X (1962–1963): Anxiety*, trans. A. R. Price (Cambridge: Polity, 2014), 264.
26 Ibid.
27 Ibid., 265.
28 Ibid.
29 Ibid., 265, 269.
30 Ibid., plates 1–2.
31 Ibid., 53–4.
32 See, for example, Melanie Klein, "Early Stages of the Oedipus Conflict," in *Love, Guilt and Reparation and Other Works 1921–1945* (New York: The Free Press, 1975), 187.
33 Max Horkheimer and Theodor Adorno, *Dialectic of Enlightenment: Philosophical Fragments*, trans. Edmund Jephcott (Stanford, CA: Stanford University Press, 2002), 26.
34 Ibid.
35 See, for instance, Hannah Arendt, *The Origins of Totalitarianism* (New York: Harcourt Brace Jovanovich, 1951).
36 Jacques Lacan, *The Seminar of Jacques Lacan, Book XI (1963–1964): The Four Fundamental Concepts of Psychoanalysis*, trans. Alan Sheridan (New York: Norton, 1998), 41.
37 Ibid.

38 On this point, see Judith Butler, "To Preserve the Life of the Other," Tanner Lectures (unpublished manuscript), Yale University, October 2016, 22ff.
39 Melanie Klein, "On the Theory of Anxiety and Guilt," in *Envy and Gratitude and Other Works 1946–1963* (New York: The Free Press, 1975), 25–42.
40 Ibid., 39.
41 Ibid.
42 Ibid.
43 Ibid., 39–40.
44 See Jacques Lacan, "The Phallic Phase and the Subjective Import of the Castration Complex," in *Feminine Sexuality: Jacques Lacan and the École Freudienne*, ed. Juliet Mitchell and Jacqueline Rose (New York: Norton, 1985), 99–122.
45 On this point, see also Rose, "Negativity in the Work of Melanie Klein"; and Catalina Bronstein, "Corporeality and Unconscious Phantasy: The Role of the Body in Kleinian Theory," in *The New Klein-Lacan Dialogues*, ed. Julia Borossa, Catalina Bronstein, and Claire Pajaczkowska (London: Karnac, 2015), 109–18.

Chapter 4

1 Sara Ahmed, *Willful Subjects* (Durham, NC: Duke University Press, 2014), 160, 246n45.
2 See Eve Sedgwick, "Paranoid Reading and Reparative Reading, or, You're So Paranoid, You Probably Think This Essay Is About You," in *Touching Feeling: Affect, Pedagogy, Performativity* (Durham, NC: Duke University Press, 2003), 123–51.
3 Lee Edelman, *No Future: Queer Theory and the Death Drive* (Durham, NC: Duke University Press, 2004); Lauren Berlant and Lee Edelman, *Sex, or the Unbearable* (Durham, NC: Duke University Press, 2014).
4 Rita Felski, *The Limits of Critique* (Chicago: University of Chicago Press, 2015); *Critique and Postcritique*, ed. Elizabeth Anker and Rita Felski (Durham, NC: Duke University Press, 2017); Heather Love, "Close but Not Deep: Literary Ethics and the Descriptive Turn," *New Literary History* 41, no. 2 (2010): 371–91.
5 I want to thank Prathna Lor for having underlined this point for me.
6 Sara Ahmed, *The Promise of Happiness* (Durham, NC: Duke University Press, 2010); Love, "Close but Not Deep"; Berlant and Edelman, *Sex, or the Unbearable*, 36–61; Ann Cvetkovich,

    Depression: A Public Feeling (Durham, NC: Duke University Press, 2012); Sianne Ngai, *Ugly Feelings* (Cambridge, MA: Harvard University Press, 2005).
7   David Eng and Shinhee Han, "A Dialogue on Racial Melancholia," in *Loss: The Politics of Mourning*, ed. David Eng and David Kazanjian (Berkeley, CA: University of California Press, 2003), 343–71; David Eng, *The Feeling of Kinship: Queer Liberalism and the Racialization of Intimacy* (Durham, NC: Duke University Press, 2010).
8   Angela Davis, *Women, Race & Class* (New York: Vintage, 1983); Audre Lorde, *Sister Outsider: Essays and Speeches* (Berkeley, CA: Crossing Press, 2007); Gloria Anzaldúa, *Borderlands/La Frontera: The New Mestiza* (San Francisco, CA: Aunt Lute Books, 1987); bell hooks, *Feminist Theory: From Margin to Center* (New York: Routledge, 2015).
9   Sedgwick, "Paranoid Reading and Reparative Reading," 130–1.
10 Jacques Lacan, *The Seminar of Jacques Lacan, Book VII (1959–1960): The Ethics of Psychoanalysis*, trans. Dennis Porter (New York: Norton, 1992).
11 Ibid., 278.
12 Kathleen Stewart, *Ordinary Affects* (Durham, NC: Duke University Press, 2007); Lauren Berlant, *Cruel Optimism* (Durham, NC: Duke University Press, 2011); Cvetkovich, *Depression*.
13 Carl Schmitt, *The Concept of the Political*, trans. George Schwab (Chicago: University of Chicago Press, 1996), 58.
14 Sigmund Freud, "Civilization and Its Discontents (1930)," in *The Standard Edition of the Complete Psychological Works of Sigmund Freud*, vol. XXI, ed. James Strachey (London: Vintage Press, 2001), 57–146, 111.
15 Maurice Florence, "Foucault," in Michel Foucault, *Essential Works of Foucault, Volume 2: Aesthetics, Method, and Epistemology*, ed. James Faubion (New York: The New Press, 1998), 459–64, 461.
16 Ibid.
17 Ibid., 462.
18 For a helpful rearticulation of psychoanalytic drive theory along these lines, see Benjamin Fong, *Death and Mastery: Psychoanalytic Drive Theory and the Subject of Late Capitalism* (New York: Columbia University Press, 2016).
19 For a more detailed discussion of the connections between Lacan and Foucault, see Mari Ruti, *The Ethics of Opting Out: Queer Theory's Defiant Subjects* (New York: Columbia University Press, 2017), 162–8.
20 Jacques Derrida, "Cogito and the History of Madness," in *Writing and Difference*, trans. Alan Bass (Chicago: University of Chicago Press, 1978), 31–63.

21 See Michel Foucault, "Critical Theory/Intellectual History," in *Critique and Power: Recasting the Foucault/Habermas Debate*, ed. Michael Kelly (Cambridge, MA: MIT Press, 1994), 109–38, 126–7.
22 Jacques Lacan, *The Seminar of Jacques Lacan, Book II (1954–1955): The Ego in Freud's Theory and in the Technique of Psychoanalysis*, trans. Sylvana Tomaselli (New York: Norton, 1991), 272.
23 Axel Honneth, *The Struggle for Recognition: The Moral Grammar of Social Conflicts*, trans. Joel Anderson (Cambridge, MA: MIT Press, 1995).
24 I'm grateful to Nicole Yokum, who is currently working on a dissertation on critical theory and affect theory, for bringing this connection to my attention.
25 Mari Ruti, *The Call of Character: Living a Life Worth Living* (New York: Columbia University Press, 2013), 141–58.
26 Ngai, *Ugly Feelings*.
27 See Melanie Klein, "Envy and Gratitude," in *Envy and Gratitude and Other Works 1946–1963* (New York: The Free Press, 1975), 181.
28 Ibid., 202.
29 Ibid., 181.
30 Ibid., 187.
31 Ibid.
32 Jacques Lacan, *The Seminar of Jacques Lacan, Book X (1962–1963): Anxiety*, trans. A. R. Price (Cambridge: Polity, 2014), 14.
33 Teresa Brennan, *The Transmission of Affect* (Ithaca, NY: Cornell University Press, 2004).
34 Melanie Klein, "Notes on Some Schizoid Mechanisms," in *Envy and Gratitude and Other Works 1946–1963* (New York: The Free Press, 1975), 22.
35 Michael Feldman, "Splitting and Projective Identification," in *Clinical Lectures on Klein and Bion*, ed. Robin Anderson (New York: Routledge, 1992), 74–88, 78.
36 Ibid., 82–3.
37 Jacques Lacan, *The Seminar of Jacques Lacan, Book VII (1959–1960): The Ethics of Psychoanalysis*, trans. Dennis Porter (New York: Norton, 1997), 106.
38 Ibid.
39 Jacques Lacan, *The Seminar of Jacques Lacan, Book I (1953–1954): Freud's Papers on Technique*, trans. John Forrester (New York: Norton, 1988), 68.
40 Ibid.
41 Ibid., 85.
42 Ibid.
43 Ibid., 68.

44 Alain Badiou, "What is Love?," in *Sexuation*, ed. Renata Salecl (Durham, NC: Duke University Press, 2000), 263–81.
45 Slavoj Žižek, *The Parallax View* (Cambridge, MA: MIT Press, 2006), 310.
46 For a more detailed argument to this effect, see Amy Allen, "Foucault, Psychoanalysis, and Critique: Two Aspects of Problematization," *Angelaki: Journal of the Theoretical Humanities* 23, no. 2 (2018): 170–86.
47 Melanie Klein, "Early Stages of the Oedipus Conflict," in *Love, Guilt and Reparation and Other Works 1921–1945* (New York: The Free Press, 1975), 187.
48 Melanie Klein, "Symposium on Child Analysis," in *Love, Guilt and Reparation and Other Works 1921–1945* (New York: The Free Press, 1975), 165.
49 Ibid., 167.

Chapter 5

1 Melanie Klein, "Mourning and Its Relation to Manic-Depressive States," in *Love, Guilt and Reparation and Other Works 1921–1945* (New York: The Free Press, 1975), 353.
2 See Melanie Klein, "Envy and Gratitude," in *Envy and Gratitude and Other Works 1946–1963* (New York: The Free Press, 1975), 192.
3 Melanie Klein, "The Oedipus Complex in the Light of Early Anxieties," in *Love, Guilt and Reparation and Other Works 1921–1945* (New York: The Free Press, 1975), 410.
4 Melanie Klein, "The Theory of Anxiety and Guilt," in *Envy and Gratitude and Other Works 1946–1963* (New York: The Free Press, 1975), 36.
5 Ibid., 35–6.
6 Ibid., 36.
7 Melanie Klein, "Love, Guilt and Reparation," in *Love, Guilt and Reparation and Other Works 1921–1945* (New York: The Free Press, 1975), 308.
8 Ibid., 316n1.
9 Ibid., 340.
10 Jacques Lacan, *The Seminar of Jacques Lacan, Book VIII (1960–1961): Transference*, trans. Bruce Fink (Cambridge: Polity, 2015), 148.
11 See, for instance, Alain Badiou with Nicholas Truong, *In Praise of Love*, trans. Peter Bush (New York: The New Press, 2012); Alain Badiou with Fabien Tarby, *Philosophy and the Event*, trans.

Louise Burchill (Cambridge: Polity, 2014); Slavoj Žižek, *Event: A Philosophical Journey Through a Concept* (New York: Melville House, 2014); and Todd McGowan, *Capitalism and Desire: The Psychic Cost of Free Markets* (New York: Columbia University Press, 2016).
12 See Lauren Berlant, *Cruel Optimism* (Durham, NC: Duke University Press, 2011).
13 Roland Barthes, *A Lover's Discourse: Fragments*, trans. Richard Howard (New York: Hill & Wang, 2010), 25.
14 Mari Ruti, *The Singularity of Being: Lacan and the Immortal Within* (New York: Fordham University Press, 2012).
15 Jacques Lacan, *The Seminar of Jacques Lacan, Book VII (1959–1960): The Ethics of Psychoanalysis*, trans. Dennis Porter (New York: Norton, 1997), 118.
16 Bruce Fink, *Lacan on Love: An Exploration of Lacan's Seminar VIII, Transference* (Cambridge: Polity, 2016).
17 Ibid., ix.
18 Jacques Lacan, *The Seminar of Jacques Lacan, Book XI (1963–1964): The Four Fundamental Concepts of Psychoanalysis*, trans. Alan Sheridan (New York: Norton, 1998), 263–76.
19 Lacan, *Seminar VIII*, 137–8.
20 Ibid., 138.
21 Ibid., 39–40.
22 Ibid., 154.
23 Ruti, *The Singularity of Being*; Mari Ruti, *Distillations: Theory, Ethics, Affect* (New York: Bloomsbury Press, 2018).
24 Lacan, *Seminar VIII*, 163.
25 Ibid., 154.
26 Ibid., 157.
27 Melanie Klein, "Some Theoretical Conclusions Regarding the Emotional Life of the Infant," in *Envy and Gratitude and Other Works 1946–1963* (New York: The Free Press, 1975), 64.
28 Judith Butler, "To Preserve the Life of the Other," Tanner Lectures (unpublished manuscript), Yale University, October 2016, 24.
29 Melanie Klein, "A Contribution to the Psychogenesis of Manic-Depressive States," in *Love, Guilt and Reparation and Other Works 1921–1945* (New York: The Free Press, 1975), 288.
30 Klein, "Some Theoretical Conclusions Regarding the Emotional Life of the Infant," 67.
31 Lacan, *Seminar VIII*, 143.
32 Ibid.
33 Ibid., 144.
34 Ibid., 397; emphasis added.
35 See, for instance, Judith Butler, *Giving an Account of Oneself* (New York: Fordham University Press, 2005).

36 Berlant, *Cruel Optimism*.
37 Lacan, *Seminar VII*, 184.
38 Ibid.
39 Ibid., 185.
40 Ibid., 185–6.
41 Ibid., 186.
42 Slavoj Žižek, "Neighbors and Other Monsters: A Plea for Ethical Violence," in Slavoj Žižek, Eric Santner, and Kenneth Reinhard, *The Neighbor: Three Inquiries in Political Theology* (Chicago: University of Chicago Press, 2005), 134–90, 162.
43 Angela Davis, *Are Prisons Obsolete?* (New York: Seven Stories Press, 2011).
44 David McIvor, *Mourning in America: Race and the Politics of Loss* (Ithaca, NY: Cornell University Press, 2016). See also Michael Rustin, "Klein on Human Nature," in *Other Banalities: Melanie Klein Revisited*, ed. Jon Mills (New York: Routledge, 2006), 25–44, and David Eng, "Reparations and the Human," *Columbia Journal of Gender and Law* 21, no. 2 (2011): 561–83.
45 McIvor, *Mourning in America*, 143.
46 Ibid., 149.

Chapter 6

1 Friedrich Nietzsche, *The Gay Science*, trans. Walter Kaufmann (New York: Vintage, 1974); Michel Foucault, *The Care of the Self: Volume 3 of The History of Sexuality*, trans. Robert Hurley (New York: Vintage, 1988).
2 Jacques Lacan, *The Seminar of Jacques Lacan, Book VII (1959–1960): The Ethics of Psychoanalysis*, trans. Dennis Porter (New York: Norton, 1992), 106.
3 Ibid.
4 Ibid.
5 Ibid., 106–7.
6 Ibid., 107.
7 Ibid.
8 Ibid.
9 Melanie Klein, "Love, Guilt and Reparation," in *Love, Guilt and Reparation and Other Works 1921–1945* (New York: The Free Press, 1975), 306–43; Melanie Klein, "Mourning and Its Relation to Manic-Depressive States," in *Love, Guilt and Reparation and Other Works 1921–1945* (New York: The Free Press, 1975), 344–69.

10 See Sigmund Freud, "Mourning and Melancholia (1917)," in *The Standard Edition of the Complete Psychological Works of Sigmund Freud*, vol. XIV, ed. James Strachey (London: Vintage, 2001), 237–58, 245–9.
11 Sigmund Freud, "The Ego and the Id (1923)," in *The Standard Edition of the Complete Psychological Works of Sigmund Freud*, vol. XIX, ed. James Strachey (London: Vintage, 2001), 1–66, 28.
12 Ibid., 29.
13 Ibid.
14 Klein, "Mourning and Its Relation to Manic-Depressive States," 345.
15 Mari Ruti, *The Call of Character: Living a Life Worth Living* (New York: Columbia University Press, 2013).
16 Melanie Klein, "On the Development of Mental Functioning," in *Envy and Gratitude and Other Works 1946–1963* (New York: The Free Press, 1975), 245.
17 Thomas Ogden, *The Primitive Edge of Experience* (Lanham, MD: Rowman and Littlefield, 2004), 29.
18 Ibid., 30.
19 Ibid.
20 Klein, "Love, Guilt and Reparation," 311–12n1.
21 Melanie Klein, "Envy and Gratitude," in *Envy and Gratitude and Other Works 1946–1963* (New York: The Free Press, 1975), 201.
22 Melanie Klein, "The Origins of Transference," in *Envy and Gratitude and Other Works 1946–1963* (New York: The Free Press, 1975), 56.
23 Klein, "Envy and Gratitude," 220–1.
24 Hanna Segal, "A Psychoanalytic Approach to Aesthetics," in *Reading Melanie Klein*, ed. Lyndsey Stonebridge and John Phillips (New York: Routledge, 1998), 203–22.
25 Ibid., 219.
26 Joel Whitebook, *Freud: An Intellectual Biography* (Cambridge: Cambridge University Press, 2017), 349–50.
27 Ibid., 121.
28 Ibid., 118.
29 Ibid., 112.
30 Ibid., 114.
31 Mari Ruti, *The Singularity of Being: Lacan and the Immortal Within* (New York: Fordham University Press, 2012).
32 Whitebook, *Freud*, 118.
33 See Jacques Lacan, *The Seminar of Jacques Lacan, Book XXIII (1975–1976): The Sinthome*, trans. A. R. Price (Cambridge: Polity, 2016).
34 Segal, "A Psychoanalytic Approach to Aesthetics," 219.
35 Ibid., 208–9.

36 Theodor Adorno, *Minima Moralia: Reflections on a Damaged Life*, trans. E. F. N. Jephcott (London: Verso, 2005), 15.
37 Theodor Adorno, *History and Freedom: Lectures 1964–1965*, ed. Rolf Tiedemann (Cambridge: Polity, 2006), 129.
38 Theodor Adorno, "The Actuality of Philosophy," *Telos* 31 (1977): 120–33, 127.
39 Ibid., 130.
40 Adorno, *History and Freedom*, 134.
41 Roberto Harari, *How James Joyce Made His Name: A Reading of the Final Lacan*, trans. Luke Thurston (New York: Other Press, 2002), 141.
42 Michel Foucault, *History of Madness*, ed. Jean Khalfa (Abingdon: Routledge, 2006).
43 Ibid., 28.
44 For a brilliant example of this reading which is also in other respects extremely compelling, see Lynne Huffer, *Mad for Foucault: Rethinking the Foundations of Queer Theory* (New York: Columbia University Press, 2010).
45 Gilles Deleuze and Félix Guattari, *Anti-Oedipus: Capitalism and Schizophrenia*, trans. Robert Hurley, Mark Seem, and Helen Lane (London: Bloomsbury Press, 2013).
46 Amy Allen, "Feminism, Foucault, and the Critique of Reason: Re-reading the History of Madness," *Foucault Studies* 16 (2013): 15–31.
47 Ibid., 25.
48 This theme runs through Butler's writings on ethics. See, for instance, Butler's *Precarious Life: The Powers of Mourning and Violence* (New York: Verso, 2004); *Giving an Account of Oneself* (New York: Fordham University Press, 2005); *Frames of War: When Is Life Grievable?* (New York: Verso, 2009); and *Dispossession: The Performative in the Political*, with Athena Athanasiou (New York: Polity, 2013).
49 Klein, "Envy and Gratitude," 233.
50 See R. D. Hinshelwood, "Melanie Klein and Countertransference: A Note on Some Archival Material," *Psychoanalysis and History* 10, no. 1 (2008): 95–113.

Chapter 7

1 See, for example, Jürgen Habermas, *The Philosophical Discourse of Modernity: Twelve Lectures*, trans. Frederick Lawrence (Cambridge, MA: MIT Press, 1987), 294–326.

2. Even though Habermas's early work contains a problematically rationalist reading of Freud, it's a substantial engagement. See Jürgen Habermas, *Knowledge and Human Interests*, trans. Jeremy Shapiro (Boston: Beacon Press, 1971). For an insightful discussion of Habermas's break with psychoanalysis and its implications for his critical theory, see Joel Whitebook, *Perversion and Utopia: A Study in Psychoanalysis and Critical Theory* (Cambridge, MA: MIT Press, 1996).
3. Axel Honneth, "The Work of Negativity: A Recognition-Theoretical Revision of Psychoanalysis," in *The I in We: Studies in the Theory of Recognition*, trans. Joseph Ganahl (Cambridge: Polity, 2012), 193–200.
4. Ibid.
5. Judith Butler, "To Preserve the Life of the Other," Tanner Lectures (unpublished manuscript), Yale University, October 2016, 14–15.
6. Ibid., 20.
7. Ibid., 22.
8. Noëlle McAfee, *Fear of Breakdown: Politics and Psychoanalysis* (New York: Columbia University Press, 2019).
9. I address this concern in my *Between Levinas and Lacan: Self, Other, Ethics* (New York: Bloomsbury Press, 2015) and *The Ethics of Opting Out: Queer Theory's Defiant Subjects* (New York: Columbia University Press, 2017).
10. McAfee, *Fear of Breakdown*, 40.
11. See Amy Allen, "Emancipation without Utopia: Subjection, Modernity, and the Normative Claims of Feminist Critical Theory," *Hypatia* 30, no. 3 (2015): 513–29.
12. Bruce Fink, *The Lacanian Subject: Between Language and Jouissance* (Princeton, NJ: Princeton University Press, 1995), 78.
13. Jacques Lacan, *The Seminar of Jacques Lacan, Book VII (1959–1960): The Ethics of Psychoanalysis*, trans. Dennis Porter (New York: Norton, 1992), 183–4, 207–8.
14. Sigmund Freud, "The Psychotherapy of Hysteria from Studies on Hysteria (1893–95)," in *The Standard Edition of the Complete Psychological Works of Sigmund Freud*, vol. II, ed. James Strachey (London: Vintage, 2001), 253–305, 305.
15. Jacques Lacan, *The Seminar of Jacques Lacan, Book II (1954–1955): The Ego in Freud's Theory and in the Technique of Psychoanalysis*, trans. Sylvana Tomaselli (New York: Norton, 1991), 326.
16. Eric Santner, *On the Psychotheology of Everyday Life: Reflections on Freud and Rosenzweig* (Chicago: University of Chicago Press, 2001), 7.
17. Paul Eisenstein and Todd McGowan, *Rupture: On the Emergence of the Political* (Evanston, IL: Northwestern University Press, 2012), 36.

18 Sara Ahmed, *Differences that Matter: Feminist Theory and Postmodernism* (Cambridge: Cambridge University Press, 2004), 95–118; Sara Ahmed, *Willful Subjects* (Durham, NC: Duke University Press, 2014), 160, 246; Maggie Nelson, *The Argonauts* (Minneapolis: Graywolf Press, 2015), 75–6.
19 Michael Hardt and Antonio Negri, *Multitude: War and Democracy in the Age of Empire* (New York: Penguin, 2004), xv; Michael Hardt and Antonio Negri, *Commonwealth* (Cambridge, MA: Belknap Press, 2009).
20 See, for instance, Edward Said, *Culture and Imperialism* (New York: Vintage, 1994); Homi Bhabha, *The Location of Culture* (Abingdon: Routledge, 2004); and Paul Gilroy, *The Black Atlantic: Modernity and Double Consciousness* (London: Verso, 1993).
21 For my critique of Žižek, see my *Between Levinas and Lacan*.
22 Ruti, *The Ethics of Opting Out*.

INDEX

Adorno, Theodor W. 72, 95, 99, 107, 176–7, 189
affect 95
  repression, absence 121
affect theory 95, 97, 113, 212–13
  inflection (Foucault) 106
  problem 103–4
ágalma/agálmata 139
agency, demolition 182
aggression 130–1, 151, 165, 186
  alleviation 72
  anxiety, connection 70
  anxiety, mutual reinforcement (elaboration) 71
  centrality, emphasis 160
  destructiveness 65
  external causes 89
  importance 151–2
  instincts 70
  perception (Freud) 59
  primacy 2, 7, 86
  sublimation 159, 165
  targets 90
aggressiveness
  ineradicability, recognition 194
  share 106–7
aggressive phantasies 131
aggressivity 151, 164
  display 155
  level, elevation 69
  palliative 152
ahistorical structuralism 122
Ahmed, Sara 95, 97, 206
Alcibiades 139–41, 143, 147, 172
alienation
  acceptance 203
  forms 115
almightiness, fomentation 79
ambivalence 191
  types 142
ambivalence/ambiguity, toleration/tolerance 28, 120, 130, 133
amor fati type 29
amorous event, ambivalence 143
anal phase, potty training 46–7
analysand 159, 184–5
  enabling 26–7
  love/care 26
analysand, creativity 167
  enhancement 164
analysis, goal 8
  opposition 26–7
analysis. *See* psychoanalysis
  objective 21
analyst, role 185
analytic transference 86
anatomy, destiny (contrast) 52
annihilation, fear 2–3
antagonisms, elimination 212
anthropological universals
  envisioning 108, 111
  rejection 107
Antigone, reading/presentation 100, 103
antinormativity 103, 105–6, 197
anti-ontology 58–9
anxiety 63, 81, 131, 186

INDEX

absence 27
admiration 92
aggression, connection 70
aggression, mutual reinforcement (elaboration) 71
alleviation 84–5
analysis (Lacan) 93
common-place 78
conception (Klein) 117
creativity, connection 117
depression, coexistence 65
depressive response 84
diminishment 166–7
external causes 89, 91
generation 47
intrapsychic phenomenon 91
processing, notion 85
response 93
role 24
seminar 85–6
surplus anxiety 93
theorization (Lacan) 77
toleration, capacity 6
valorization 116, 118
Anzaldúa, Gloria 97
archaic mother 37
Arendt, Hannah 83
artistic beauty 55
authenticity, degree 48
autonomy 104, 209

bad breast
demonization 64
part-object 68
Badiou, Alain 95, 100, 133, 147, 205
amorous event 143
event theorization/ understanding 109–11
badness, representations 51
Balint, Michael
critique (Lacan) 39–40
doctrine, contradiction 40

Barthes, Roland 19, 134
being
nothingness/emptiness 89–90
singularity, representation 135–6
being-toward-death 67
Benhabib, Seyla 189
Benjamin, Jessica 113
Benjamin, Walter 95, 177
Berlant, Lauren 97, 103
Beyond the Pleasure Principle (Freud) 168, 202
Bhabha, Homi 208
biological essentialism, endorsement (Klein) 3
biological reductionism 92
biologism 123
dangers 122
Bion, Wilfred 47
biopolitical forces 90–1
biopolitics 96, 112–13
Bluest Eye, The (Morrison) 13
body
explanation 1
openings 47
bourgeois capitalism 114–15
bourgeois subjectivity 107
breast
deprivation, experience 88
discussion (Klein) 52
fantasy 49
infant asymmetrical dependence 120
purity 48
splitting 4
spoiling 119
Brennan, Teresa 121
brute reality, realm 43
Butler, Judith 108, 142, 183

capitalism 96, 112, 187
Capitalism and Desire (McGowan) 75–6
capitalism, logic (replication) 76

caregivers, dependence 53
castration
   acceptance 169, 203
   anxiety, causes 47
   image 80
   lack-in-being, relationship 20–1
   symbolic castration, result 59–60
catastrophe, avoidance 72–3, 75
character, construction 162–3
che vuoi 47, 81
childhood, paradise 54
children
   anxiety, blame 66
   defining, tendency (Balint) 41
   formative expediencies, idealization 33
   insertion 42
   persecutory fantasy 66
   perversion 40
   phantasy 124
   play, interpretations (Klein) 124
   primary object, relationship 68
   real-life other, relationship 49
   subjective structure 112
   superego, harshness 127
Civilization and Its Discontents (Freud) 151
coldness 114–15, 183–4
communication 104
complexity, gain 65
concrete mother, immediacy 51
concretion (Klein) 123
conflict
   elimination 191
   tolerance 28
conflictual drive impulses, existence (toleration) 9
consciousness
   subject, truth 15
   unhappiness 177
consensus building 195–6

constitutional factors 24–5
constitutive deformation/dislocation 115
constitutive lack, negation 91
context-specific factors, predictability 90
context-transcendent ethics 209
contextualism 209
continental philosophy 95
corruption 134
countertransference 186
creative activity 67
creativeness, manifestation 166
creativity 84
   anxiety, connection 117
   lack, relationship 169–70
   loss 169
   paranoid-schizoid position, value 61
   precondition 163
   psychosis, relationship 174
   source 64
critical social theory (Frankfurt School) 23
culture, erasure 208
Cvetkovich, Ann 97, 103

das Ding (the Thing) 123, 141, 172–3
   central place 49
   characterization (Lacan) 54
   context 51
   detail 52
   dignity 171–2
   loss 7–8, 14, 34
   mother, body (placement) 50
   murder 13
   nonobject 170–1
   partial substitute 56
   replacement 122–3
   retroactive fantasy 31, 57
   sublimation, connection 158
Dasein 67, 92

Davis, Angela 97, 154
death drive 59, 91–2, 108, 128
　absence 61
　action 67
　beginning 60
　centrality/ineliminability 28
　elimination 178
　energy, harnessing 164
　equivalence (Klein) 68
　expression 28–9, 60
　function, differences 111
　fundamental fantasy,
　　relationship 29
　impact 16
　importance 153, 164
　internal/external manifestations
　　67
　internal operation, defenses 45
　jouissance, uncoupling (Lacan)
　　58
　materialization 100–1
　persistence 72
　primacy 7
　recognition/reckoning 194
　sublimation 102
　theory 190
　undead 70
　valorization 20
death, valorization (Lacan) 58
de Beauvoir, Simone 92
deformation, acceptance 169, 203
Deleuze, Gilles 13, 180, 182
deliberative ethics 198
deliberative politics 199
democratic theory, psychoanalytic
　intervention 199
dependence, asymmetrical
　relations 120
depression 155
　anxiety, coexistence 65
depressive anxiety 117
　action 69
　complication 65
　distinction 63
　emergence 64
　guilt, relationship 87
　impact 64
depressive feelings 131
depressive position 1, 27–8, 73,
　84, 95, 130
　achievement 168–9
　approach 24
　commentary 66
　examination 30
　failure 175
　guilt, relationship 5
　melancholy strain 30
　mourning/melancholia, linkage
　　162
　paranoid-schizoid position,
　　relationship 5
　working through/overcoming
　　5–6
　working through, subject
　　formation (impact) 6
derailment 129, 134
Derrida, Jacques 19, 110
desire
　annihilation 111
　frustration 53
　functions 147
　sentimentalization 146
　workings, *objet a*
　　(explanations) 145
destiny
　anatomy, contrast 52
　destiny-defining fulcrum 50
destructiveness 193, 195
　healing, reparation (usage) 117
　mitigation 99
Dialectic of Enlightenment
　(Horkheimer/Adorno) 82
die Not des Lebens (Freud) 54, 58
difference 192
　toleration/tolerance 130, 133
　violence 73

disharmony, elimination 191
disintegration, goal 16
dislocation, forms 115
diversity, non-totalizing/open-
    ended togetherness 74
drive energy, too-muchness 54

Edelman, Lee 95–6, 100, 182
Eden, Christian notion
    (replication) 55–6
ego
    aversion (Lacan) 20
    burning off 15
    core 84
    critique (Lacan) 15–16, 26
    destructive impulses,
        integration 163
    development, analysand ability
        184
    formation 17–18
    imaginary ego, narcissism/
        inauthenticity 10
    inception 18–19
    integration 9, 87, 192
    libido, relationship 15
    mirror stage, connection 18–19
    resistances, dissolving 15
    strengthening 8–9, 130
    term, change 30
Ego and the Id, The (Freud) 161–2
ego psychology 10, 26
    critique (Lacan) 14
Einstein, Albert 144
Eisenstein, Paul 41, 109–10, 205
End of Progress, The 19
energy, excess (impact) 58–9
Eng, David 212
Enlightenment 19, 100, 106
envy 118, 186
    experience 120
Envy and Gratitude 53
episteme, term (usage) 108–9, 111,
    201

erection, loss 77
eros
    binding power, usage 68
    social bond 86
erotic drive, impact 36–7
erotic stance 68
erotogenic zones (Freud) 47
Erscheinung 173
essentialism, dangers 122
ethical standards 188
ethics
    context-transcendent notion
        205
    definition 101
ethnic studies 206
Europe, fascism/Holocaust
    (descent) 74–5
event, account (Badiou) 101
evolution, process 109
excessive autonomy 19
existentialism 116
external/internal danger-situations,
    persistence 88
external objects, internal objects
    (contrast) 38
external other 47–8
external persecutory object 64
external stressors, escape 118

failure, repetition 41–2
Fairbairn, Ronald 63, 112
Fanon, Frantz 12, 15
fantasy 22–3
    fabrications 34–5
    life 78
    notion (Lacan) 21–2
    relationships 35
    retroactive fantasy 44
fear
    decrease 87
    hatred, reinforcement 71
Fear of Breakdown (McAfee) 195
feeling, management 122

Feldman, Michael 122
Felski, Rita 96
feminist theory 206
Fink, Bruce 137, 201
Forst, Rainer 189
Fort-da, impossibility 80–1
Foucault, Michel 106–11, 179–80
foundationalism 209
fragility/fracture, lines
    (illumination) 179
fragmentation, experience 176
Frankfurt School 9, 19, 89, 95,
    104, 113
    critical social theory 23, 182,
    187, 195
    critical theorists, impact 33–4
    psychoanalysis reception 107
Fraser, Nancy 189
free association 84
freedom, conceptualizations 116
French poststructuralism 58–9,
    95–6
French revolution, ideals 209
Freud, Anna 127, 193
Freud, Sigmund 2, 195
    description (Whitebook) 168
    insight 28
    Oedipal story 18
    paradigm, death drive 59
    primary narcissism conception 3
    psychosexual development,
        model 17
    Whitebook reading 160
fundamental fantasy 21
    death drive, relationship 29
fusion 33
    biological characteristic 35
    dialectic 81–2
    fantasy 57
    idea 46
    infantile expression 36
    love, intersubjectivity
        (generation) 40
    moments 36
    mother-infant fusion,
        idealization 82
    primary fusion (Winnicott) 34
    psychoanalytic story,
        acceptance (Klein) 82
    theory (Honneth) 54
    threatening aspects 82
    undifferentiated fusion 45

Galileo 144
Gay Science, The (Nietzsche) 176
gender discrimination 79
genocide, absolute integration 73
Gilroy, Paul 208
good breast
    introjection 144–5
    loss 162
    purity, phantasy 163
    role 184
good life 173
goodness, representations 51
good object, internalization 56
gratification, source 64
greed
    experience 120
    involvement 118–19
Guattari, Félix 180, 182
guilt 131
    depressive anxiety, impact 64
    depressive anxiety, relationship
        87
    depressive position,
        relationship 5
    Nietzschean/Freudian model 87

Habermas, Jürgen 113, 188, 195
Harari, Roberto 178
Hardt, Michael 206–7
hate 186
    anxiety/guilt, impact 66–7
hatred
    experience 120
    fear, reinforcement 71
    healing, reparation (usage) 117

Hegel, Georg Wilhelm Friedrich 23, 207
Heidegger, Martin 67, 92
heteropatriarchical symbolic order 101–2
heteropatriarchy, social problems (personification) 83
heterosexism 112
heterosexuality, image 78
historical progress, Eurocentric narrative 200
historicism, question 106–7
History of Madness (Foucault) 110, 179–81
homophobia 211
  social problems, personification 83
Honneth, Axel 34–5, 39, 189
  challenges 36
hooks, bell 97
Horkheimer, Max 95, 189
human beings
  animals, distinction (Lacan) 41
  becoming 1
  deformity, idea 71
  image 38
  masculine character, creation 82
  negative/realistic view, adoption (necessity) 72
  wrong form 71–2
human life
  affective valences 197
  prelapsarian vision 34
  starting point 46
  status quo 41–2
  tragedies 14
human nature
  features 111
  negative assessment 66
human subjectivity/social relationships 99

ideality, loss 196–7
idealization 43–4, 102, 191
  defenses 64
  persecutory defenses 126
  phantasies, destructiveness (analysis) 198
  skepticism 44
idealization/demonization, dualities 142
identification, reparative trajectory 194
identity, nonidentity 74
id, impulses 127
imaginary ego, narcissism/inauthenticity 10
immanent transcendence 188
immortality, desire 160–1
infancy, paradise 54
infantile experience, fusion basis 36
infants
  breast introjection 4–5
  breast perception (paranoid-schizoid position) 48
  inferior power/asymmetrical dependence 120
  object relation 38
  psychic experiences, dissociation 25
  relationships 23–4
inhuman, allusion 41–2
injunction to enjoy, analysis (Žižek) 125
innate aggressivity 24
inner turmoil, feeling 69
instinct, term (usage) 59–60
instinctual endowments 106–7
instinctual reductionism 92
integrated ego 28
  desire 8
intellectual beauty 55
internal ambivalence 192
internal anxiety 88

internal differentiation, gain 65
internal good object,
    establishment 167
internalized introjections, basis 6
internal objects, external objects
    alignment 127
    contrast 38
internal psychic conflicts 74
intersubjective 90
    intrapsychic, relationship/
        alignment 52, 90–1, 149–50
    suspicions 56–7
    term, usage 23
    version, counterpoint 33–4
intersubjectivity
    account, absence (Lacan) 47–8
    generation 40
    importance 76
    sense 11
intrapsychic 90, 113
    dynamics 56–7, 190
    intersubjective, relationship/
        alignment 52, 90–1, 149–50
    priority 56–7
introjection 102
    dynamic 64
    process 72–3
Irigaray, Luce 19
irrationality, forces 188
ISIS, fundamentalism 196

jouissance 10, 14, 33, 101, 134
    acceptance 29
    death drive, uncoupling
        (Lacan) 58
    drive 42
    evil jouissance 156
    focus 173–4
    heart 152
    love, thunderbolt 137–8
    loving 152–3
    signifier, commingling 175
    site 46

surplus 78
understanding (Lacan) 61
jouissance in the Other 47

Kierkegaard, Søren 92
Kjar, Ruth 171
Klein, Melanie
    attitude, divergence 8
    breast, splitting 4
    position theory 2
    resonance 28
    subject formation 1
Kohlberg, Lawrence 189
Kristeva, Juila 18, 19, 165, 167
    lack-in-being, loss (connection)
        31

Lacan, Jacques
    attitude, divergence 8
    constructivism 92
    contextualization 20
    death, valorization 58
    ego critique 15–16
    ego psychology critique 14
    ethics 153
    interpretation 29
    mentality, *amor fati* type 29
    mirror stage 5
    narrative 10
    objet a (analysis) 147
    objet a (importance) 144
    paradigm 16–17
    perspective, sense 6–7
    subject, melancholy 8
    thinking, complexity 57–8
Lacan on Love (Fink) 137
lack 116
    acceptance 169, 203
    constitutive lack, negation 91
    creativity, relationship 169–70
    deprivation 76–7
    embryonic state 13
    intimation 13

primary site 171
suffering frequency 31
lack-in-being 27, 89–90
   castration, relationship 20–1
   constitutive lack-in-being 79
   cure, absence 23
   introduction 13
   loss, connection 31
language acquisition 11
Levinas, Emmanuel 19
libido 112
   ego, relationship 15
life
   antithesis 203
   emergency 58
   life/death, conflict 3
   register, engagement 72
lines of fragility 110
Loewald, Hans 2, 10
Lorde, Audre 97
loss
   emphasis 30
   experience 7, 176
   inevitability 126–8
   lack-in-being, connection 31
   mourning, capacity 196
   reality 212
   suffering frequency 31
lost paradise, fantasy 55–6
love 129
   absence 86
   adulation 132
   ambivalence 132
   capacity 68
   conception, idealization 86
   discussion 55–6
   love/support/gratification, relationship 26–7
   mature love 142
   paradigm (Klein) 38–9
   paternal/maternal love 138
   reduction, anxiety/guilt (impact) 66–7
   relationships 149–50
   romance, distinction 133
   source 64
   thunderbolt 137–8
   unpredictability, impact 135
love/hate, dualities 142
Love, Heather 97

madness 180
   glorification/absence 181
   valorization 20
maladaptation 177
   acceptance 169, 203
manic reparation 30
Marasco, Robyn 168
Marcuse, Herbert 107, 189
Marx, Karl 23
maternal body, repair 164
maternal function, idea (Winnicott) 52–3
mature love 142
McAfee, Noëlle 114, 195
McGowan, Todd 41, 75, 109–10, 133, 205
McIvor, David 154
meaning, creation 168
mediated relationships 34
Meehan, Johanna 114
melancholia 31
   contrast (Freud) 161
   depressive position, connection 162
   external causes 90
   pathologization 161–2
   self-fashioning, connection 162–3
melancholy tropes 177–8
mental illness, transformation 179
message, mediation 46
metaphorical castration 77
Minima Moralia (Adorno) 176
mirror recognition, experience 12

INDEX 241

mirror stage 11–12, 18
  ego, connection 18–19
  Lacan account 5
  lack, embryonic state 13
  symbolic predating 43
misogyny, social problems
  (personification) 83
misrecognition 13
morality 96
Morrison, Toni 13, 15
mother
  body, relationship 50
  concrete mother, immediacy 51
  mother-infant fusion,
    idealization 82
  psychological/physical
    condition 43–4
mother-child bond
  idealization (Honneth) 53–4
  naturalization 40–1
mother-child dyad (breakup) 39
mother-child harmony, vision
  39–40
mother-child love 151–2
mother-child relationship 18, 44–5
  idealization 83
mourning 198
  depressive position, connection
    162
Mourning in America (McIvor)
  154
mourning, reparative work 126
Muselmann 155

Name of the Father (phallus) 39
narcissism 10
  development (impedance),
    social inequalities (impact)
    13
  emergence, difficulty 12–13
narcissistic satisfaction, analysis
  (Fanon) 12–13
narrativization 84

naturalization, dangers 122
near-psychosis 178
necropolitical forces 90–1
necropolitics 112–13
negation, forms 115
negative affects, projection 122
negative dialectics (Adorno) 74
Negri, Antonio 206–7
Nelson, Maggie 206
neoliberal academic establishment,
  anti-theoretical (theory-
  phobic) impulse 96
neoliberalism 96, 106
neurotic anxiety 88
Ngai, Sianne 97, 118
Nietzsche, Friedrich 29, 176
nihilistic capitulation 75–6
Nirvana principle, ontological
  version (Freud) 57
nonidentity 74
nonobject 49, 170–1
non-violent ethics, conception 192
normalization 125–6
normative, conception 102
normative ethics 197
normative limits, demolition 182
normative transcendence 188–9
normativity 96, 105–6, 187, 191
  antinormativity 103
nourishment, source 64
Nullpunkt (zero point) 34

object
  destruction, fear 88
  external objects, internal
    objects (contrast) 38
  good object, internalization 56
  loss 80
  love/hate 65
  object-relations theory 63
  partial object 45, 57, 145
  part-object 26–7, 68, 144–5
  phantastic aspects 67

radical dependence 53
"refound" object 136
whole object 145
objective danger-situation 88
object relations 10, 25
 importance 138
object-relations analysts, grouping 54
objet a 14, 24, 35, 115, 136
 analysis (Lacan) 147
 associations, pleasure 55
 cathecting 85
 deposit (Alcibiades) 139
 description 56–7
 equivalence 55
 fantasmatical mediation 57
 importance 138, 144
 mediation 55
 paradigm (Lacan) 56
 partial substitution 56
 power 143
 pursuit 169–70
 reading, vacillation 138
 relationships 35
 task 143
 trace 136
 usage (Lacan) 139–40, 145
oceanic feeling, notion (Freud) 37
Oedipal conflicts 54
Oedipal myth, verbalization 123
Oedipal story (Freud) 18
Oedipus tendencies, awakening 127
Ogden, Thomas 98, 164
ontology, purity 42
orgasm, imagining 85
Other (other) 77, 193
 attachment, irrationality 148–9
 awareness 12
 demands 166
 demonization 193
 message mediation 46
 overproximity 81
 recognition 183–4

relationship, envelopment 47–8
representation 15
separate entity, recognition 10–11
outsiders, demonization 207

paranoia 98
paranoid, label 58
paranoid/reparative reading practices, distinction 95–6
paranoid-schizoid position 1–2, 27–8
 animating force 68
 characterization 4–5, 56
 creativity, connection 164
 depressive position, relationship 5
 human life, starting point 46
 infants, breast perception 48
 literalizations 58
 movement 24
 organization 38
 persecutory anxiety, combination 63–4
 splitting characteristic 74
 subject formation, starting point 3–4
 value, emphasis 98–9
partial object 45, 57, 144–5
 function 145
 translation 145
partial substitute 56
particularity, violence 73
part-object 26–7, 68, 144–5
penis, androcentric perspective 112
perfectionism 165
persecutory anxiety 44, 82
 action 69
 defenses 64
 distinction 63
 notion (Klein) 65–6
 paranoid-schizoid position, combination 63–4

persecutory entity, experiences 4
personality
　enhancement 146
　enrichment 16, 67, 166–7
　integration 125–6, 192
phallic power, claim 79
phallocentric nature, challenge 18
phallus
　psychoanalysis, interest 79
　temporary erection 78
phallus (Name of the Father) 39
phantasized projection 47–8
phantasy 21–2
　account 23
　basis 120–1
　centrality, downplaying 22
　idea 48
　impact 22
　life 163
　loss 142
　unconscious phantasy 67, 92
philosophical anthropology
　　(Honneth) 114
philosophy, task 176–7
Piaget, Jean 189
Plato 139
pleasure principle
　impact 50
　operation 37
pleasure, retroactive fantasy 57–8
plenitude, retroactive fantasy 57–8
political conflicts, mitigation
　　86–7
politics 187
position
　term, usage 1
　theory (Klein) 2
postcolonial theory 206
postcritique 96
post-traumatic stress disorder
　　(PTSD) 89
potty training 46–7
power, external networks 91

power, relations 201
precarity, ethics 196–7
prelinguistic child,
　intersubjectivity 11
prelinguistic child (reality),
　symbolic intervention
　(Lacan) 43
pre-natal state 43–4
primary aggression
　cessation 9
　denial 42
primary fusion
　account (Honneth) 37
　break-up 36, 120
　idea, resistance 43–4
　possibility 44
　psychoanalytic story 39
primary fusion (Winnicott) 34
primary narcissism
　conception (Freud) 3
　idea, challenge 37–8
primary object 118
　children, relationship 68
　relation, phantasmatic aspects
　　160
　relationship 7, 53
primordial fusion 59
progress
　backward-looking notion 200
　negativistic conception 72–3,
　　99
progressive critical theory 199,
　　204
progress narratives, pursuit 76
projection 102, 191
　dynamic 64
　process 72–3
projective identification, account
　　(Klein) 121
prosocial bond, assumption 36–7
Proust, Marcel 176
psyche, psychotic core 6–7
psychic constitution 10

psychic experiences, dissociation 25
psychic life 46
  infiltration 83
psychoanalysis 189
  dark form 198
  goal/aim 3, 16, 131, 141–2
  normalization 126
  role 71
  transference 166
  unconscious, role 9–10
  value 104, 112–13
Psycho-Analysis of Children 54
psychoanalytic approaches 14
  criticism (Adorno) 73
psychoanalytic concepts, domestication 198
psychoanalytic theory 108
  phallocentric nature, challenge 18
psychological development, goal 141–2
psychological disturbance, modality 1–2
psychosexual development, model (Freud) 17
psychosis 46, 61
  near-psychosis 178
psychotic incoherence 190
psychotic, real (relationship) 178

queer affect theory 97
queer theory 206
quilting points 178

racism 112, 211
radical disruption 44
radical historical rupture, idea (Foucault) 109
radical, term (redefining) 100
rational agreement 104
rationality 180–1
rational learning process 109

real 116
  bits, bite 178
  conceptualization (Lacan) 109–10
  jouissance 33
  psychotic, relationship 178
  real-life other, children (relationship) 49
  signifiers, commingling 173
reality (perception), phantasy (impact) 22
real other 47–8
reason
  demolition 182
  relationship (Foucault) 181
recognition
  struggles, motivation 36
  term, usage (avoidance) 34–5
  zero point 37
reconciliation 154
  hope, absence 72–3
reflexive sociality, passage 199
"refound" object 136
relationality 48, 96
  valorization 183
relational scenarios 149
relationships
  impedance 48
  possibility, emphasis (Klein) 48
reparation 101, 130–1
  affiliation 100
  attempts 69
  connections 154
  corrective 97–8
  drive 86
  involvement 30
  manic reparation 30
reparative powers 166
reparative/restorative justice, theories 192
repetition compulsion 21, 128
  breaking 99
  death drive expression 28–9

description 69–70
self-destructiveness 58
singularization 43
usage 22–3
repression, notion (replacement) 17
reproductive futurism 96
resignation, perspective (Whitebook) 160–1
ressentiment 118
retroactive fantasy 8, 31, 44, 57
Rimbaud, Arthur 83
romance
  alignment 137–8
  critique 136
  love, distinction 133
Rose, Jacqueline 213
rudimentary ego, fragmentation/incoherence 45
rupture, definition 205–6
Rupture: On the Emergence of the Political (Eisenstein/McGowan) 41
rupture, term (usage) 108–9

Said, Edward 208
Sartre, Jean-Paul 92
schizophrenia, valorization 20, 180
Schmitt, Carl 104
Sedgwick, Eve 95–6, 98
Segal, Hannah 1, 24, 47, 69, 98, 167, 175–8
self
  boundaries, dissolution 59
  image 13
  social view 190
  split-off parts, instability 164
self-absorption 134–5
self-aggrandizing fantasies 18–19
self-alienation 129
self-beratement 87
  feelings 161

self-congratulation 199–200
self-destructive (destructive) asociality 182
self-destructiveness 58
self-dissolution 60
self-fashioning 166
  melancholia, connection 162–3
self-improvement, insistence 77
self-integration 180
self-laceration 87
self-recognition, moment 13
self-shattering, process 59
Seminar I (Lacan) 10–11, 39–40, 124
  criticism 123
Seminar II (Lacan) 13, 15, 26, 112
  argument 28
  child, insertion 42
  impossibility 71
  integration, idea 29–30
  prelinguistic child (reality), symbolic intervention (Lacan) 43
Seminar VII (Lacan) 44, 59, 122–3, 138, 159
  critique 157
  theme 202
  vase, discussion 170
  wording 174
Seminar VIII (Lacan) 129, 138–9
  basis 137
  support 140
Seminar X (Lacan) 11–12, 42, 76–8
Seminar XI (Lacan) 85, 138
Seminar XX (Lacan) 78
Seminar XXIII (Lacan) 21, 174
sex, importance 125
sexism 211
sexuality, account (Klein) 123
sexuation 125

signification
    forms 174
    processes 84
signifiers 49, 81, 91, 145
    cut 92
    fashioning 170
    gaps 171
    jouissance, commingling 175
    meddling 60–1
    real, commingling 173
    significance, insistence 50
sinthome 21
    discussion 29
Smith, Jada Pinkett 79
social bond 86
social change, recommendations 103
social conflicts, mitigation 86–7
social inequalities 204
    collective situations 81
    impact 13
social normalization, implication 126
social order 73
    change 74
    resistance 193
social reality 177
    adaptation 126
social structure 96
sociocultural order 105
socioeconomic differences, leveling 207
Socrates 139–41, 143, 147, 172
sovereign self, critique 58–9
spiritual beauty 55
splitting 102, 191
    characteristic 74
    defenses 64
    mechanism 26–7
    persecutory defenses 126
    process 72–3
Stewart, Kathleen 103
Studies on Hysteria (Freud) 202

subject
    anxiety, responsibility 89
    becoming 1
    conception (Habermas) 114
    constitutive lack-in-being 79
    destiny, repetition compulsion (usage) 22–3
    destruction/pulverization 19–20, 143
    disorientation 135
    emergence 28
    fundamental fantasy 21
    melancholic structure 161
    melancholy 8
    personality, enrichment 166
    psychic constitution 10
    psychic experience, mediation 24
    self-alienation 129
    self, sense 10–11
    self-understanding 21
    truth 15
    whole personality 10
subject formation
    anxiety, necessity 63
    impact 6
    lack, intimation 13
    starting point 3–4
    thinking, contrast 30
    understanding 1
subjective destitution 16
subjectivity 1, 96
    intersubjective account 39
    psychic/social dimensions 104–5
    theory 200
sublimation 84, 86, 157–60
    das Ding (connection) 158
    description 171–2
subsumptive logic 73
suffering
    context-specific (circumstantial) forms 210–11
    frequencies 31

suicide, death drive expression 60
surplus anxiety 93
symbolic castration, result 59–60
symbolic/imaginary/real, trinity
 (interaction) 10
symbolic order 13
 entry 13–14
symbolic order, static conception
 105
symbolic representative 53
symbolization 167
 result 84
Symposium (Plato) 139

tension
 absence 57
 reduction (Freud) 57–8
Thing. *See das Ding*
totalization, dialectic 145
transcendence 188
 desire 160–1
 fantasy, relinquishment 163
 Thing representation 172–3
transference 27, 167
 love 136
transference, analysis 17
 goal 66–7
transitional object, notion
 (Winnicott) 45
transphobia 211
traumatization 129, 134, 204
 context-specific forms 210–11
 lacerating place 70
 scenarios 113
Trump, Donald (rallying) 196
truth and reconciliation
 commissions (TRCs) 154

unconscious
 awareness, description (Segal)
 176
 blocking 14
 discourse 14

ego expense 16
 formative 25
 role 9–10
 subject 14
unconscious phantasy 92
 life, implication 67
undeadness 69–70, 72
undifferentiated fusion 45
universal human nature,
 metaphysical/ahistorical
 conception 104
universalism 209
 deconstruction 206–7
 reformulation 210
 renegotiation 207
unpredictability, impact 135
unreason
 analysis (Foucault) 180
 conceptualization (Foucault)
 109–10
utopia, conceptions (problem) 75

van Gogh, Vincent (visions) 179
violence 101–2
 external causes 89
 healing, reparation (usage) 117
virtual fracture 110
Vorstellung(en) 50
 goodness/badness,
 representations 51

Western metaphysics, middle
 ground 20
Western subjectivity, malaise
 112–13
Whitebook, Joel 2, 9–10, 39, 75,
 113
 Freud biography 37
white masculinist bias 206
wholeness
 rejection 56
 retroactive fantasy 57–8
whole object 145

Winnicott, Donald 25, 144, 189, 195
  maternal function 52–3
  primary fusion 34
  transitional object 45
worthlessness, feelings 161
wounding, forms 115

young infants, developmental phases 17–18

zero point (Nullpunkt) 34, 37
Žižek, Slavoj 13, 58, 60, 95, 100, 133, 205
  ethical argument 153
  problems 210
  symptom, enjoyment 28–9
Zurbarán, Francisco de 79–80